The Review of
Austrian Economics

The Review of Austrian Economics

Volume 1

Edited by
Murray N. Rothbard
University of Nevada, Las Vegas

The
Ludwig von Mises
Institute

Auburn University/Washington, D.C.

Lexington Books
D.C. Heath and Company/Lexington, Massachusetts/Toronto

HB
98
.R4
v.1

The Review of Austrian Economics

Murray N. Rothbard, Editor
University of Nevada, Las Vegas

Walter Block, Senior Associate Editor
Fraser Institute

EDITORIAL BOARD

Sudha Shenoy
University of Newcastle, Australia

Mark Skousen
Rollins College

Gene Smiley
Marquette University

Jack Sommer
University of Texas, Dallas

T. Alexander Smith
University of Tennessee

Thomas C. Taylor
Wake Forest University

Richard K. Vedder
Ohio University

Leland Yeager
Auburn University

Albert H. Zlabinger
Carl Menger Institute

Published simultaneously in Canada
Printed in the United States of America
Casebound International Standard Book Number: 0-669-12892-9
International Standard Serial Number: 0889-3047

The paper used in this publication meets the minimum requirements of American National Standard for Information Sciences—Permanence of Paper for Printed Library Materials, ANSI Z39.48-1984.

87 88 89 90 8 7 6 5 4 3 2 1

Contents

Introductory Editorial

Murray N. Rothbard
Walter Block

D emand calls forth supply in the world of economic journals as much as in the "real" economic world. The proliferation of new journals since World War II has been a function of the increasing number of Ph.D.s and of the acute exigencies of "publish or perish." But there is another category of new journals more relevant to this one: periodicals that function as a nucleus and a sounding board for schools of economic thought partially or wholly outside the prevailing neoclassical paradigm.

The *Review of Austrian Economics* arrives in just this spirit. We believe that the Austrian tradition, the Austrian paradigm, is only imperfectly represented within the present neoclassical synthesis, and that the best way to rectify this situation is with the creation of a new review. Hence, the *Review of Austrian Economics.*

The *Review of Austrian Economics* has two broadly conceived objectives: (1) to promote the development and extension of Austrian economics and (2) to promote the analysis of contemporary issues in the mainstream of economics from an Austrian perspective.

The first objective is fundamental. The existence of the *Review of Austrian Economics* will resolve some dilemmas now faced by Austrian-oriented researchers who attempt to publish in the mainline journals. Articles that simply assume a familiarity on the part of the profession with methodological norms and theoretical developments within the Austrian tradition are unlikely to be published; the profession, by and large, has no such familiarity. Articles that devote substantial space to stating and defending the methodological norms and retracing the theoretical development are also unlikely to be published; they are seen, and correctly so, as unoriginal. Articles whose backgrounds are extensive in absolute terms but brief in relation to the remainder of the article do not constitute a workable compromise; they are rejected on the basis of length. These constraints do not totally preclude the publication of Austrian-oriented articles in mainline journals, but they make such events much more difficult. The *Review of Austrian Economics* will allow the praxeologically oriented researcher to assume a certain familiarity with the Austrian literature on the part of its readers. This will allow scholars to make an original contribution without requiring that they reiterate material already available.

The second objective, creating a dialog between Austrian and non-Austrian economists, is essential to the long-term success of the *Review of Austrian Economics*—and of Austrian economics itself. The first objective, if pursued by itself, could easily lead to a self-imposed isolation of the Austrian school. Contemporary issues (the national debt, monetary reform, industrial policy, for example) are common denominators linking the Austrian school with other schools of thought. By providing an Austrian analysis of these issues and contrasting it with more orthodox analyses, the contributors to the *Review of Austrian Economics* can build bridges—two-way bridges—between the Austrian and other schools. Articles that fulfill this second objective will attract a wider readership and will enlarge the number of potential contributors of articles to the *Review of Austrian Economics*. Likewise, articles of this type may pave the way for similar publications in the mainline journals. The long-term success of the *Review of Austrian Economics* will thus depend upon the contributors' ability and willingness to publish in both the *Review of Austrian Economics* and the mainline journals.

We propose to explore the rich tapestry of the Austrian tradition. But we also propose to help build and refine the great edifice of Austrian theory itself, as well as to apply that theory to the events of human history, past and present. We are therefore interested in articles that build Austrian theory, explore its traditions and its practitioners, or apply the theory to historical events or situations.

It is one of our prime purposes to help nurture and expand the number and the output of Austrian economists in the United States and elsewhere, but we intend to assess each potential contribution without regard to the author's credentials as an Austrian economist. Any article that helps to build or explore aspects of Austrian economics will be welcome, whether or not the author considers himself or herself an Austrian in any sense.

We have also been appalled that the pressures of demand upon supply have led inexorably to shorter and shorter articles in the journals. As an annual, we can afford to relax greatly the requirements of space. We welcome articles short, medium-sized, or long to the point of being virtual monographs; the overriding consideration is, as it should be, quality and not length.

Finally, we must define what we mean by Austrian economics. It obviously has nothing to do with the economy of Austria or even with economists who happen to have lived or worked in that country. It is noncontroversial that Austrian economics means that body of theory founded by Carl Menger in 1871 in his path-breaking *Principles of Economics*. But Austrian economics is not a monolith, and there have been many competing and even clashing traditions and schools, each of which claims Carl Menger as its founder. The *Review of Austrian Economics* hopes to play a part in building that theory as well as in calling attention to the importance of that structure.

The *Review of Austrian Economics* will publish manuscripts dealing with methodology, Austrian theory, business cycles, history of thought, monetary theory, microeconomics, public policy, and indeed with all traditional economic areas. We define our interests, concerns, and perspective in the broadest possible manner. The *Review* is to be inclusive of all strands of Austrian economics, such as market process, subjectivism, emphasis on entrepreneurship, and praxeology. We most certainly welcome articles incorporating non-Austrian and even anti-Austrian viewpoints, provided only that they are of relevance to the Austrian perspective, broadly understood.

The Review of
Austrian Economics

Editorial:
The Inflationary Chaos Ahead

Henry Hazlitt

T he monetary outlook for the United States—and for the world—was never darker than it is today. The federal budget is unbalanced by some $200 billion a year, and the prospect of getting it back to a balance even five years from now is very dim. At the moment of this writing, the president and the Senate majority leadership have worked out a courageous spending reduction schedule for fiscal year 1986, but congressional Democrats have decided to oppose this plan even if a Senate majority agrees to it, on the ground that it lacks "compassion." Huge deficits will probably continue.

What is happening in the United States is happening in most other countries. Governments have practically all adopted the welfare state, and the political forces within each country seem to ensure its continuance. Scores of pressure groups, from people on unemployment insurance to people on Social Security, insist on the continuance of the payments they have become accustomed to, and on their automatic increase with every increase in the cost of living. But this means that the greater the past or present inflation, the greater must be future inflation. It was estimated in the *New York Times* on April 28, 1985, that in Israel inflation was running at about 1,000 percent a year. It was reported the day before that the inflation in Argentina was expected to reach an annual rate of more than 900 percent that month.

And so it goes. While there is no single source, to my knowledge, where one can find a day-to-day calculation of the latest annual or monthly rates of inflation of each of the world's principal currencies, a mere listing from the daily foreign exchange table of the rates at which some of them now exchange for a U.S. dollar (which is itself depreciating against commodities) indicates what has been happening. A dollar (as of April 26, 1985) bought 4,900 Brazilian cruzeiros, 1,186 Indonesian rupiahs, 932 Israeli shekels, 2,001 Italian lire, 253 Japanese yen, 246 Mexican pesos, 8,688 Peruvian soles, and 495 Turkish lire.

It may be thought that what happens to the currency in other countries is irrelevant to the prospects for future inflation in the United States or chances for returning to a gold standard. But it is not so. Bad currencies depress better currencies.

This was illustrated by the Bretton Woods system set up in 1944 and 1945. The framers of that system, after explicitly permitting not only devaluations at any time by individual countries, but also *uniform* devaluations of member currencies by agreement, paid obeisance to the gold standard by providing that one country, the United States, would keep the dollar convertible into a fixed weight of gold and accept other currencies (at their official rates) in exchange for the dollar.

When the dollar was thrown off gold on August 15, 1971, the result was blamed on President Nixon, who made the announcement. Mr. Nixon must of course bear part of the blame, but his was far from the sole guilt. On the day he stopped gold payments, U.S. gold reserves amounted to only about 2 percent of outstanding currency and demand and time bank deposits. There was only $2.23 in gold to redeem every $100 of U.S. paper promises.

But this takes no account of outstanding Eurodollars or even of the outstanding currency and bank deposits of all the foreign signatories to Bretton Woods (who were entitled under the agreement to turn in their currencies for conversion into dollars or gold). The ultimate gold reserves on which the conversion burden could legally fall under the system must have been only some fraction of 1 percent of the total paper obligations against them. The Bretton Woods system was inherently impossible to maintain. Even if Mr. Nixon had not closed the gold window on August 15, 1971, he would probably have been forced to close it a week or so later for lack of further gold reserves to pay out.

What in 1971 was a run on gold has become in 1986 a run on the dollar. In terms of its exchange rate against goods, the dollar continues to depreciate. But it is considered the world's least unsafe currency of which there is a substantial supply. Therefore, businesspeople and wealthier citizens of foreign countries buy it as an international currency to do business with each other and as a store of value—or at least a better hedge against inflation than their own currencies. This temporarily has increased the demand for dollars and therefore their exchange rate against other currencies. But it has also tended to increase the supply of dollars further—partly to meet the increased demand, and partly because the increased supply of dollars is not immediately or proportionately reflected in the inflation rate.

But the process is ominous. It means that, in a world in which every currency is on a paper basis, the citizens of the countries whose currencies are depreciating fastest will try to exchange them for a major currency that is depreciating least, and therefore make the stronger currency in turn tend to depreciate faster. The worst will pull down the better.

I wish I could foresee a stopping point to this process—a point that would at least lead to the emergence of political responsibility. I regret that I cannot envisage this now. I cannot imagine how democratic politicians, with their eyes fastened on the next election two years or two months away, can bring themselves to substantially reduce, not to whisper abolish, most of the handouts to pressure groups that now make up the welfare state.

One more point needs to be clarified. There is only one workable currency reform—a return by all the leading economic nations to the old-fashioned gold standard. There are no trick reforms that would "economize" the use of gold. Such reforms, as economists have found, merely lead to renewed inflation, and eventually break down. But there is no use even in talking about a return to a gold standard until the United States has abolished the deficit in the federal budget and has kept it balanced or overbalanced for a couple of years.

When will the world learn, after the countless credit booms and busts throughout history, after the American Continentals of the 1776 Revolution, the French assignats of 1789, the German mark disaster of 1918–23, and the world monetary disorder promoted by the Bretton Woods agreement, that inflation is not the main remedy for economic ills but is instead the main cause of them?

Why Subjectivism?

Leland Yeager

Insights and Exaggerations

Economists of the Austrian school put special emphasis on subjectivism. This article reviews why subjectivist insights are important, but it also warns against exaggerations. The latter part, while briefer, particularly warrants attention in Austrian circles.

Various writers define subjectivism in ways that, though not necessarily inconsistent, do seem quite different. Empirical concepts (as opposed to mathematical concepts, like "triangle") necessarily have an "open texture" (Waismann 1965). An open-textured concept just cannot be defined so precisely and comprehensively as to rule out the possibility of an unforeseen situation or case or example that would require modifying the previously framed definition. I feel no duty, then, to start with a definition. Instead, the meaning of subjectivism will emerge from the topics covered and from contrasts with non-subjectivist attitudes.

Materialism versus Subjectivism in Policy

Subjectivist insights contribute to positive economics—to understanding how the world works (or would work with circumstances changed in specified ways). They do not bear primarily on policy. As an expository device, however, it is convenient to begin by considering subjectivism being applied—or being ignored—in policymaking.

Perhaps the broadest subjectivist insight is that economics deals with human choices and actions, not with mechanistically dependable relations. The economy is no machine whose "structure" can be ascertained and manipulated with warranted confidence. Economics knows nothing comparable to Avogadro's number, atomic weights and numbers, the speed of light in a vacuum,

The author thanks Roger Garrison and two anonymous referees for valuable suggestions.

and similar constants of nature (Mises 1963, p. 55). Or if such constants do exist, an economist could earn a great reputation by demonstrating a few of them. No amount of cleverness with econometrics can make the nonexistent exist after all.

One reason why no enduring "structural parameters" characterize the economic system is that the way people behave in markets, as in other aspects of life, depends on their experiences and expectations and on what doctrines they have come to believe. (Here is one area of overlap between Austrian economics and the rational-expectations school currently, or recently, in fashion.)

The circumstances mentioned are inherently changeable. One implication warns against policies whose success presupposes unrealistic kinds of degrees of knowledge. It warns against overambition in attempting detailed central control of economic life.

Subjectivist economics points out, for example, what is lost when policy makes simplistic distinctions between necessities and luxuries or when, unlike voluntary transactions, policy fails to take account of subtle differences between the circumstances and tastes of different people. (My discussion passes over personal rights, not because they are unimportant but only because my present topic is, after all, rather different.)

Examples abound, in Third World countries and elsewhere, of attempts to conserve scarce foreign-exchange earnings for "essentials" by exchange controls, multiple exchange rates, import quotas, and selective import duties designed to limit or penalize the waste of foreign exchange on "luxury" imports and other "nonessential" uses.

The arguments offered for such controls, like arguments for consumer rationing in wartime, are not always sheer nonsense. But subjectivist considerations severaly qualify them. It is impossible to make and implement a clear distinction between luxuries and essentials. Suppose that a government tightly rations foreign exchange for pleasure cruises and travel abroad but classifies oil as an essential import. Some of the oil may go for heating at domestic resorts operating on a larger scale than if the cruises had not been restricted. The restrictions may in effect divert factors of production from other activities into providing recreation otherwise obtainable at lower cost through foreign travel. Because of poor climate at home, it may well be that the marginal units of foreign exchange spent on imported oil go to satisfy wants of the same general sort—while satisfying them less effectively—as wants otherwise satisfied by foreign travel. Restricting travel and supposedly nonessential imports is likely to promote imports of their substitutes and also divert domestic and imported resources or materials into home production of substitutes. The diversions may also impede exports that earn foreign exchange.

It is particularly dubious to try to distinguish between essential and frivolous imports according to whether they serve production (or "economic growth") or mere consumption. All production supposedly aims at satisfying human wants, immediately or ultimately. Producing machinery or building factories is no more inherently worthy than producing restaurant meals or nightclub entertainment, for the machinery or factories are pointless unless they can sooner or later yield goods or services that do satisfy human wants. To favor production-oriented (or export-oriented) imports over consumption-oriented imports is to prefer a roundabout achievement of ultimate consumer satisfactions to their more direct achievement merely because of the greater roundaboutness. It is to confuse ends and means.

People obtain their satisfactions in highly diverse ways (even altruistic ways). Some policymakers evidently do not understand how the price system brings into play the dispersed knowledge that people have about their own tastes and circumstances. A journalist illustrated such misunderstanding when badgering Alan Greenspan, then Chairman of the Council of Economic Advisers, with questions about whether business firms would continue producing essential goods when frivolous goods happened to be more profitable. As Greenspan properly replied (in Mitchell 1974, pp. 74–76), people differ widely in their tastes. Some choose to buy extraordinary things and deliberately deprive themselves of other things generally counted as necessities.

One might conceivably—which is not to say conclusively—urge controls as correctives for specific market distortions. Barring such identified distortions, the idea naturally occurs to subjectivist economists of letting ultimate consumers appraise "essentiality." Sweeping philosophical comparisons are unnecessary. People can act on their own comparisons of the satisfactions they expect from additional dollar's worths of this and that. Consumers and businessmen can judge and act on the intensities of the wants that various goods can satisfy, either directly or by contributing to further processes of production.

Standard theoretical reservations about this suggestion—standard arguments for government discriminations in favor of some and against other particular goods and services—invoke the concepts of externalities, of merit wants and goods, and of income redistribution. Yet how can policymakers be confident that supposed externalities are genuine and important, that supposed merit wants really deserve cultivation, or that discriminating among goods will accomplish the desired redistribution of real income? Any one of many goods, considered by itself, might seem deserving of special favor; yet how *relatively* deserving different goods are may remain highly uncertain, particularly when no one knows just how severely the diversion of resources into particular lines of production will impair production in other lines that might even be more meritorious by the policymaker's criteria. (Tunnel vision is a failing of policymakers not thoroughly familiar with the idea of general economic interdependence.)

More fundamentally, particular goods do not possess qualities deserving special consideration globally, or by their very nature. On the contrary, usefulness or desirability is a relation between things and human wants. The usefulness of something—specifically, its marginal utility—is the smaller the more abundant the thing is. Ideally, decisions about adjusting quantities of various things should consider their usefulness *at the margin*. It is easy to imagine circumstances in which an additional dollar's worth or an additional ounce of penicillin or polio vaccine would contribute less to human satisfaction than an additional unit of orchids.

The concept of priorities does not properly apply in the contexts considered here. For the reasons mentioned, and also in view of how the political process works and of ample experience with controls, it is unrealistic to expect the government to choose "social priorities" reasonably. Consider, for example, the botch of energy policy, including the long record of subsidizing energy consumption in travel and transport (through the underpricing of road and airport facilities) and also including tax exemptions and subsidized loans granted to rural electric cooperatives, even while government officials plead for energy conservation.

Policies adopted or advocated during the energy crises of 1974 and 1979 betray ignorance of subjectivist insights. Examples are rationing of gasoline not so much by price as by the inconvenience and apprehension of having to hunt around for it and wait in long lines to buy it, or being allowed to buy gasoline only on odd- or even-numbered days according to one's license-plate number. A former chairman of Inland Steel Company (Joseph L. Block in Committee for Economic Development in 1974, pp. 79–80) suggested requiring each car owner to choose one day of the week when he would be forbidden to drive. That prohibition, enforced with appropriate stickers, would supposedly have eliminated some needless driving and encouraged use of public transportation. Another example was a decision by the California Public Utilities Commission banning natural-gas heating of new swimming pools (Charlottesville, Va., *Daily Progress,* 29 February 1976, p. E11).

Such measures and proposals underrate the value of freedom and flexibility. Aribtrary measures burden some people lightly and others heavily because different people's lives afford different scopes of substituting away from the restricted consumption and make advance scheduling of activities difficult and unrestricted flexibility important in widely differing degrees. In unrestricted voluntary transactions, by contrast, people can allow for such differences.

A narrowly technological outlook is often linked with puritanical moralizing. (I am reminded of my maternal grandmother, who used to bewail the waste of using a teabag only once if it could be made to serve twice and of using and washing a large plate if the food could be crammed onto a small plate.) Recovery techniques left too much oil and gas in the ground, natural gas on the continental shelf was flared, and the prevailing practice in coal mining left half of a seam in the ground merely because it was needed there as a supporting column or because getting it all out was too expensive—so went one complaint (Freeman 1974, pp. 230–232). Energy has been wasted by "too little" insulation of buildings.

Yet so-called waste was probably sensible at the lower energy prices of the past. There can be such a thing as too much conservation; for example, producing aluminum for storm windows installed under tax incentives even consumes energy in other directions. Ample heat and air conditioning brought comfort, and fast driving saved valuable time. Not having to concentrate on ferreting out ways to conserve energy saved mental capacity for other purposes. Now, at today's higher prices, a dollar spent on energy no longer buys as much comfort or saves as much time or thought as before; and people respond accordingly. Conceivably, of course, the energy prices of the past, distorted downward by interventions, may have led people to consume more energy than they would have done at free-market prices; but if so, the specific distortions should have been identified and addressed. Moralizing about ways of consuming less was off the track.

Such moralizing almost regards waste as something perpetrated only with material resources, not with people's time or comfort or peace of mind. Ironically, this strand of materialism sometimes occurs among people who announce Galbraithian scorn for the alleged materialism of the affluent society. Another apparent strand sometimes found in the attitude of such people is self-congratulation on heroic hard-headedness in recognizing necessary austerities. (Speaking at a conference in Beverly Hills on 26 April 1975, Senator Gaylord Nelson welcomed the challenge of helping to create the new and simpler lifestyles of the future.)

Materialistic energy-conservation proposals illustrate a kind of thinking related to what F.A. Hayek (1952) has called *scientism*. It is something quite different from science or the scientific outlook. A full definition is unnecessary here, but one aspect is the feeling that results somehow do not count unless they have been deliberately arranged for. A person with the scientistic attitude does not understand how millions of persons and companies, trading freely among themselves, can express and arrange for satisfying the wants they themselves consider most intense. He does not appreciate self-adjusting processes, like someone's decision to forgo a gas-heated swimming pool, or any pool at all, in view of the prices to be paid. He assumes that a grandmotherly state must take charge, and he performs feats of routine originality in thinking of new ways for it to do so—as by requiring that cars get 30 miles to the gallon, by imposing standards for building insulation, or by banning pilot lights in gas appliances. Tax gimmicks and ideas are a dime a dozen—incentives for storm windows and solar heating and the plowback of profits into oilfield development and what not. The current, or recent, vogue for partial national economic planning under the name of "industrial policy" provides further examples.

Subjectivist insights illuminate the issue of the military draft. (For early discussions by University of Virginia Ph.D. graduates and graduate students, see Miller 1968.) Many persons have advocated the draft on the grounds that an all-volunteer force is too costly. They understand cost in an excessively materialistic and accounting-oriented way. In truth, costs are subjective—unpleasantnesses incurred and satisfactions foregone—in keeping down monetary outlays, the draft conceals part of the costs and shifts it from the taxpayers being defended to the draftees compelled to serve at wages inadequate to obtain their voluntary service. Furthermore, the draft increases total costs through inefficiency. It imposes unnecessarily large costs on draftees who find military life particularly unpleasant or whose foreclosed civilian pursuits are particularly rewarding to themselves and others. At the same time it wastes opportunities to obtain relatively low-cost service, meaning service at costs subjectively appraised as relatively low, from men who happen to escape the draft but would have been willing to serve at wages below those necessary to obtain voluntary service from men in fact drafted. The opposite method—recruiting the desired number of service men and women by offering wages adequate to attract them as volunteers—brings to bear the knowledge that people themselves have of their own abilities, inclinations, and alternative opportunities. So doing, the market-oriented method holds down the true, subjectively assessed, costs of staffing the armed forces. (Of course, considerations in addition to these also figure in the case against the military draft.)

Subjectivist insights help one understand why compensation at actual market value for property seized under eminent domain probably will not leave the former owner as well off as he had been. His having continued to hold the property instead of having already sold it suggests that he valued it more highly than the sales proceeds or other property purchasable with those proceeds.

Neglect of subjectivism is central to the fallacy of "comparable worth." According to that doctrine, currently fashionable among feminists and interventionists, the worth of work performed in different jobs can be objectively ascertained and compared. People performing different jobs that are nevertheless judged alike, on balance, in their arduousness or pleasantness, their requirements in ability and training, the degrees of responsibility involved, and other supposedly ascertainable characteristics should receive the same pay; and government, presumably, should enforce equal pay. Formulas should replace wage-setting by voluntary agreements reached under the influences of supply and demand.

This idea ducks the questions of how to ration jobs sought especially eagerly at their formula-determined wages and how to prod people into jobs that would otherwise go unfilled at such wages. It ducks the questions of what kind of economic system and what kind of society would take the place of the free-market system, with its processes of coordinating decentralized voluntary activities. (Though writing before comparable worth became a prominent issue, Hayek, 1960, chapter 6, aptly warned against displacing market processes by nonmarket assessments of entitlements to incomes.) The comparable-worth doctrine neglects the ineffable individual circumstances and subjective feelings that enter into workers' decisions to seek or avoid particular jobs, employers' efforts to fill them, and consumers' demands for the goods and services produced in them. Yet wages and prices set through market processes do take account of individual circumstances and personal feelings (a point I'll say more about later on).

Subjectivist economists recognize the importance of intangible assets, including knowledge, a kind of "human capital." They recognize the scope for ingenuity in getting around government controls of various kinds, whereas the layman's tacit case for controls involves a mechanistic conception of the reality to be manipulated, without due appreciation of human flexibility. Controls, and responses to them, destroy human capital by artificially hastening the obsolescence of knowledge; they impose the costs of keeping abreast of the artificially changing scene and divert material and intellectual resources, including inventiveness, from productive employments. Credit-allocation measures and other controls on financial institutions, for example—even reserve requirements and interest-rate ceilings—have bred innovations to circumvent them. Managers have to be trained and other start-up costs borne for new institutions and practices, and customers must spend time and trouble learning about them. Price and wage controls and energy-conservation rules provide further illustrations of such wastes.

Arbitrariness and unfairness figure among the costs of controls intended to buck market forces. As controls become more comprehensive and complex, their administrators are less able to base their decisions on relatively objective criteria. Bureaucratic rules become more necessary and decisions based on incomplete information less avoidable. Multiplication of categories entitled to special treatment invites the pleading of special interests. Even morality, another intangible asset, is eroded.

The complexity of detailed monitoring and enforcement suggests appealing for voluntary compliance, compliance with the spirit and not just the letter of the regulations. (Controls over foreign trade and payments for balance-of-payments purposes, such as President Johnson attempted in the mid-1960s, provide still further examples; see Yeager 1965.) Whether compliance is avowedly voluntary, or whether ease of evasion makes compliance voluntary in effect, such an approach tends to penalize public-spirited citizens who do comply and gives the advantage to others. Exhorting people to act against their own economic interest tends to undercut the signaling and motivating functions of prices. How are people to know, then, when it is proper and when improper to pursue economic gain? To exhort people to think of compliance as in their own interest when it plainly is not, or to call for self-sacrifice as if it were the essence of morality, is to undercut the rational basis of morality and even undercut rationality itself.

A kind of perverse selection results. Public-spirited car owners who heed appeals for restraint in driving thereby leave more gasoline available, and at a lower price than otherwise, to less public-spirited drivers. Sellers who do comply with price ceilings or guidelines must consequently turn away some customers unsatisfied, to the profit of black-marketeers and other less scrupulous sellers. Eventually such effects become evident, strengthening the idea that morality is for suckers and dupes.

Subjectivists know better than to erect efficiency, somehow conceived, into the overriding criterion either of particular processes or institutions or of entire economic systems. The principle of comparative advantage discredits the idea that each product should necessarily be produced wherever it can be produced most efficiently in the technological sense. No presumption holds, furthermore, that any particular line of production necessarily should be carried on in the technologically most advanced way; for the resources required in such production are demanded by other industries also, where they may well contribute more at the margin to consumer satisfactions, as judged by what consumers are willing to pay.

Efficiency in the sense of Pareto optimality is often taken as a criterion of policy. Pareto efficiency is indeed a useful concept in the teaching and study of microeconomic theory. It is useful in contemplating outcomes of the market process in the form of particular—but abstractly conceived—allocations of resources and goods. Economists seldom if ever face an occasion or opportunity to appraise concrete, specific allocations, in the real world. As Rutledge Vining properly emphasizes, legislators and their expert advisors necessarily are choosing among alternative sets of legal and institutional constraints rather than among alternative specific results or allocations. (See Vining 1985 and Yeager 1978.) Such constraints are rules of the game within which people strive to make the most of their opportunities amidst ceaseless change in wants, resources, and technology. The very point of having rules and institutions presupposes their having a certain stability and dependability, which would be undermined by continual efforts to make supposedly optimal changes in them.

What is useful in policy discussions, then, is not the supposed benchmark of Pareto efficiency but rather comparison of what alternative sets of rules add up to in terms of alternative economic and social systems. If we must have a standard against which to appraise reality, we might well adopt the view of a competitive market economy as a collection of institutions and practices for gathering and transmitting information and incentives concerning not-yet-exhausted opportunities for gains from trade (including "trade with nature" through production or rearrangements of production).

Knowledge and Coordination

Subjectivists recognize the many kinds of information that market prices and processes bring to bear on decisions about production and consumption. These kinds include what F.A. Hayek (1945) called "knowledge of the particular circumstances of time and place," knowledge that could hardly be codified in textbooks or assembled for the use of central planners, knowledge that can be used, if at all, only by numerous individual "men on the spot." It includes knowledge about all sorts of details of running business firms, including knowledge of fleeting local conditions. It includes what people know about their own tastes and particular circumstances as consumers, workers, savers, and investors. Subjectivist economists recognize how such factors not only underlie the prices that consumers are prepared to pay for goods but also underlie costs of production.

Each consumer decides how much of each particular good to buy in view of the price of the good itself, the prices of other goods, his income and wealth, and his own needs and preferences. Subject to qualifications about how possible and how worthwhile precise calculation seems, he leaves no opportunity unexploited to increase his total satisfaction by diverting a dollar from one purchase to another. Under competition, the price of each good tends to express the total of the prices of the additional inputs necessary to supply an additional unit of that good. These resource prices tend, in turn, to measure the values of other marginal outputs sacrificed by diversion of resources away from their production. Prices therefore tell the consumer how much worth of other production must be foregone to supply him with each particular good. The money values of forgone alternative production tend, in turn, to reflect consumer satisfactions expectedly obtainable from that foregone production. (I say "reflect"—take account of—in order not to claim anything about actual measurement of what is inherently unmeasurable. I speak only of tendencies, furthermore, for markets never fully reach competitive general equilibrium.)

With prices bringing to their attention the terms of choice posed by the objective realities of production possibilities and the subjective realities of other persons' preferences, consumers choose the patterns of production and resource use that they prefer. Their bidding tends to keep any unit of a resource from going to meet a less intense willingness to pay for its productive contribution (and thus the denial of a more intense willingness). Ideally—in competitive equilibrium, and subject to qualifications still to be mentioned—no opportunity remains unexploited to increase the total value of things produced by transferring a unit of any resource from one use to another. Changes in technology and consumer preferences always keep creating such opportunities afresh, but the profit motive keeps prodding businessmen to ferret them out and exploit them.

To determine how resources go into producing what things in what quantities, consumers need freedom to spend their incomes as they wish, unregimented by actual rationing. But they need more: opportunities to make choices at unrigged prices tending to reflect true production alternatives.

We could speak then of "consumers' sovereignty," but the term is a bit narrow. Insofar as their abilities permit, people can bring their preferences among occupations as well as among consumer goods to bear on the pattern of production. In fact, investors' preferences, including notions about the morality and the glamor of different industries and companies, also have some influence; and we might speak of "investors' sovereignty" as well. (See Rothbard 1962, p. 452, n. 12, and pp. 560–562 on what Rothbard calls "individual sovereignty.")

Suppose that many people craved being actors strongly enough to accept wages below those paid in other jobs requiring similar levels of ability and training. This willingness would help keep down the cost of producing plays, and cheap tickets would draw audiences, maintaining jobs in the theater. Suppose, in contrast, that almost everyone hated to mine coal. The high wages needed to attract miners would enter into the production cost and price of coal, signaling power companies to build hydroelectric or nuclear or oil-burning rather than coal-burning plants and signaling consumers to live in warmer climates or smaller or better-insulated houses than they would do if fuel were cheaper. Such responses would hold down the number of distasteful mining jobs to be filled. The few workers still doing that work would be ones whose distaste for it was relatively mild and capable of being assuaged by high wages.

No profound distinction holds between workers' sovereignty and consumers' sovereignty or between getting satisfactions or avoiding dissatisfactions in choosing what work to do and in choosing what goods to consume. Consumer goods are not ultimate ends in themselves but just particular means of obtaining satisfactions or avoiding dissatisfactions. People make their personal tastes and circumstances count by how they act on the markets for labor and goods alike.

Our broadened concept of consumers' and workers' sovereignty by no means upsets the idea of opportunity cost. We need only recognize that people choose not simply among commodities but rather among *packages* of satisfactions and dissatisfactions. The choice between additional amounts of A and B is really a choice between satisfactions gained and dissatisfactions avoided by people as consumers and. producers of A and satisfactions gained and dissatisfactions avoided by people as consumers and producers of B. Choosing package A costs forgoing package B. Ideally, the prices of products A and B indicate the terms of exchange, so to speak, between the entire combinations of satisfactions gained and dissatisfactions avoided at the relevant margins in connection with the two products. Prices reflect intimately personal circumstances and feelings as well as physical or technological conditions of production and consumption.

None of this amounts to claiming that different persons' feelings about goods and jobs (and investment opportunities) can be accurately measured and compared in terms of price or in any other definite way. However, people's feelings do count in the ways that their choices are expressed and their activities coordinated through the price system, and changes in their feelings do affect the pattern of production in directions that make intuitively good sense.

Clearly, then, economic theory need not assume that people act exclusively or even primarily from materialistic motives. Pecuniary considerations come into play, but along with others. As the laws of supply and demand describe, an increase in the pecuniary rewards or charges—or other rewards or costs—attached to some activity will increase or decrease its chosen level, other incentives and disincentives remaining unchanged. Money prices and changes in them can thus influence behavior and promote coordination of the chosen behaviors of different people, even though pecuniary considerations do not carry decisive weight and perhaps not even preponderant weight.

Value Theory

The role of subjectivism in solving the diamond-and-water paradox, replacing the labor theory or other real-cost theories of value, and accomplishing the marginalist revolution of the 1870s, is too well known to require more than a bare reminder here. Subjectivism must be distinguished from importing psychology into economics (Mises 1963, pp. 122–127, 486–488). Diminishing marginal utility is a principle of sensible management rather than of psychology: a person will apply a limited amount of some good (grain, say, as in Menger 1950, pp. 129–130) to what he considers its most important uses, and a larger and larger amount will permit its application to successively less important uses also.

Subjectivists do not commit the error of John Ruskin, who thought that "Whenever material gain follows exchange, for every plus there is a precisely equal minus" (quoted in Shand 1984, p. 120). They recognize that wealth is produced not only by physically shaping things or growing them but also by exchanging them. In the words of Henry George (1898/1941,pp. 331–332), who independently achieved several Austrian insights, "Each of the two parties to an exchange . . . [gets] something that is more valuable to him than what he gives. . . . Thus there is in the transaction an actual increase in the sum of wealth, an actual production of wealth."

Subjectivists recognize nonmaterial elements in costs as well as demands. Every price is determined by many circumstances classifiable under the headings of "subjective factors" and "objective factors" (or "wants" and "resources and technology"). An alternative classification distinguishes between demand factors and supply factors. This alternative is not equivalent to the first classification because there is no reason to suppose that subjective factors operate only on the demand side of a market while objective factors dominate the supply side.

On the contrary, subjective factors operate on both sides. The supply schedule of a good does not reflect merely the quantities of inputs technologically required for various amounts of output, together with given prices of the inputs. The input prices are themselves variables determined by bidding among various firms and lines of production in the light of the inputs' capabilities to contribute to producing goods valued by consumers. Consumers' subjective feelings about other goods thus enter into determining the money costs of supplying quantities of any particular product.

Subjective factors operate in both blades of Marshall's scissors. (Misleadingly, Marshall 1920, pp. 348, 813ff., had referred to a utility blade and a cost blade, as if utility and cost were quite distinct.)

By the logic of a price system, then, money cost brings to the attention of persons deciding on production processes and output volumes in any particular line—and utlimately to the attention of its consumers—what conditions prevail in all other sectors of the economy, including persons' attitudes toward goods and employments. Money prices and costs convey information about subjective conditions outside the direct ken of particular decisionmakers.

At this point the subjectivism of Austrian economists reinforces their awareness of general economic interdependence and their concern with coordination among the plans and actions of different people. They are wary (as many textbook writers seem not to be) of focusing so narrowly on the choices of the individual household and individual firm as to detract attention from the big picture.

Recognizing the subjective aspects of cost, we gain insights into the dubiousness of expecting prices to correspond to costs in any precise way. Costs represent values of forgone alternatives: costs are intimately linked with acts of choice.

Cost curves are no more objectively given to business firms than are demand curves for their products. A large part of the task of entrepreneurs and managers is to learn what the cost (and demand) curves are and to press the cost curves down, so to speak, through inspired innovations in technology, organization, purchasing, and marketing. Outsiders are in a poor position to second-guess their decisions.

Subjectivists appreciate the role of expectations. Well before the recent vogue of "rational expectations" in macroeconomics, Ludwig von Mises (1953/1981, pp. 459–460) recognized that an inflationary policy could not go on indefinitely giving real "stimulus" to an economy; people would catch on to what was happening, and the supposed stimulus would dissipate itself in price increases. Von Mises also argued (1963, p. 586) that disorders such as the corn–hog cycle would be self-corrective. Unless the government protected farmers from the consequences of unperceptive or unintelligent behavior, farmers would learn about the cycle, if it did in fact occur; and by anticipating it would forestall it. (Those who did not learn would incur losses and be eliminated from the market.)

Much expressed nowadays are notions such as "the market's" expectation of some future magnitude—the dollar–mark exchange rate in three months, or whatever. Subjectivists are skeptical. They understand that "the market" does not form expectations or change light bulbs ("How many right-wing economists does it take to change a light bulb?") or do anything else. *People* do form expectations while acting and interacting on markets. Since expectations are formed by people, they are understandably loose, diverse, and changeable.

All this intertwines with the inherent unpredictability of future human affairs. It is not even possible to make an exhaustive list of all possible outcomes of some decision, let alone attach probability scores to outcomes (Shackle 1972, especially p. 22). Policymakers should take this point to heart and restrain their optimism about being able to control events.

This is not to deny that some predictions can be made with warranted confidence, notably the if-this-then-that predictions of economic theory and of science in general. Foretelling the future is quite another matter. Economists, like other people, have only limited time and energy. It is reasonable for each one to stick to work exploiting his own comparative advantages and hunches about fruitfulness and not let himself be badgered into foretelling the unforetellable.

Further Policy Implications

The ultrasubjectivist view of cost put forward by James Buchanan (1969) and writers in the London School tradition (some of whose articles are reprinted in Buchanan and Thirlby 1981) has been largely adopted by Austrian economists (Vaughn 1980 and 1981, Seldon 1981).

In examining this view, we must avoid false presuppositions about how words relate to things. It is not true that each word has a single definite and unequivocal meaning and that it labels a specific thing or action or relation objectively existing in the real world. On the contrary, many words have wide ranges of meaning. One way to learn what writers mean by a word is to see what implications they draw from propositions containing it.

This is true of "cost" as interpreted by Buchanan and the London economists. Those writers associate particular policy positions with the fuzziness that they attribute to cost. They heap scorn on cost-oriented rules for managing enterprises.

Advocates of such rules typically attribute important welfare properties to them. Probably the most prominent such rule is the one requiring the output of an enterprise to be set at such a level that price equals marginal costs. (In the same general cost-oriented family, however, would be rules like the one that total revenue should just cover total cost.) One strand of argument for socialism, in fact, is that socialized enterprises could be made to follow such rules, unlike unregulated private enterprises. Even under capitalism, such rules supposedly might be useful in the framing of antimonopoly policy and the regulation of public utilities. They might also figure in other government economic interventions and in the simulation of market results in nonmarket settings, as in tort settlements.

The case for socialism and milder government economic interventions can be weakened, then, by discrediting the measurability and even the conceptual definiteness of "cost." This, I conjecture, is a clue to the ultrasubjectivist view of the concept. "Cost," says Buchanan (1969, pp. 42–43), "is that which the decisionmaker sacrifices or gives up when he makes a choice. It consists in his own evaluation of the enjoyment or utility that he anticipates having to forego as a result of selection among alternative courses of action." If cost can thus be portrayed as a thoroughly subjective concept or magnitude, if no one but the individual decisionmaker (entrepreneur or manager) can know what cost is or was, and if such knowledge is ineffable and practically incommunicable, then no outside authority can reasonably impose cost-oriented rules on him. The case for displacing or overriding the market dissolves.

This line of argument has merit. In particular, as already observed, cost curves do not objectively exist. Instead, business decisionmakers have the task of discovering or inventing them and modifying them by happy innovations. Unfortunately, as a later section of this article shows, Buchanan and the London economists carry their subjectivist line too far and so tend to discredit it.

Subjectivist insights about expectations have other notable policy implications. The history of energy policy, and of politicians' demagogy, provides reason for expecting future repetition of past infringements on property rights. Firms and investors must recognize that if they make decisions that turn out in some future energy crisis to have been wise—for example, stockpiling oil, cultivating nonconventional energy sources, adopting conservation measures, or building flexibility into their facilities and operations so as to be able to cope relatively well with energy squeezes—then they will not be allowed to reap exceptional profits from their risk bearing, their correct hunches, and their good luck. They will be victimized by seizure of oil stocks, by adverse treatment under rationing schemes, by price controls, or in other ways. Government reassurances, even if made, would nowadays not be credible. The benefits of diverse private responses to diverse expectations about energy supplies are thus partly forestalled.

This example reminds subjectivists of a broader point about remote repercussions of particular policies, repercussions remote in time or in economic sector affected. A violation of property rights may seem the economical and expedient policy in the individual case. Yet in contributing to an atmosphere of uncertainty, it can have grave repercussions in the long run.

Because expectations influence behavior, a policy's credibility conditions its effectiveness, as the rational-expectations theorists, and William Fellner (1976) before them, have emphasized. The question of the withdrawal pangs of ending an entrenched price inflation provides an example. When money-supply growth is slowed or stopped, the reduced growth of nominal income is split between price deceleration and slowed real production and employment. Expectations affect how favorable or unfavorable this split is. If the anti-inflation program is not credible—if wage negotiators and price-setters think that the policymakers will lose their nerve and switch gears at the first sign of recessionary side-effects—then those private parties will expect the inflation to continue and will make their wage and price decisions accordingly; and the monetary slowdown will bite mainly on real activity. If, on the contrary, people are convinced that the authorities will persist in monetary restriction indefinitely no matter how bad the side-effects, so that inflation is bound to abate, then the perceptive price-setter or wage-negotiator will realize that if he nevertheless persists in making increases at the same old pace, he will find himself out ahead of the installed inflationary procession and will lose customers or jobs. People will moderate their price and wage demands, making the split relatively favorable to continued real activity.

It is only superficially paradoxical, then, that in two alternative situations with the same degree of monetary restraint, the situation in which the authorities are believed ready to tolerate severe recessionary side-effects will actually exhibit milder ones than the situation in which the authorities are suspected of irresolution. Subjectivists understand how intangible factors like these can affect outcomes under objectively similar conditions.

Capital and Interest Theory

Capital and interest theory is a particular case or application of general value theory, but its subjectivist aspects can conveniently occupy a section of their own.

Subjectivist insights help dispel some paradoxes cultivated by neo-Ricardians and neo-Marxists at Cambridge University. These paradoxes seem to impugn standard economic theory (particularly the marginal-productivity theory of factor remuneration), and by implication they call the entire logic of a market economy into question.

Reviewing the paradoxes in detail is unnecessary here (see Yeager 1976 and Garrison 1979). One much-employed arithmetical example describes two alternative techniques for producing a definite amount of some product. They involve different time-patterns of labor inputs. In each technique, compound interest accrues, so to speak, on the value of invested labor. Technique A is the cheaper at interest rates above 100 percent, B is cheaper at rates between 50 and 100 percent, and A is cheaper again at rates below 50 percent.

If a decline of the interest rate through one of these two critical levels brings a switch from the less to the more capital-intensive of the two techniques, which seems normal enough, then the switch to the other technique as the interest rate declines through the other switch point is paradoxical. If we view the latter switch in the opposite direction, an increased interest rate prompts a more intensive use of capital. Capital intensity can respond perversely to the interest rate.

Examples of such perversity seem not to depend on trickery in measuring the stock of capital. The physical specifications of a technique, including the timing of its inputs and its output, stay the same regardless of the interest rate and regardless of whether the technique is actually in use. If one technique employs physically more capital than the other in relation to labor or to output at one switch point, then it still employs more at any other interest rate. This comparison remains valid with any convention for physically measuring the amount of capital, provided only that one does not change measurement conventions in mid-example. If the capital intensities of the two techniques are such that the switch between them at one critical interest rate is nonparadoxical, then the switch at the other must be paradoxical—a change in capital intensity in the *same* direction as the interest rate. We cannot deny perversity at both switch points—unless we abandon a purely physical conception of capital.

The paradox-mongers commit several faults. They slide from comparing alternative static states into speaking of *changes* in the interest rate and of *reponses* to those changes. They avoid specifying what supposedly determines the interest rate and what makes it change.

The key to dispelling the paradoxes, however, is the insight that capital—or whatever it is that the interest rate is the price of—cannot be measured in purely physical terms. One must appreciate the value aspect—the subjective aspect—of the thing whose price is the interest rate. It is convenient to conceive of that thing as a factor of production. Following Cassel (1903, pp. 41ff. and passim), we might name it "waiting." It is the tying up of value over time, which is necessary in all production processes. (This conceptualization is "convenient" not only because it conforms to reality and because it dispels the paradoxes but also because it displays parallels between how the interest rate and other factor prices are determined and what their functions are: it brings capital and interest theory comfortably into line with general microeconomic theory.)

In a physically specified production process, a reduced interest rate not only is a cheapening of the waiting (the tying up of value over time) that must be done but also reduces its required value-amount. It reduces the interest element in the notional prices of semifinished and capital goods for whose ripening into final consumer goods and services still further waiting must be done. Increased thrift is productive not only because it supplies more of the waiting required for production but also because, by lowering the interest rate, it reduces the amount of waiting required by any physically specified technique.

The amounts of waiting required by alternative physically specified techniques will in general decline in different degrees, which presents the possibility of reswitching between techniques, as in the example mentioned. When a decline in the interest rate brings an apparently perverse switch to a technique that is less capital-intensive by some physical criterion, the explanation is that the decline, although reducing the waiting-intensities of both techniques, reduces them differentially in such a way as to bring a larger reduction in the overall expense of producing by the adopted technique.

Preconceived insistence on measuring all factor quantities and factor-intensities in purely physical terms clashes with the fact of reality—or arithmetic—that the amount of tying up of value over time required in achieving a physically specified result does indeed depend on that factor's own price. Not only the waiting-intensity of a physically specified processes but also the relative waiting-intensities of alternative processes really are affected by the interest rate. When a switch of technique occurs, the technique adopted really is the more economical on the whole, the inputs, waiting included, being valued at their prices. When a rise in the interest rate triggers a switch of techniques, the displace done has become *relatively* too waiting-intensive to remain economically viable. It is irrelevant as a criticism of economic theory that *by some other, inapplicable, criterion* the displaced technique counts as less capital-intensive.

Further discussion of the supposed paradoxes would display parallels between reswitching and the conceivable phenomenon of multiple internal rates of return in an investment option, which is hardly mysterious at all (Hirshleifer 1970, pp. 77–81). Already, though, I've said enough to show how a subjectivist conceptualization of the factor whose price is the interest rate can avoid fallacies flowing from a materialist or objective conceptualization.

"I Am More Subjectivist than Thou"

On a few points, some Austrian economists may not have been subjectivist enough. Murray Rothbard (1962, pp. 153–154) seems to think that a contract under which no property has yet changed hands—for example, an exchange of promises between a movie actor and a studio—is somehow less properly enforceable than a contract under which some payment has already been made. Blackmail is a less actionable offense than extortion through application or threat of physical force (1962, p. 443, n. 49). If a villain compels me to sell him my property at a mere token price under threat of ruining my reputation and my business by spreading vicious but plausible lies, his action is somehow less of a crime or tort than if he had instead threatened to kick me in the shins or trample one of my tomato plants (Rothbard 1982, especially pp. 121–127, 133–148, and personal correspondence). The material element in a transaction or a threat supposedly makes a great difference.

I may be at fault in not grasping the distinctions made in these examples, but it would be helpful to have further explanation of what superficially seems like an untypical lapse from subjectivism into materialism.

Far more common is the lapse into overstating the subjectivist position so badly as to risk discrediting it. F.A. Hayek is not himself to blame, of course, but a remark of his (1952, p. 31) has been quoted *ad nauseam* (for example by Ludwig Lachmann in Spadaro 1978, p. 1; Walter Grinder in his introduction to Lachman 1977, p. 23; and Littlechild 1979, p. 13). It has had a significance attributed to it that it simply cannot bear. "It is probably no exaggeration to say that every important advance in economic theory during the last hundred years was a further step in the consistent application of subjectivism."

This proposition of doctrinal history could be strictly correct without its implying that every subjectivist step was an important advance. Moreover, past success with extending subjectivism in certain degrees and directions does not imply that any and all further extensions constitute valid contributions to economics.

A theorist is not necessarily entitled to take pride in being able to boast, "I am more subjectivist than thou." More important than subjectivism for its own sake is getting one's analysis straight.

The most sweeping extensions of subjectivism occur in remarks about a purely subjective theory of value, including a pure time-preference theory of the interest rate. Closely related remarks scorn the theory of mutual determination of economic magnitudes, the theory expounded by means of systems of simultaneous equations of general equilibrium. The ultrasubjectivists insist on monocausality instead. Causation supposedly runs in one direction only, *from* consumers' assessments of marginal utility and value and the relative utilities or values of future and present consumption *to* prices and the interest rate and sectoral and temporal patterns of resource allocation and production (Rothbard 1962, pp. 302–303).

Taken with uncharitable literalness, the ultrasubjectivist slogans imply that people's feelings and assessments have *everything* to do and the realities of nature, science, and technology have *nothing* to do with determining prices and interest rates and all interrelated economic magnitudes. Actually, these objective realities do interact with people's tastes. They condition how abundant various resources and goods are, or could be made to be, and so help determine *marginal* utilities.

For two reasons I know that the ultrasubjectivists do not really believe all they say. First, the propositions in question, taken literally, are too preposterous for *anyone* to believe. Second, subjectivist writings sometimes discuss production functions, the principle of diminishing marginal physical product, and other physical relations, conceding some importance to such matters.

What I am objecting to, then, is not so much substantive beliefs as, rather, the willful use of misleading language, language that sometimes misleads even its users, language adopted on the presupposition that subjectivism is good and more of it is better.

Subjectivists may contend that physical reality counts only *through* people's subjective perceptions of it and the valuations they make in accord with it. But that contention does not banish the influence of objective reality.

Businessmen (and consumers) who perceive reality correctly will thrive better on the market than those who misperceive it. A kind of natural selection sees to it that objective reality does get taken into account.

Full-dress argument for purely subjective value and interest theory and for unidirectional causality appears rarely in print, probably because such notions are not defensible. They do keep being asserted in seminars, conversation, and correspondence, however, as I for one can testify and as candid Austrians will presumably acknowledge. Furthermore, such assertions do appear in authoritative Austrian publications. (For example, see Rothbard 1962, pp. 117, 122, 293, 307, 332, 363–364, 452, n. 16, 455, n. 12, 457, n. 27, 508, 528, 557, 893, n. 14; Rothbard, introduction to Fetter 1977; Taylor 1980, pp. 26, 32, 36, 47, 50; and Shand 1984, pp. 23, 44, 45, 54, 56. Garrison 1979, pp. 220–221, avoids the word "pure" in recommending a time-preference theory of interest and a subjectivist theory of value in general, but he does contrast them favorably with what he calls "eclectic" theories, such as the "standard Fisherian" theory of interest. For outright avowal of a pure-time-preference interest theory, see Kirzner's manuscript.)

The point repeatedly turns up in Austrian discussions that goods that people consider different from each other are indeed different goods, no matter how closely they resemble each other physically. This point is not downright fallacious, but the significance attributed to it is excessive, and its use in question-begging ways is likely to repel mainstream economists. An example is the contention that when a manufacturer sells essentially the same good under different labels at different prices, he is nevertheless not practicing price discrimination; for the goods bearing the different labels are considered by the consumers to be different goods, which *makes* them different goods in all economically relevant senses. The manufacturer is supposedly just charging different prices for different things.

Quite probably his practice is not one that perceptive economists and social philosophers would want to supress by force of law; but we should not let our policy judgments, any more than our subjectivist methodological preconceptions, dictate our economic analysis or remove certain questions from its scope. It may be more fruitful to recognize that price discrimination is indeed going on, with the different labels being used to separate customers according to their demand elasticities.

Crypticism sometimes accompanies insistence on pure subjectivism. An example is a line of attack taken against mainstream interest theory, which enlists considerations of intertemporal transformability (that is, the *productivity* of investment) as well as the subjective time-preference element. This theory is epitomized by Irving Fisher's diagram (1930, pp. 234ff., Hirshleifer 1970, passim) showing a transformation curve between present and future goods (or consumption), as well as a map of indifference curves between present and future goods. A familiar Austrian objection is to insist that the diagram, specifically the transformation curve, fails to make the required distinction between physical productivity and value productivity.

If not deliberate obscurantism, this objection does indicate misunderstanding of Fisher's theory (or impatience with or prejudice against it). Of course, some technological change that increases the physical productivity of investment in some specific line of production, say widgets, may not increase the value productivity of such investment. The increased physical amount of future widgets obtainable for a given present sacrifice may indeed have a reduced total value in terms of other goods and services in general (the future demand for widgets may be price-inelastic). Some of the new opportunities created by technological change will indeed be unattractive to investors. In invoking the greater productivity of more roundabout methods of production, Böhm-Bawerk (1959, II, 82–84, III, 45–56) was referring to "well-chosen" or "skillfully chosen" or "wisely selected" methods; and a similar stipulation applies to the present case. Technological changes that increase the physical productivity of particular roundabout methods broaden the range of opportunities among which investors can exercise wise choice, and implementing some of those choices does add to the demand for waiting, tending to bid up the interest rate.

The ultrasubjectivist objection is open to another strand of reply. It is illegitimate to invoke a contrast between physical productivity and value productivity by restricting the discussion to examples of sacrificing *specific* present goods to get more future goods of the same kind. What is conveyed by borrowing and lending (and other transactions in waiting) is not command over investable resources that would otherwise have gone into producing specific present goods but command over resources in general. It *is* legitimate to do what Fisher's diagram helps us to do: to conceive of present goods in general being sacrificed for larger amounts of future goods in general.

With their admirable general emphasis on process and on the decisions and actions of individual persons, Austrian economists should not rest content with attacks on mainstream capital and interest theory that rely on cryptic allusions to a distinction between physical productivity and value productivity (or, similarly, to assertions that factor prices will adjust). They should defend their pure subjectivism on this topic, if they can, with a detailed process analysis of how persons act.

Next I turn to exaggerations in the subjectivist cost doctrines of Buchanan and the London school. These terrorists interpret the cost of a particular course of action as the next-best course perceived and forgone by the decisionmaker. Ronald Coase (quoted with approval in Buchanan 1969, p. 28) says that "The cost of doing anything consists of the receipts which would have been obtained if that particular decision had not been taken. . . . To cover costs and to maximize profits are essentially two ways of expressing the same phenomenon."

Well, suppose the best course of action open to me is, in my judgment, to open a restaurant of a quite specific type in a specific location. The next-best course, then, is presumably to open a restaurant identical in all but some trivial detail, such as the particular hue of green of the lampshades. If so, the cost of the precise restaurant chosen is presumably an all but identical restaurant worth to me, in my judgment, almost fully as much. Generalizing, the cost of a chosen thing or course of action is very nearly the full value that the decisionmaker attributes to it.

My counterexample to the Coase-Buchanan cost concept may seem frivolous, but it raises a serious question. How far from identical to the chosen course of action must the next best alternative be to count as a distinct alternative? The point conveyed by questions like this is that either radical error or sterile word-jugging is afoot. (Nozick, 1977, especially pp. 372–373, expresses some compatible though not identical doubts about subjectivist concepts of cost and preference.)

More ordinary concepts of cost, however, are meaningful, including the interpretation of money cost in a particular line of production as a way of conveying information to decisionmakers in it about conditions (including personal tastes) in other sectors of the economy.

Buchanan (1969, p. 43) draws six implications from his choice-bound conception of cost, and Littlechild (in Spadaro 1978, pp. 82–83) quotes them all with apparent approval. I'll quote and comment only on the first, second, and fifth.

1. Most importantly, cost must be borne exclusively by the decisionmaker; it is not possible for cost to be shifted to or imposed on others.
2. Cost is subjective; it exists in the mind of the decisionmaker and nowhere else.
5. Cost cannot be measured by someone other than the decsionmaker because there is no way that subjective experience can be directly observed.

As for the first word and second implications, of course cost can be imposed on others in quite ordinary senses of those words; it is not always kept inside the mind of the decisionmaker. What about adverse externalities—smoke damage and the like? What about losses imposed on stockholders by an incompetent business management? What about the costs that a government imposes on a population by taxation or inflation (or its command of resources, however financed)? Isn't it notoriously true that a government official need not personally bear all the costs of his decisions? What about involuntarily drafted soldiers? Even an ordinary business decision has objective aspects in the sense that the resources devoted to the chosen activity are withdrawn or withheld from other activities.

Of course the costs incurred in these examples have subjective aspects also—in the minds or the perceptions of the draftees and of persons who would have been consumers of the goods from whose production the resources in question are competed away. What is odd is the contention that no cost occurs except subjectively and in the mind of the decsionmaker alone.

As for the fifth implication, it is true that cost cannot be measured—not measured precisely, that is, whether by the decisionmaker or someone else. But measureability itself is evidently what is at issue, not the admitted imprecision of measurement of cost, as of other economic magnitudes. The money costs of producing a definite amount of some product, or the marginal money cost of its production, can indeed be estimated. Estimates of money cost take into account, in particular, the prices multiplied by their quantities of the inputs requried to produce specified amounts of marginal amounts of the good in question. True cost accounting has no objective and infallible rules and must employ conventions. For this and other reasons, estimates of money cost are just that—estimates. But they are not totally arbitrary; they are not meaningless.

Money costs of production, as well as the input prices that enter into estimating them, play a vital role in conveying information to particular business decisionmakers about conditions in other sectors of the economy. Money costs and prices reflect—do not measure precisely, but reflect—the values and perhaps even the utilities attributed by consumers to the goods and services whose production is foregone to make the required inputs available to the particular line of production whose money costs are in question. (Money costs and factor prices also reflect, as noted above, the preferences and attitudes of workers and investors.)

It is therefore subversive to the understanding of the logic of a price system to maintain that cost is entirely subjective, falls entirely on the decisionmaker, and cannot be felt by anyone else.

Perhaps this risk of subversiveness is being run in a good cause. A healthy skepticism is in order about socialism, nationalization, and the imposition of cost rules on nationalized and private enterprises. However, we should beware of trying to obtain substantive conclusions from methodological preconceptions. Sound conclusions and policy judgments incur discredit from association with questionable verbal maneuvers.

Valid subjectivist insights join with the fact that general equilibrium never actually prevails in recommending skepticism about policies that would unnecessarily impose imitation markets or the mere feigning of market processes. The fact of disequilibrium prices does not, of course, recommend junking the market system in favor of something else. Market prices, although not precise indicators of the trade-offs posed by reality, are at least under the pressures of supply and demand and entrepreneurial alertness to become more nearly accurate measures.

The recommended skepticism does have some application, however, with regard to compensation for seizures under eminent domain, damage awards in tort cases, and the development of case law. It also has some application with regard to benefit–cost studies. Personal rights, not such exercises, should of course dominate many policy decisions.

Again, though, I want to warn against overstatement. Admittedly, costs and benefits are largely subjective, market prices are at disequilibrium levels, and other bases of making estimates are innaccurate also. But what is to be done when some decision or other has to be made—about a new airport, a subway system, a dam, or a proposed environmental regulation? Does one simply ramble on about how imponderable everything is, or does one try in good faith to quantify benefits and costs? Of course the estimates will be crude, even very crude, but perhaps the preponderance of benefits or costs will turn out great enough to be unmistakable anyway. In any case, expecting the advocates of each of the possible decisions to quantify their assertions and lay them out for scrutiny will impose a healthy discipline on the arguments made. It will weaken the relative influence of sheer poetry, oratory, demagogy, and political maneuvering.

My last example of subjectivism exaggerated and abused is what even some members of the Austrian school have identified as a "nihilism" about economic theory. Nihilistic writings stress the unknowability of the future, the dependence of market behavior on divergent and vague and ever-changing subjective expectations, the "kaleidoscopic" nature of the economic world, and the poor basis for any belief that market forces are tending to work toward rather than away from equilibrium (if, indeed, equilibrium has any meaning). Some of these assertions are relevant enough in particular contexts, but ultrasubjectivists bandy them sweepingly about as if willing to cast discredit not merely on attempts to foretell the future but even on scientific predictions of the if-this-then-that type. It is hard to imagine why an economist who thus wallows in unknowability continues to represent himself as an economist at all. (One hunch, he may think he has an all-purpose methodological weapon for striking down whatever strand of analysis or policy argument he happens not to like. But then his own analysis and arguments—if he has any—would be equally vulnerable.)

There is no point trying to conceal from knowledgable Austrian readers what economist I particularly have in mind, so I'll refer to the writings of Ludwig Lachmann listed in the references (including his articles in Dolan 1976 and Spadaro 1978), as well as Lachmann's admiration of Shackle's writings on the imponderability of the future. Also see O'Driscoll's refreshing criticism (in Spadaro 1978, especially pp. 128–134) of Lachmann for practically repudiating the concepts of the market's coordinating processes and of spontaneous order.

Most recently, Lachmann has shown evident delight in the phrase "dynamic subjectivism." "[A]t least in the history of Austrian doctrine, subjectivism has become progressively more dynamic" (1985, p. 2). "To Austrians, of all people, committed to radical subjectivism, the news of the move from static to dynamic subjectivism should be welcome news" (1985, pp. 1–2).

The word "committed" is revealing. Instead of the scientific attitude, Lachmann evidently values commitment—commitment to a doctrine or to a methodology. Recalling Fritz Machlup's essay on "Statics and Dynamics: Kaleidoscopic Words" (1959/1975), I wish Machlup were alive today to heap onto "dynamic subjectivisum" the ridicule it deserves.

Concluding Exhortations

As Gustav Cassel wrote in a book first published over sixty years ago, it was an absurd waste of intellectual energy for economists still to be disputing whether prices were determined by objective factors or subjective factors (1967, p. 146). Referring to interest theory in particular, Irving Fisher (1930, p. 312) called it "a scandal in economic science" that two schools were still crossing swords on the supposed issue. Prices, including interest rates, are determined by factors of both kinds. As noted earlier, saying so does not mean identifying objective factors with the supply side and subjective factors with the demand side of markets, nor vice versa. Both sorts of factors operate on both sides.

For a grasp of how subjective and objective factors thoroughly intertwine in a system of economic interdependence, a study of the simplified general-equilibrium equation system presented in Cassel's (1967) chapter 4 is well worthwhile. The reader should pay attention, among other things, to the role of the technical coefficients, that is, coefficients indicating the amounts of each input used in producing a unit of each product. Cassel does not need to suppose, of course, that these coefficients are rigidly determined solely by nature and technology. On the contrary, an elaboration of his system can take account of how many of these coefficients are themselves variable and subject to choice in response to prices, which are themselves determined in the system of mutual interdependence.

Study of Cassel's chapter (or similar expositions) should also disabuse the open-minded reader of any lingering belief in unidirectional causality. Mutual determination of economic variables is a fact of reality; and no blanket prejudice against general-equilibrium theory, which does afford important insights, should blind one to that fact.

Of course, when one investigates the consequences of a specified change—say in tastes, technology, taxes, or a fixed exchange rate—it is not enough (nor, realistically, is it possible) to solve a general-equilibrium equation system with one or more parameters changed and then compare the new and old solutions. An adequate analysis traces out, perhaps even sequentially, the reactions of the persons invloved and shows the reasonableness of their theorized reactions from their own points of view. But insisting on such a causal analysis does not presuppose belief in monocausality. The specified disturbance does indeed impinge on a system of mutual determination. Both the new and old constellations of economic activities result from multidirectional interactions of a great many subjective and objective factors.

Austrian economists have important messages to convey about subjective elements that, on all sides, pervade market behavior, signals, and outcomes. Their insights have important implications for policy. It is a shame to impede communication by remarks about purely subjective value theory, pure-time-preference interest theory, and the alleged fallacy of multidirectional causality.

Austrians cannot really mean what such remarks, taken literally, convey. They mislead and repel people outside the inner circle. The main goal of the Austrians is presumably not to recite slogans that reinforce cozy feelings of camaraderie among members of an elite. Instead, their goal, shared with other economists who wish well for mankind, is presumably to gain and communicate understanding of economic (and political) processes in the world as it is, has been, and potentially could be. They want to extend and communicate such knowledge so as to increase whatever chance there may be that man's deepest values will ultimately prevail. Respect for the straightforward meanings of words will aid in that endeavor.

Besides shunning deceptive slogans, Austrian economists should beware of surrounding their doctrines with a fog of methodological preachments, preachments suggestive, moreover, of pervasive sniping and sour grapes (as, for example, about the elegant formal theory that some other economists rightly or wrongly delight in). Above all, Austrians should avoid discrediting the sound core of their doctrine by contaminating it with bits of downright and readily exposable error (or what comes across as error on any straightforward reading of the words used). Austrians have positive contributions to make and should make them.

References

James M. Buchanan. *Cost and Choice.* Chicago: Markham, 1969.

James M. Buchanan and G.F. Thirlby, eds. *L.S.E. Essays on Cost.* New York: New York University Press, 1981 (first published 1973).

Gustav Cassel. *The Nature and Necessity of Interest.* New York: Kelley, 1971 (first published 1903).

Gustav Cassel, *The Theory of Social Economy.* Trans. by S.L. Barron from fifth German edition, 1932. New York: Kelley, 1967 (reprint of 1932 English edition).

Committee for Economic Development. *Achieving Energy Independence.* New York: CED, 1974

Edwin G. Dolan, ed. *The Foundations of Modern Austrian Economics* (includes, among others, articles by L.M. Lachmann and Murray Rothbard). Kansas City: Sheed & Ward, 1976.

William Fellner. *Towards a Reconstruction of Macroeconomics.* Washington, D.C.: American Enterprise Institute, 1976.

Frank A. Fetter. *Capital, Interest, and Rent.* Edited with an introduction by Murray N. Rothbard. Kansas City: Sheed Andrews and McMeel, 1977.

Irving Fisher. *The Theory of Interest.* New York: Kelley, 1970 (first published 1930).

S. David Freeman. *Energy: The New Era.* New York: Walker, 1974.

Roger Garrison, "Waiting in Vienna," pp. 215–226 in Mario J. Rizzo, ed., *Time, Uncertainty, and Disequilibrium.* Lexington, Mass.: Lexington Books, 1979.

Henry George. *The Science of Political Economy.* New York: Schalkenbach Foundation, 1941 (first published in 1898).

Friedrich A. Hayek. *The Constitution of Liberty.* Chicago: University of Chicago Press, 1960.

Friedrich A. Hayek. *The Counter-Revolution of Science.* Glencoe, Ill.: Free Press, 1952.

Friedrich A. Hayek. "The Use of Knowledge in Society." *American Economic Review* 35, September 1945, pp. 519–530.

J. Hirshleifer. *Investment, Interest, and Capital*. Englewood Cliffs, N.J.: Prentice-hall, 1970.

Israel M. Kirzner. "Pure Time Preference Theory: A Post Script to the 'Grand Debate.'" New York: New York University, manuscript, undated but early 1980s.

Ludwig M. Lachmann. *Capital, Expectations, and the Market Process*. Edited with an introduction by Walter E. Grinder. Kansas City: Sheed Andrews and McMeel, 1977.

Ludwig M. Lachmann. Review of Gerald P. O'Driscoll and Mario J. Rizzo, *The Economics of Time and Ignorance* (1985). *Market Process* (newsletter of Center for the Study of Market Processes, George Mason University), 3, Fall 1985, pp. 1–4, 17–18.

Stephen C. Littlechild. *The Fallacy of the Mixed Economy*. San Francisco: Cato Institute, 1979.

Fritiz Machlup. "Statistics and Dynamics: Kaleidoscopic Words." *Southern Economic Journal* 26, October 1959. Reprinted in his *Essays in Economic Semantics*, pp. 9–42. New York: New York University Press, 1975.

Alfred Marshall. *Principles of Economics*. Eighth edition. London: Macmillan, 1920, reprinted 1947.

Carl Menger. *Principles of Economics*. Trans. by J. Dingwall and B.F. Hoselitz. Glencoe, Ill.: Free Press, 1950 (first published in German 1871).

James C. Miller III, ed. *Why the Draft? The Case for a Volunteer Army*. Baltimore: Penguin, 1968.

Edward J. Mitchell, ed. *Dialogue on World Oil*. Washington, D.C.: American Enterprise Institute, 1974.

Robert Nozick. "On Austrian Methodology." *Synthese* 36, November 1977, pp. 353–392.

Murray N. Rothbard. *The Ethics of Liberty*. Atlantic Highlands, N.J.: Humanities Press, 1982.

Murray N. Rothbard, *Man, Economy, and State*. Two volumes. Princeton: Van Nostrand, 1962.

James R. Seldon. "The Relevance of Subjective Costs: Comment." *Southern Economic Journal* 48, July 1981, pp. 216–221.

G.L.S. Shackle. *Epistemics and Economics*. New York: Cambridge University Press, 1972.

Alexander H. Shand. *The Capitalist Alternative: An Introduction to Neo-Austrian Economics*. New York: New York University Press, 1984.

Louis M. Spadaro, ed. *New Directions in Austrian Economics* (includes, among others, articles by L.M. Lachmann, Gerald P. O'Driscoll, Jr., and S.C. Littlechild). Kansas City: Sheed Andrews and McMeel, 1978.

Thomas C. Taylor. *The Fundamentals of Austrian Economics*. San Francisco: Cato Institute, 1980.

Karen I. Vaughn. "Does It Matter That Costs Are Subjective?" *Southern Economic Journal* 46, January 1980, pp. 702–715.

Karen I. Vaughn. "The Relevance of Subjective Costs: Reply." *Southern Economic Journal* 48, July 1981, pp. 222–226.

Rutledge Vining. *On Appraising the Performance of an Economic System*. New York: Cambridge University Press, 1985.

Eugen von Bohm-Bawerk. *Capital and Interest.* Trans. by G.D. Huncke and H.F. Sennholz. Three volumes. South Holland, Ill.: Libertarian Press, 1959 (first published in German 1884, 1889, 1909–12).

Ludwig von Mises. *Human Action.* Second edition. New Haven: Yale University Press, 1963.

Ludwig von Mises. *The Theory of Money and Credit.* Trans. by H.E. Batson. Indianapolis: Liberty Classics, 1981 (reprint of 1953 edition).

Friedrich Waismann. "Verifiability," pp. 122–151 in Antony Flew, ed., *Logic and Language.* Anchor edition. Garden City, N.Y.: Doubleday, 1965.

Leland B. Yeager. "Balance-of-Payments Cure Worse than the Disease." *Commercial and Financial Chronicle* 202, no. 2 September 1965, pp. 3, 29.

Leland B. Yeager. "Pareto Optimality in Policy Espousal." *Journal of Libertarian Studies* 2, no. 3, 1978, pp. 199–216.

Leland B. Yeager. "Toward Understanding Some Paradoxes in Capital Theory." *Economic Inquiry* 14, September 1976, pp. 313–346.

Wages, Prices, and Employment: Von Mises and the Progressives

Lowell Gallaway
Richard K. Vedder

T here was a watershed in the history of economic ideas in the twentieth century, particularly ideas dealing with the relationships, in the aggregate, between money wage rates, price levels, and employment. This watershed occurred not quite a third of the way through the century and was derivative from the dramatic sequence of events known as the Great Depression. Economic thinking, in general, has never been the same since those years, especially in the United States, where, between 1929 and 1933, the unemployment rate rose from 3.2 to 24.9 percent, while output, in real terms, fell by about one-third.[1] Because of these developments, the Great Depression is often cited as a classic example of the failure of a capitalist economy to provide full employment of its resources, especially labor. Not surprisingly, that alleged failure triggered one of the most vigorous debates in the history of economic affairs, a debate that can be understood more fully if it is considered in the context of the state of thinking about the causes of unemployment on the eve of the Great Depression.

As the decade of the 1920s wound down, the dominant explanation for the occurrence of unemployument was the classical one, perhaps best represented in the writings of the British economist A.C. Pigou who, in his *Industrial Fluctuations* (1927), states that sufficiently flexible wages would "abolish fluctuations of employment altogether."[2] Even more explicit (although published in 1933 after the onset of the depression) is a passage from his *Theory of Unemployment* in which he argues:

> With perfectly free competition . . . there will always be at work a strong tendency for wage rates to be so related to demand that everybody is employed. . . . The implication is that such unemployment as exists at any time is due wholly to the fact that changes in demand conditions are continually

A substantial portion of the work presented here was accomplished while the authors were Liberty Fund Fellows in residence at the Institute for Humane Studies, Menlo Park, California. This article is being expanded considerably into a book, *Unemployment and the State*, to be published by the Pacific Institute for Public Policy Research in San Francisco.

taking place and that frictional resistances prevent the appropriate wage adjustments from being made instantaneously.[3]

With the Pigovian, or classical, argument lay the germ of the controversy to follow. The relationship between wage rates and employment envisaged by Pigou implied that unemployment was the result of real wage rates being too high (greater than their equilibrium level), suggesting that the solution to high levels of unemployment was a reduction in money (and real) wage rates.[4]

As a generalized explanation of the source of and remedy for unemployment, the classical analysis was found objectionable by many, some contesting it on theoretical grounds and others objecting for moral reasons. For example, within the broad fraternity of economists, there were those who felt that when dealing with the overall, or aggregate, economy, postulating an inverse relationship between real wage rates and employment was totally inappropriate in that it reversed the true direction of response. This argument, one variant of a long line of underconsumptionist ideas, had a wide range of appeal. The British economist John A. Hobson had espoused underconsumptionism beginning in the late nineteenth century; in 1923, he restated his position in *The Economics of Unemployment,* noting with disapproval that, "in depressed trade, with general unemployment, businessmen have considerable support from economists in calling for cuts in real wages."[5] In declaiming against the notion of wage cuts during times of high unemployment, Hobson emphasized the importance of the functional distribution of income in the determination of levels of output and employment, arguing that higher levels of wage rates were necessary to insure the existence of the level of consumption required to produce the full employment of labor. Thus, the cutting of wage levels in a time of depression would actually worsen the unemployment problem according to Hobson.

We should add that Hobson's was not the only form of underconsumptionist theory. W.T. Foster and W. Catchings proposed another variant, as did the famous Major Douglas.[6] However, Hobson was the most explicit in emphasizing the importance of wage rates as a determinant of levels of consumption. Thus, his theorizing stands in sharpest contrast to the classical view.

Underconsumptionism such as Hobson's would be expected to have had a rather substantial degree of popularity among trade unionists and the political left. In addition, though, it also had a remarkable vitality among American businessmen and supposedly, conservative politicians. Murray Rothbard has argued that:

As early as the 1920's, "big" businessmen were swayed by "enlightened" and "progressive" ideas, one of which . . . held that American prosperity was *caused* by the payment of high wages instead of the other way around. . . . By the time of the depression . . . businessmen were ripe for believing that lowering wage rates would cut "purchasing power" (consumption) and worsen the depression.[7]

Supporting Rothbard's view are the public pronouncements of certain major American business figures when faced with the prospect of the Great Depression. Henry Ford, for one, speaking in late November 1929, said:

> Nearly everything in this country is too high priced. The only thing that should be high priced in this country is the man who works. Wages must not come down, they must not even stay on their present level; they must go up.
>
> And even that is not sufficient of itself—we must see to it that the increased wages are not taken away from our people by increased prices that do not represent increased values.[8]

Ford's remarks were made in conjunction with a meeting of himself and other American business leaders at a White House conference convened by President Herbert Hoover. The meeting's conclusions were summarized in the following press release quoted in the *New York Times*:

> The President was authorized by the employers who were present at this morning's conference to state on their individual behalf that they will not initiate any movement for wage reductions, and it was their strong recommendation that this attitude should be pursued by the society as a whole.
>
> They considered that, aside from the human consideration involved, the consuming power of the country will thereby be maintained.[9]

The conference from which these statements emerged was one of a series Hoover convened in November and December 1929, for the purpose of instituting what he perceived to be a new departure in dealing with the phenomenon of the business cycle—in his own words, a "program unparalleled in the history of depressions in any country and any time." Hoover believed in the efficacy of the federal government as a mechanism for the coordination of economic activity. He was an interventionist who, among other things, found morally and intellectually unacceptable the classical means of dealing with earlier incidents of depressed economic conditions. He termed it the "liquidation" of labor and he opposed it on two grounds. First, "labor was not a commodity: it represented human bones." Second, he found the underconsumptionist doctrines attractive; they had captured his mind.[10]

While the underconsumptionist hypotheses are intriguing, during the 1930s, the strongest attack on the classical view of the way to deal with unemployment came from within the orthodox economics establishment. In his *General Theory*, John Maynard Keynes challenged whether adjustments in money wage rates could be relied on to achieve full employment of labor.[11] The basis of this challenge was twofold. First, he questioned whether what Pigou called "frictional resistances" and what he treated as downward money wage rigidity would ever permit the money wage rate adjustments necessary to restore full employment. More important, though, Keynes and his explicators, perhaps most notably Abba Lerner, argued that even if this were not the case, whatever money wage adjustments took place would induce corresponding decreases in prices, leaving real wages (and output and employment) unchanged.[12]

If that were not enough, in an almost incestuous fashion, the Keynesian repudiation of the role of money wage rates as an adjustment mechanism at the aggregate level was capable of producing another round of underconsumptionist thought. As Paul Sweezy recalls, his reaction to the Keynesian argument in 1936 was that:

> [The] reasoning depended on the assumption of pure competition. . . . I asked myself how it would be affected if one dropped this assumption and substituted the more realistic one of generalized oligopoly. . . . [It] was here that the kinked demand curve came into the picture. I was not too much concerned with the demand curve as with the associated marginal revenue curve which of course would show not a kink but a gap. If the relevant cost curve passed through this gap, it could be raised or lowered without affecting output or employment. The next step was that higher incomes owing to a wage increase would then cause an increase in effective demand and hence in employment.[13]

Ultimately, the Keynesian attack on classicism took a variety of forms, such as liquidity traps and perfectly inelastic investment demand functions, but fundamental to all these were the already established premises that (1) the only important thing is aggregate effective demand and (2) money wage rates can be ignored.[14] The latter notion became enshrined in "progressive" economic thought of the post-World War II era in the United States. An almost classic statement of this position can be found in Peter Temin's 1976 attempt at assessing the relative importance of monetary forces in the Great Depression. In a brief, error-plagued discussion of the role of wage rates, he states:

> In the postwar debate over the Keynesian system, one of the dominant questions was whether an unemployment equilibrium was possible. *The consensus now seems to be accepted that in the long run it is not* (emphasis added).[15]

What Temin appears to mean, here, is that there is no unique equilibrium level of employment (or unemployment). Any money (or real) wage rate is potentially an equilibrium one. This position can be thought of as a neo-Keynesian view, for, to be fair to Keynes, he never would have espoused such a line of thought. In the *General Theory*, he specifically accepts the classical notion that unemployment is the result of real wage rates being too high.[16] Keynes's attack on the importance of wage rates centered on money wage rates usefulness as policy and not on whether there was an equilibrium real wage rate. The whole Keynesian framework, as envisaged by Keynes, was oriented toward prescribing ways in which the classical labor market equilibrium could be attained without relying on the money wage rate adjustment mechanism. It is the neo-Keynesians, such as Temin, who dismiss the concept of labor market equilibrium out of hand.

The neo-Keynesian or "progressive" view achieved rather widespread acceptance quite quickly. For example, when his classic *The Theory of Money and Credit* was republished in 1953, Ludwig von Mises felt compelled to address this issue in a section of an epilogue ("Monetary Reconstruction") which he wrote for the volume. In one of the more remarkable passages in the history of economic ideas, he addressed the subject, which he called "the full-employment doctrine," in a fashion that is succinct, cogent, and prescient, foretelling in an almost uncanny fashion the path the U.S. economy would follow beginning some ten years later. The passage is a mere three pages in length and one hesitates to quote selectively from it for fear of losing a portion of its full flavor. Yet, for the purposes of this article, one brief paragraph is especially important:

> The most characteristic feature of the full-employment doctrine is that it does not provide information about the way in which wage rates are determined on the market. To discuss the height of wage rates is taboo for the "progressives." When they deal with unemployment, they do not refer to wage rates. As they see it, the height of wage rates has nothing to do with unemployment and must never be mentioned in connection with it.[17]

Von Mises's complaint was registered just prior to the high tide of the neo-Keynesian view, which was to come in the 1960s, with the popularization of the Phillips curve. Interestingly, von Mises anticipated the Phillips curve discussion in his treatment of the full-employment doctrine by describing exactly what would happen in a world in which price levels were shocked upward by monetary policy and money wage rates adjusted upward, but with a lag. Specifically, he argued that as prices move upward more rapidly than money wage rates, real wage rates will fall and observed unemployment will decline, suggesting a negative relationship between the rate of change in prices and the unemployment rate—what would become known in a few years as a Phillips curve. However, von Mises viewed the fall in unemployment that results from this as a temporary aberration, arising out of a movement of real wage rates below their equilibrium level, a circumstance that will disappear as money wage rates fully adjust to the new level of prices and the equilibrium real wage rate is reestablished. This view anticipated Milton Friedman's 1967 Presidential Address to the American Economic Association.[18]

The von Misesian interpretation of the relationship between prices, wages, and unemployment was, of course, almost totally foreign to the mainstream of macroeconomic thinking when the Phillips curve relationship was announced to the world, primarily because of the prevalence of the view that there was no unique equilibrium wage rate in the labor market. In such a context, the "discovery" of the Phillips curve seemed to offer the possibility of empirically determining the "menu of policy options" available to the economy. In the mainstream view, every point on the Phillips curve was an equilibrium one. All that remained was to select the appropriate combination of unemployment and price inflation, presumably a political choice, and let the economists prescribe the set of macroeconomic policies necessary to achieve it. What with the burgeoning growth of modern high-speed data processing facilities, larger and larger macroeconometric models could be constructed and the process of producing the required sets of policy recommendations could be reduced to a simple mechanical procedure of running it through the model. The millenium had arrived. Or had it? Subsequent events, marked by the simultaneous existence of high rates of unemployment and price inflation, call into question the "optimistic" view that pervaded the 1960s.

The foregoing discussion suggests the extent of variation in perceptions of the relationship between wage rates and unemployment. Within the confines of economic orthodoxy, it took less than a half century for the pendulum to swing all the way from the classical view that, ceteris paribus, money wage rates and unemployment are positively associated with the Phillips curve notion that the more rapidly money wage rates are rising, the lower will be the level of unemployment. And, very recently, there is some evidence of a resurgence of interest in the role that money wage rates play in determining levels of unemployment.[19] About midway through this scenario of changing ideas, von Mises reaffirmed the classical view with his critique of the full-employment doctrine, an assessment that we find to be remarkably accurate. The remainder of this article will be devoted to presenting arguments to support our contention.

Wages in the von Misesian Framework

The basic concepts contained in the von Misesian view of the role of money wage rates are relatively straightforward. To begin, two forms of labor markets must be considered, one focusing on real wages and another dealing with money wage rates. In the real wage version, the demand for labor is determined by the marginal productivity of labor schedule, which derives from an aggregate production function relating output to the quality of capital and labor inputs. The supply of labor in the real wage labor market is determined by the leisure-real income preferences of individuals in the society and has the conventional positive slope. The real wage version of the labor market is depicted in panel B of figure 1.

On the money wage side, the demand and supply functions for labor are simple transformations of the real wage relationships. Assuming competitive commodity markets, the money wage labor demand curve is obtained by multiplying the real wage labor demand function by the price level, P. Similarly,

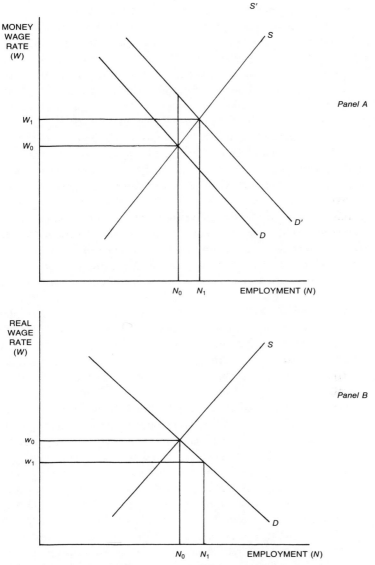

Figure 1. Wages in the von Misesian Framework

the real wage labor supply function can be translated into a money wage relationship by multiplying it by the price level workers *expect* to prevail, designated
as P_e, in the period of employment. If the actual price level and the expected
price level are identical, the money wage labor market equilibrium level of
employment will coincide with the real wage equilibrium level of employment.
These relationships are shown in panel A of figure 1.

Suppose, though that the actual price level deviates from the expected price level (that is, unanticipated price inflation or deflation occurs). In such a case, the money wage labor market equilibrium level of employment will not be consistent with equilibrium in the real wage labor market. For example, imagine a burst of totally unanticipated inflation which shifts the *money wage* labor demand function to the right (To D' in panel A of figure 1), increasing the level of employment from N_0 to N_1. The impact in the *real wage* labor makret, holding the technological conditions of production (the production function) constant, will be a movement down the labor demand curve to the level of employment, N_1, consistent with the *money wage* labor market equilibrium and the reduction in the *real wage* rate implicit in the inflation's being unanticipated. The new real wage rate is w_1 in panel B of figure 1.

If there were no subsequent adjustment in the money wage labor supply function, the new money wage equilibrium could be sustained indefinitely. However, such an assumption implies the existence of a permanent money illusion on the part of workers and a shift in the real wage labor supply function that will produce an equating of the quantities demanded and supplied of labor in that market. The more likely response is one in which the expected price level, P_e, adjusts upward, shifting the money wage labor supply function to the left, and moving the money wage equilibrium level of employment back toward its initial position. In fact, if P_e adjusts until it is equal to P, the money-wage supply function will have shifted to S' and the original equilibrium will have been restored, albeit at a higher price and money wage level.

From the standpoint of better understanding the discussion of the variety of notions about the role of money wage rates in macroeconomic affairs that introduced this article, this theoretical paradigm is quite useful. The complete adjustment process where P_e becomes equal to P can be thought of as the von Misesian-classical view of the way in which labor markets function. By contrast, the various forms of the "progressive," or neo-Keynesian perception of the world can be derived from a situation in which money wage rates remain unchanged or P_e either does not respond to movements in P or responds incompletely. The no-money-wage response case corresponds to the pure-money-wage rigidity hypothesis, while a lack of adjustment or partial adjustment between P_e and P implies that both money and real wage rates adjust, ex post, to create an equilibrium that is both different from the previous equilibrium and consistent with the new value of P. In short, in a world of incomplete adjustment between P_e and P, the equilibrium levels of both money and real wage rates as well as *the level of unemployment* are determined by the price level.

ERRATA

Page 6, line 27: FOR severaly qualify READ severely qualify
Page 8, line 27: FOR (Charlottesvilla, VA., Daily Progress.
READ (Charlottesville, Daily Progress,
Page 10, line 3: FOR satisfactions foregone READ satisfactions
forgone
Page 16, line 9: FOR utlimately to READ ultimately to
Page 16, line 43 and Page 17, line 1: FOR People do form
expectations while acting and interacting READ People do.
People acting and interacting
Page 22, line 39: FOR (Paragraph) Businessmen (and consumers)
READ (No parpgraph break) Businessmen (and consumers)
Page 24, line 19: FOR over investable READ over investible
Page 24, line 31: For These terrorists interpret READ These
theorists interpret
Page 26, line 3: FOR True cost accounting READ True, cost
accounting
Page 27, line 10: FOR the "kaleidoscopic" nature READ the
"kaleidic" nature
Page 27, line 17: FOR (One hunch, he READ (One hunch: he
Page 27, line 38: FOR "dynamic subjectivism" READ "dynamic
subjectivism"
Page 81, line 19: FOR Karl Menger READ Carl Menger
Page 82, line 27: FOR Economics systems READ Economic

$$\overline{\frac{P}{M}} \overset{=}{=} \overline{\frac{P}{R}} \qquad \frac{P}{M} = \frac{P}{R}$$

Page 93, line 8:   FOR $P_{M,is}$ $\frac{1}{P_r}$ READ $P_{M,is}$ $\frac{1}{P_R}$

Page 93, equation (2):   FOR $\frac{1}{P_R}$ READ $\frac{1}{P_R}$

Page 93, line 13:   FOR equation 1 READ equation (1)
Page 93, line 14:   FOR would aldo equal READ would also equal

Page 94, equation (4):   FOR MU_M MU_R READ MU_M MU_R
                                $\frac{1}{3} = 3.$ $\frac{1}{3} = 3.$

Page 94, equation (5):   FOR $MU_M = MU_R$ READ MU_M MU_R
                                9 9

Page 94, line 3:   FOR is explained by nothing
                   READ is explained by noting

Page 95, note 4:   FOR $\overline{T} = M$, and (ital.) $\frac{M}{P}$
                   READ $\overline{V} = \frac{M}{P}$, and (no ital.) $\frac{M}{P}$

Some Overall Empirical Evidence

The logic of the von Misesian-classical position seems clearly superior to any of the alternatives, it being difficult to envisage why a permanent money illusion on the part of workers should exist. However, the money illusion hypothesis cannot be dismissed out of hand. Rather, it needs to be evaluated by referring to the actual evidence pertaining to movements of money wages and prices. The clear implication of the von Misesian-classical framework is that, in a world in which the technological conditions of production and workers' leisure income preferences are constant, the continual adjustment of P_e to bring it into equality with P would result in the maintenance of a stable real wage rate. In effect, over time, the rate of change in the level of money wage rates would exactly equal the rate of change in the price level.

Through time, though, technological progress alters the conditions of production. With a reasonable set of assumptions about the nature of the aggregate production function, the impact of technical progress in the labor market is reflected in changes in the average productivity of labor.[20] Consequently, if the real wage rate moves in consonance with the average productivity of labor, there is a clear indication that P_e responds and adjusts in the von Misesian-classical manner to changes in the price level. Table 1 presents statistical measures describing the behavior of real wage and average productivity levels in the United States for various time periods during the twentieth century. What these data show is that for substantial time periods, real wage rates and productivity levels have moved virtually in unison, that is, in accord with the predictions of the von Misesian-classical view of labor markets. In all fairness, though, extended intervals can be found in which this relationship is not as precise as suggested by the wider time frames. In particular, during the 1930s, real wage rates advanced more rapidly than productivity. The period since 1973 has also been marked by a greater increase in real wage rates than in average productivity. The detailed movements are shown in table 2. Both of these periods are marked by a substantial escalation of the observed unemployment rate, exactly what the von Misesian-classical model of labor markets argues should occur. The clear suggestion is that there is a systematic relationship between the level of real wages (adjusted for productivity change) and the level of unemployment.

The real wage–unemployment relationship for the United States can be explored more fully through the application of standard multivariate statistical analysis techniques. Table 3 describes the relationship between the level of unemployment and the real wage rate that emerges from such an analysis for the periods 1901–41 and 1949–80.[21] In general, it appears that a 1 percent movement in the index of average real wage rates, adjusted for productivity change, will be associated with about a seven-tenths of one percentage point

Table 1

Behavior of Wage and Productivity Measures, Various Periods, United States, 1901–73

Time Period and Wage or Productivity Measure	Index at End of Period (Beginning = 100)
1901–29: Average of annual and hourly real wage series	155.9
1901–29: Average of annual and hourly productivity series	156.0
1949–73: Bureau of Labor Statistics compensation per hour (real) series	203.0
1949–73: Bureau of Labor Statistics output per hour series	204.1

Table 2

Behavior of Wage and Productivity Measures, Various Periods, United States, 1929–82

Time Period and Wage or Productivity Measure	Index at End of Period (Beginning = 100)
1929–41: Average of annual and hourly real wage series	142.1
1929–41: Average of annual and hourly productivity series	124.0
1973–82: Bureau of Labor Statistics compensation per hour (real) series	110.1
1973–82: Bureau of Labor Statistics output per hour series	106.5

Table 3

Estimates of Statistical Relationship between Unemployment and Productivity-Adjusted Real Wage Rate, United States, 1901–80

	Change in Unemployment Rate Associated with a 1 Percent Change in Index of Adjusted Average Real Wage Rate
1901–41	0.73
	(0.08)
1949–80	0.72
	(0.12)

Source: Statistical appendix to this article.

Note: Values in parentheses are standard errors of the cited statistic.

change in the same direction in the unemployment rate. Thus, the greater the productivity-adjusted real wage rate, the greater the level of unemployment.

Historical Example (1): The 1920–22 Cycle

The von Misesian-classical paradigm is a useful one for interpreting and understanding several rather disparate periods in the history of U.S. economic affairs in the twentieth century. Begin with the sharp post-World War I recession, the business cycle of 1920–22. Measured by the Federal Reserve Board series on factory employment, this downturn begins in the second quarter of 1920.[22] By the third quarter of 1921 (six quarters into the cycle), factory employment levels have fallen to 71.1 percent of what they were in the first quarter of 1920. Beyond that point, employment begins to rise, by the fourth quarter of 1922, returning to 85.6 percent of its first quarter 1920 level. The annual national unemployment rates for 1920, 1921, and 1922 are 4.0, 11.9, and 7.6 percent, respectively.[23] By 1923, full recovery has been achieved and the overall unemployment rate averages 3.2 percent.

What happened in this business cycle? Basically, the productivity-adjusted real wage rate $w_r{}^*$) rose quite rapidly.[24] With first quarter 1920 equal to 100,, $w_r{}^*$ in the manufacturing area soared to 150.3 by second quarter 1921, primarily because the price level fell precipitously between 1920 and 1921. The Bureau of Labor Statistics (BLS) wholesale price index fell by 36.5 percent in this interval, a decline that was only partially matched by a fall in money wage rates. BLS data indicate manufacturing hourly wage rates fell by only about 13 percent between 1920 and 1921. The sharp rise in real wage rates produced by this combination of price and money wage rate changes was only partially offset by a rise in the average annual productivity of labor of 3.3 percent.[25]

Midway through 1921, the price level stabilized and the recovery began as money wage rates continued to fall, in a lagged response to the drop in the price level, while productivity rose, lowering the productivity-adjusted real wage rate. Figure 2 shows the behavior of $w_r{}^*$ and employment in the manufacturing sector of the economy. The pattern is clear. As real wage rates begin to move back toward their equilibrium level, employment begins to rise. It is an almost classic case of labor markets responding to and correcting a substantial disequilibrium that was introduced by a destablizing shock to the price level.

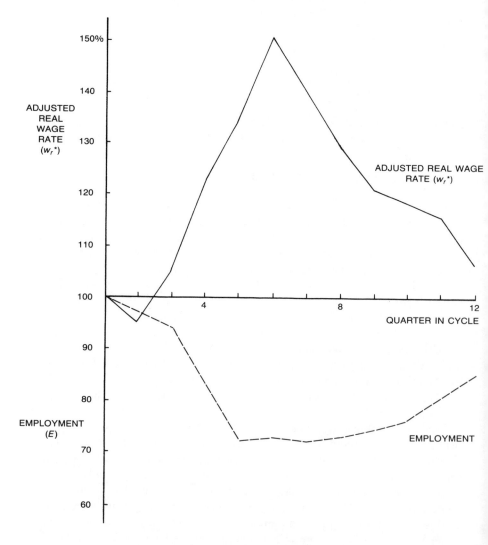

Figure 2. The 1920–22 Business Cycle

Historical Example (2): The Great Depression

If the von Misesian-classical labor market adjustment mechanism worked so well in 1921 in correcting the employment disequilibrium generated by the shock of an unanticipated large fall in prices, what happened during the Great Depression beginning at the close of 1929? Why did the unemployment rate rise as much as it did and why did the Depression persist as long as it did? The Great Depression began innocently enough with a combination of events that shocked labor markets out of equilibrium by increasing the productivity-adjusted real wage rate, w_r^*. On the one hand, the price level fell in 1930—not nearly as much as in 1921, only 3 percent—but, nevertheless, it fell. However, at the same time, the average productivity of labor also declined, by about 4 percent, unlike the 1920–21 downturn when it rose.[26] The combination of the productivity and price declines necessitated a compensating decline in money wage rates if a fall in employment was to be avoided. However, money wage rate decreases lagged developments in the price level and productivity sectors, much as in 1920, falling by less than 3 percent.[27] This operated to produce a disequilibrium in the real wage rate of 5 to 6 percent in 1930, depending on which money wage rate and productivity data series are used. (See table 4.) Predictably, unemployment rose from 3.2 to 8.7 percent.

It is interesting to speculate on how President Hoover's insistence on not cutting wage rates contributed to the emerging labor market disequilibrium. Rhetoric is one thing, but actual behavior may be something else. Indeed, some chroniclers of the history of this disturbed period have concluded that the public pronouncements of the Fords and Hoovers of the world did not have the effect of preserving wage stability. Perhaps betraying a predilection for underconsumptionism, Broadus Mitchell claims that, "The obligation [of industry] not to cut wages was . . . widely dishonored," and Arthur Schlesinger, Jr., states that, "The entire wage structure was apparently condemned to disintegration."[28]

Table 4
Unemployment Rate and Indexes of Consumer Prices, Money Wages, Productivity, and Productivity-Adjusted Real Wages, United States, 1929–33

		Indexes (1929 = 100)						
			Money Wages		Productivity		Productivity-Adjusted Real Wage	
	Unemployment Rate	Consumer Prices	Annual	Hourly	Annual	Hourly	Annual	Hourly
1929	3.2 %	100.0	100.0	100.0	100.0	100.0	100.0	100.0
1930	8.7	97.3	97.4	98.4	94.8	96.3	106.7	105.0
1931	15.9	88.6	90.4	94.4	94.4	97.1	111.4	109.7
1932	23.6	79.6	80.1	82.4	81.8	93.4	118.5	110.1
1933	24.9	75.4	73.3	82.6	87.6	91.6	117.0	119.6

That wages fell, ultimately, is not to be questioned. The Hoover policies could not be pursued indefinitely. What is more important is the timing of the wage decreases. The issue is whether the Hoover recipe delayed the onset of money wage adjustments sufficiently to exacerbate the disequlibrium and increase the severity of the Great Depression. The evidence is persuasive that this is the case. The average hourly earnings of production workers in manufacturing declined from 56 cents in 1929 to only 55 cents in 1930; in bituminous coal mining, average hourly earnings stayed constant at 66 cents in 1930; and in both the building and printing trades, union wage scales actually increased in 1930.[29] At a more detailed level, a monthly wage index compiled by the Federal Reserve Bank of New York (reported by Lionel Robbins) shows almost no movement in money wage rates from the fourth quarter of 1929 through the second quarter of 1930.[30]

Contrast this pattern with that of the 1920–21 downturn. In both cycles, industrial production peaked at midsummer before the onset of the decline. In both cycles, the decline was precipitous, 27.5 percent from July 1920 to July 1921 and 21.3 percent from June 1929 to July 1930.[31] However, as noted earlier, in the 1920–21 case, money wage rates fell by 13 percent, setting the stage for the sharp recovery that began in August 1921. One of the factors cited by Benjamin Anderson in explaining this recovery is "a drastic reduction in the costs of production."[32] How these costs were reduced is clear—money wage rates were cut, something that did not occur in the early days of the Great Depression. For example, according to data compiled by the National Industrial Conference Board, hourly wage rates for unskilled male labor fell more between 1920 and 1921 than they declined throughout the Great Depression.[33]

The clear implication seems to be that the money wage rate adjustment process was distinctly different during the Great Depression compared to the 1920–21 decline in business activity. Apparently, Herbert Hoover's goal of maintaining levels of money wage rates was achieved, at least temporarily. It is worth noting that not only did the Hoover policies call for maintaining wages in order to sustain purchasing power but, in addition, they advocated a similar departure with respect to dividends. Amazingly, at a time when corporate profits were falling rapidly, dividends were relatively unchanged, while undistributed corporate profits turned *negative*. Anderson remarks, "The poor old St. Louis and San Francisco Railroad, impressed with its duty to keep purchasing power high, proceeded to declare its preferred dividend a full year in advance—with unsatisfactory consequences."[34]

The course of the onset of the Great Depression can be traced in a more detailed fashion by employing the data series referred to in the discussion of the 1920–22 business cycle. Using Federal Reserve Board information on factory employment and estimates of productivity-adjusted real wages in manufacturing, it is possible to observe the same pattern of wage and employement changes that marked the 1920–21 downturn in the business cycle. It began in the fourth quarter of 1929. By the fourth quarter of 1930, factory employment had fallen to 78.7 percent of its third quarter 1929 level. Accompanying this was a 26.7 percent rise in adjusted real wage rates in the industrial sector.[35]

Up to this point, the 1920–21 cyclical downturn and the Great Depression are quite similar in nature. Unanticipated exogenous shocks of the price level and productivity variety have displaced the real wage rates upward from its equilibrium level, resulting in a rise in unemployment. In the case of 1921, the price level stabilized, money wage rates continued to adjust downward, and recovery began. However, during the Great Depression, the price level did not stabilize. Rather, a secondary price shock occurred that ultimately (by 1933) drove the price level down to 75 percent of its 1929 value. Milton Friedman and Anna Schwartz ascribe this secondary (as well as the primary) price shock to the policies of the Federal Reserve Board.[36]

While the Friedman-Schwartz argument is intriguing, there is an alternative explanation that builds on the contribution of Hoover's underconsumptionist policies to delaying the normal adjustment process. A good case can be made that the failure of labor markets to adjust during the first year of the Great Depression had very important second-round effects that contributed to the sharp decline in output and rise in unemployment noted in 1931 and 1932. For example, the financial crisis, beginning in full force in 1931, can easily be attributed to the failure of labor markets to adjust in 1930. In turn, that financial crisis led to an unanticipated sharp decline in the stock of money that brought about equally unanticipated deflation, deflation that complicated the process of labor market adjustment even further, and, in fact, contributed to higher real wages and interest rates in 1931 and 1932.

By maintaining money wages in the face of falling productivity and prices, businesses encountered a massive profit squeeze by mid-1930. Before-tax corporate profits fell some 63 percent from 1929 to 1930 and, given that dividends were maintained at essentially their 1929 levels, undistributed corporate profits fell from $2,820 million in 1929 to a *negative* $2,613 million the following year.[37] Whereas, in mid-1929, less than 6 percent of firms surveyed by First National City Bank of New York were losing money, by the third quarter of 1930, the proportion of losers had increased to 29 percent and a large percent of the remainder were not covering dividend payments.[38] Profits in the second quarter of 1930 are estimated to have been less than half of what they were but nine months earlier.[39]

By mid-1930, the profit squeeze was beginning to be noticed by the financial community. One immediate effect was a sharp decline in new capital financing. New capital issues averaged $810 million a month in the first half of 1930, but fell more than 55 percent to $362 million a month in the last half of the year.[40] Stock prices, which were higher in May 1930 than in November 1929, fell 36 percent between May and December, a greater decline than observed in the so-called "great crash" of late 1929.[41]

The financial squeeze that led to a decilne in demand for corporate equities led to a similar decline in the attractiveness of corporate debt. An increasing inability of buisinesses to cover debt obligations from cash flow led to growing lender hesitancy in making loans, which manifested itself in higher risk premiums on loans to business. What Ben Bernanke calls the "cost of credit intermediation" began to increase sharply.[42] Bernanke observes that the yields of middling-quality corporate debt (Baa bonds) were about 2.5 percent higher than on high-quality U.S. government bonds in both late 1929 and mid-1930, but that the differential rose more than 30 basis points every month in the last quarter of 1930, with the differential of 2.41 percentage points in September widening to 3.49 percentage points by December, and, then, to more than 4 percentage points by the summer of 1931.[43] More importantly, the deterioration in corporate balance sheets increased the proportion of firms with debt classified as being of low or middling quality and a corresponding decrease in the proportion of firms with high-quality debt ratings. As a consequence, the risk premiums paid by U.S. corporations on new debt probably rose far more than 100 basis points in 1930 and even more in 1931. The real price of financial capital was rising even faster, as accelerating deflation, beginning in late 1930, raised real interest rates substantially. Rising government borrowing to finance the Hoover fiscal program in 1931 added to interest rate pressures and the crowding out of private investment.[44]

The impact of the decline in corporate profitability on the supply of savings and loanable funds was devastating, as table 5 documents. Savings fell roughly 40 percent between 1929 and 1930, with nearly 90 percent of the decline attributable to the decrease in corporate undistributed profits. Savings fell again, by another 40 percent, in 1931, with about half the decline resulting from the worsening corporate profitability picture and 30 percent of it due to the shift in deficit financing by the federal government. The sharp fall in savings contributed to a massive increase in real interest rates and the real cost

Table 5
Savings in the United States, 1929–31
(in $ billions)

Form of Savings[a]	1929	1930	1931
Personal savings	$4.2	$3.4	$2.6
Capital consumption allowances	7.9	8.0	7.9
Corporate retained earnings	2.8	−2.6	−4.9
Net federal savings[b]	0.7	0.7	−0.6
Total	15.6	9.5	5.0

Source: U.S. Department of Commerce, Bureau of Economic Analysis.

[a]State and local governmental savings are excluded.

[b]As measured by the change in the public debt; a reduction in the national debt is viewed as positive savings.

of financial capital.[45] This helps explain the drop of 53 percent in nonresidential fixed investment between 1929 and 1931.[46]

It is important to note that the deterioration in corporate profits began long before the banking crisis emerged. The sum of bank deposits and currency in October 1930 was within 3 percent of the level prevailing in September 1929, before the stock market crash.[47] A good measure of depositor confidence is the deposit/currency ratio, which tends to fall as depositors become wary of banks and convert deposits to currency. The deposit/currency ratio in October 1930 was the second highest monthly total ever recorded.[48] Fear of banks on the part of depositors clearly had not yet developed. Yet, retained earnings already had turned negative by October 1930, and the risk premiums associated with corporate lending already were rising.

In the year after October 1930, the banking crisis began in force. The deposit/currency ratio fell more than one-third from October 1930 to October 1931, a majority of the decline observed during the whole of the Great Depression.[49] The conventional wisdom is that the failure of the Bank of the United States on December 11, 1930, and some other bank failures, triggered a decline in depositor confidence leading to the shift from deposits into currency, a move that lowered bank reserves and forced monetary contraction.[50] Our alternative hypothesis is that the deterioration in corporate profits, in part explained by the wage inflexibility of late 1929 and early 1930, led to a decrease in the market value of business loans, wiping out much—possibly all—of the net worth of many financial institutions. Growing realization that bank balance sheets (which were generally based on book values) did not reflect true market valuations of assets led to depositor withdrawals that, in turn, caused the banking crisis. In this view, the banking crisis was a consequence of labor market maladjustment rather than the cause of a deepening of the Great Depression.

Is it reasonable to assert that the decline in the quality of business loans associated with falling business earnings, and also the decline in the value of mortgages and consumer loans associated with rising unemployment, caused a dramatic deterioration in the true financial condition of banks? The answer is clearly yes, as an example can illustrate. Suppose a long-term loan were made at 6 percent interest in 1929, but had that loan been made in late 1930, an 8 percent interest rate would have been required to compensate the lender for the greater risk associated with the diminished ability of the lender to repay. A $1,000 loan made at 6 percent in 1929 with a very long maturity date would have, by late 1930, a market value approaching $750, since the $60 interest payment (6 percent of $1,000) would be 8 percent (the risk-augmented rate) of $750.[51] On a short-term obligation, the decline in the market value would have been much less, but in any case some decline in market value would occur. Assume that, by late 1930, bank loans and investments, on balance, were worth 10 percent less than their stated market value. Considering the 36 percent decline in equity prices from May to December 1930, this seems to be a reasonable estimate of the actual decline in value. For all banks, for the entire year 1930, average loans and investments of banks were stated to be $59,080 million.[52] If the true value were 10 percent less, the overstatement is $5,908 million, an amount equal to 57 percent of stated bank capital for the year.[53] In other words, true bank capital would have been far less than half the amount stated. Moreover, these are average amounts, and many banks no doubt would have had much less real capital, and, in some cases, none. In a world before deposit insurance, bank capital was a reserve providing depositor protection. As that protection became increasingly fictitious in nature, a reasonable depositor response is the flight from deposits that characterized the crisis that began in very late 1930.

We wish to emphasize that this hypothesis regarding the banking crisis is tentative. Further research needs to be done. We have not exhaustively examined either financial records or historical accounts. Indeed, some evidence might be viewed as contradicting the hypothesis.[54] On balance, however, a preliminary examination of the available data supports the contention that the banking crisis was a result of the disequilibrium in labor markets that resulted from an adherence to the underconsumptionist pleas of President Hoover and leading industrialists. This is not to deny that the banking crisis aggravated the Great Depression. Quite the contrary. On this point, the evidence of Friedman and Schwartz is rather persuasive. The cause of the banking crisis, however, needs reexamination.

Whatever its source, the secondary wave of price declines had the effect of increasing the degree of maladjustment in labor markets, partly because they were accompanied by further drops in productivity, largely due to a decline in the nation's capital stock. Between 1929 and 1933, low levels of new investment in fixed capital produced a rapid deterioration in the capital stock, as much as one-fourth according to Kuznets—less, but still significant, if other sources are believed.[55] Collectively, these additional price and productivity shocks vitiated a downward adjustment in money wage rates that began in mid-1930. Between 1930 and 1931, average annual money wage rates declined by 6.5 percent; from 1931 to 1932, by 12.1 percent; and between 1932 and 1933, by 8.4 percent. All told, in the four years from 1929 to 1933, average annual money wage rates fell by about 27 percent, or slightly more than the decline in the price level (as measured by the consumer price index). However, this was insufficient to compensate for the combined impact of the price and productivity declines and the productivity adjusted real wage rate steadily advanced until, by 1933, real wages were almost 20 percent above their equilibrium level. (See table 4 for details.)

Referring again to the quarterly data on manufacturing employment and adjusted real wages, figure 3 shows quite clearly how 1929–33 differed from 1920–22. At the six-quarter mark in the two cycles, the 1920–21 downturn was the more severe of the two. In the 1920–22 case, the adjusted real wage rate

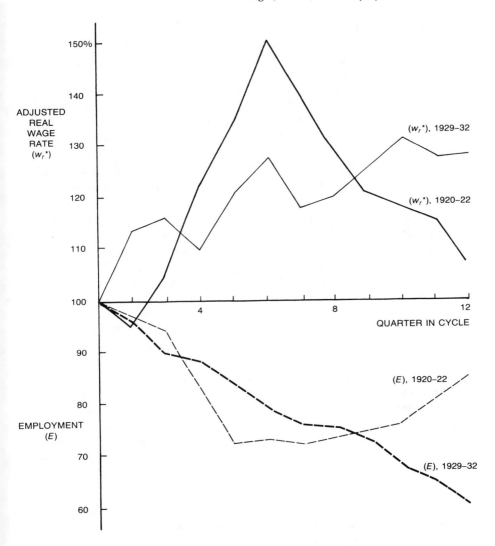

Figure 3. Comparison of 1920–22 Business Cycle with Early Years of Great Depression

began to fall at this point and continued to fall until equilibrium was restored and recovery achieved in 1923. The Great Depression, though, was marked by an aborted decline in the adjusted real wage rate. The critical point appears to be about seven to eight quarters into the Great Depression. In the seventh quarter, the adjusted real wage rate fell but, thereafter, it resumed a pattern of upward movement as the secondary price and productivity shocks impacted on the labor market. The result was that, after a brief slowing of the decline in factory employment, the economy, so to speak, "fell off the shelf" as the year 1932 began. At the twelve-quarter mark in the two cycles, recovery from the 1920–21 downturn was well under way while, in the Great Depression, the economy was still spiralling downward.

Having reached bottom in 1932–33, the U.S. economy begins to turn upward over the next four years. Unemployment falls from its 1933 high of 24.9 percent to 21.7 percent in 1934, 20.1 percent in 1935, 16.9 percent in 1936, and 14.3 percent in 1937. The speed of the recovery was slow, certainly much less rapid than in 1920–22, and this raises the question, "Why?" After 1933, the productivity decline is reversed and there are modest rises in the price level. (See table 6.) However, after a long period of declining money wage rates, they begin to rise in 1934, and, as they do, the extent of economic recovery is diminished. A simple exercise that employs the multivariate analysis of the relationship between unemployment and adjusted real wage rates reported earlier reveals that *had the real wage rate (unadjusted for productivity change) remained at its 1933 level, the unemployment rate in 1937 would have been 2.4 percent, rather than 14.3.* But, the unadjusted real wage rate did not stay constant. Between 1933 and 1937, average annual money wage rates rose by 20.5 percent (about 5 percent a year), while the price level only increased by 10.8 percent. Were it not for an 18.4 percent rise in the annual average productivity of labor, the recovery would have been even more minimal.

Why the surge in money wage rates? This is not what would be expected during a period of extremely high unemployment rates. For example, between 1936 and 1937, average annual money wage rates rose by 9.9 percent, despite unemployment rates in the 15 percent range. Some obvious possible explanations come rather quickly to mind. The period beginning in 1933 was one of substantial social and political experimentation with institutional arrangements that have an impact on labor markets. In June 1933, toward the end of the first hundred days of the New Deal, the National Industrial Recovery Act

Table 6

Consumer Price Index, Unemployment Rate, Money Wages, Productivity, and Productivity-Adjusted Real Wages, United States, 1933–38

			Wage or Price Index (1933 = 100)					
	Unemployment Rate	Consumer Prices	Money Wages		Productivity		Adjusted Real Wage	
			Annual	Hourly	Annual	Hourly	Annual	Hourly
1933	24.9 %	100.0	100.0	100.0	100.0	100.0	100.0	100.0
1934	21.7	103.5	102.0	119.1	102.7	110.1	96.0	104.5
1935	20.1	106.1	106.7	123.3	108.7	113.7	92.5	102.2
1936	16.9	107.2	109.7	125.0	117.2	119.5	87.3	97.6
1937	14.3	111.1	120.5	142.1	118.4	119.3	91.6	107.2
1938	19.0	109.2	116.8	146.1	117.9	116.9	90.8	114.5

(NIRA) was passed establishing the National Recovery Administration (NRA). At least two provisions of that legislation seem pertinent to this discussion. First, one of the conditons that was established in order for businesses to qualify for the right to display the blue eagle symbol of the NRA was adherence to a minimum wage of 40 cents per hour. Since average hourly wage rates in manufacturing in 1933 were only 44 cents, it seems likely that the minimum wage provision pushed up the wage rates of many relatively low-wage workers. Admittedly, the minimum wage rates were not a legislative mandate and, technically, were voluntary on the part of business. However, in the face of a widespread campaign urging consumers to buy at the sign of the blue eagle, the pressure on businesses to abide by such voluntary practices was substantial.[57] Certainly, the behavior of money wage rate levels in 1934 is consistent with the notion that the NRA codes had a positive impact on money wage rates. At the bottom of the Great Depression, with unemployment rates nearing 25 percent, average hourly money wage rates in manufacturing rose from 44 cents to 53 cents, slightly more than a 20 percent increase.[58]

The second portion of the NIRA with significance to labor market behavior is section 7(a), a seemingly innocuous statement guaranteeing workers the right to organize and engage in collective bargaining with employers.[59] This was the forerunner of the National Labor Relations Act of 1935 (the Wagner Act), which established as a matter of national policy the collective bargaining rights of workers. Presumably, an enhanced labor union presence will have an impact on wage levels in the unionized areas of employment. This seemingly was the expectation of the Congress. The second paragraph of section 1, the "Policy and Findings" portion of the law, reads:

> The inequality of bargaining power between employees who do not possess full freedom of association or actual liberty of contract and employers who are organized in the corporate or other forms of ownership association substantially hinders and affects the flow of commerce, *and tends to aggravate recurrent business depressions, by depressing wage rates and the purchasing power of wage earners in industry* and by preventing the stabilization of competitive wage rates and working conditions within and between industries (emphasis added).[10]

Congress was obviously under the influence of the underconsumptionist ideas of the time. However, there may be a substantial disparity between legislative intent and actual events. What evidence is there that the enactment of legislation such as the Wagner Act had any significant impact on wage levels? This issue is often debated, and there is a substantial literature dealing with the question of the effect of unionism on wage levels.[61]

Much of that literature focuses on the impact of unions on wages in the unionized sector of the labor market relative to wages in the nonunion sector. To give this research a greater historical dimension, consider the behavior since

1919 of a comprehensive measure of wage rates—compensation of full-time equivalent employees—in those private sector industries traditionally regarded as being unionized (mining, construction, manufacturing, and transportation, communications, and public utilities) vis-à-vis typically nonunionized industries (wholesale and retail trade, services, and finance, insurance, and real estate). The wage differential between these sectors, expressed as a percentage of the average wage for all workers (thus converting it into a relative wage differential), shows no trend in the decade 1919–29, averaging 4.97 percent and ranging from a low of a negative 1.91 percent (nonunion wages exceeded union wages in 1922) to a high of 7.22 percent in 1919. (See table 7.)

Over the four years that follow, the differential is negative in three, including a minus 5.89 percent in 1932. From that point, there is a consistent increase until the 1919 high is surpassed in 1936 (at 8.04 percent), followed by a 10.48 percent figure in 1937. This pattern of increases is not a transitory phenomenon.

Table 7
Union/Nonunion Wage Differential as a Percentage of Average Compensation, Full-Time Equivalent Employees, 1919–41

	Differential
1919	7.22 %
1921	5.77
1922	− 1.91
1923	5.65
1924	6.47
1925	3.97
1926	3.19
1927	6.62
1928	7.15
1929	5.60
1930	3.87
1931	− 0.23
1932	− 5.89
1933	− 0.73
1934	1.06
1935	3.65
1936	8.04
1937	10.48
1938	5.83
1939	10.32
1940	14.13
1941	23.17

Source: *Historical Statistics of the United States,* series D-685-719.

Note: In order to take account of changes in industrial mix through time, 1954 weights are used throughout to standardize the estimates of compensation per full-time equivalent employee. Thus, these estimates abstract from shifts in industrial structure.

By 1941, the measure of this differential has opened out to 23.17 percent. The trend continues after World War II to 24.45 percent in 1950 and 33.05 percent in 1960.[62] Formal statistical tests of these trends indicates a substantial change in the pattern of behavior of the union/nonunion wage differential, commencing at approximately the time the nation's basic policy with respect to trade unions shifted from being one of reluctant toleration to one of legal encouragement.

While this evidence is suggestive, a more formal statistical analysis would be reassuring. Again, multivariate statistical techniques are employed to measure the relationship between momey wage rates, on the one hand, and prices, productivity, and the extent of unionization in the labor force on the other.[63] The results confirm the existence of a statistically significant positive relationship between the portion of the labor force that is unionized and the level of money wage rates. Knowing this relationship, and knowing the impact of changes in money wage rates on unemployment (from the earlier statistical analysis of the causes of unemployment), changes in the extent of unionism can be translated into estimated changes in unemployment.[64] Table 8 presents the results of doing this for the post-1933 period. By 1938, the expansion of unionism brought about by the legislation of the mid-1930s is estimated to have caused the unemployment rate to be at least five percentage points greater than it otherwise would have been.

The rise in wage rates and unemployment attributable to the increase in trade unionization is not the only significant structural change occurring at this time. Various government policies were contributing to increasing labor costs in ways not measured by the standard wage rate statistics employed in our discussion. This was the era in which the great explosion of supplements to wages and salaries began. In 1929, supplements to wages and salaries were 1.2 percent of the total wage bill. Little change occurred in this relationship through 1935. In that year, supplements were 1.4 percent of the annual wage

Table 8
Estimates of Induced Unemployment, United States, 1934–40

	Cumulative Unemployment Attributable to		
	Growth in Unionization	Public Retirement System	Unemployment Compensation Costs
1934	0.40%	0.00%	0.00%
1935	0.91	0.00	0.00
1936	1.35	0.00	0.43
1937	4.65	0.60	1.09
1938	5.73	0.62	1.58
1939	6.28	0.66	1.55
1940	6.14	0.75	1.58

bill. In 1936, though, they rose to 2.4 percent; in 1937, to 4.2 percent; and, in 1938, to 5.1 percent.[65] At that point, supplements stabilized at about 5 percent of the total wage bill. The source of the rise in supplements is primarily in the form of employer contributions for social insurance. In 1935, they accounted for 25 percent of all supplements while, in 1938, they were 71 percent of supplements. Two new social programs old-age survivors insurance and unemployment insurance, explain this rise. The former represents about 17 percent of supplements in 1938, while the latter accounts for 43 percent of supplements. Thus, the newly emerging public retirement system produced about an 0.85 percent increase in wage costs, while the unemployment insurance system added another 2.20 percent. With the aid of the statistical model of unemployment described earlier, the impact on unemployment of these changes can be estimated.[66] Year-by-year calculations are shown in table 8. They indicate that, by the late 1930s, the impact of the increases in employer contributions for social insurance was to create about an addition. 2.2 percentage points of unemployment.

After four successive years of declining unemployment rates, 1938 saw a sharp rise in that statistic, from 14.3 to 19.0 percent. Various explanations for this reversal have been advanced, including a monetarist one focusing on the Federal Reserve Board's actions in increasing reserve requirements[67] and a fiscalist hypothesis which emphasizes tax rate increases and attempts at balancing the federal budget.[68] These are interesting possibilities, but there is an alternative of a different nature, namely, that the downturn of 1938 was, in large part, the product of movements in money wage rates in the two preceding years, particularly in 1937.[69] In that year, money wage rates rose by from 10 to 14 percent, depending on the wage measure used. A simple set of calculations illustrates the impact of these changes. If it is assumed that real wage rates had remained at their 1936 levels through 1938, not only would recovery have continued, but the unemployment rate would have been less than 10 percent in 1938.[70]

In retrospect, the von Misesian-classical framework for the interpreting macroeconomic events works remarkably well in explaining the events of the Great Depression. Just how well is indicated in figure 4, which compares the actual yearly unemployment rates with the values predicted by the statistical analysis used to evaluate the von Misesian-classical hypotheses. Clearly, these hypotheses will not only account for the initial decline in employment, but they also suggest why recovery from the Great Depression was so slow and why the economy experienced a recession in 1938.[71]

To summarize, basically, the decade of the 1930s can be characterized as a period in which the role of money wage rates as a determinant of unemployment was denigrated. Businesspeople, economists, and legislators often behaved as if money wage rates could be maintained with impunity at higher than

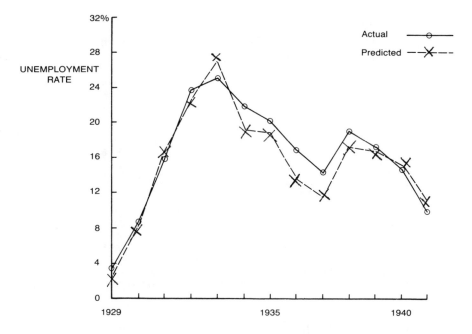

Figure 4. Unemployment during the Great Depression

von Misesian-classical equilibrium levels. That wage rates were in excess of equilibrium would seem to be beyond dispute. If the 1929 wage levels are viewed as being equilibrium ones, the data shown in table 9 indicate that wage rates were in substantial disequilibrium throughout the decade, initially largely as the result of exogenous shocks of the productivity and price level variety, but later as the product of changes in labor market institutions that imparted an upward bias to movements in money wage rates. The end result was a decade of misery for those who experienced the unemployment that ensued. However, for the more than 80 percent (on average) of the labor force who had jobs, life was not that bad. Average annual real wages rose by 10 percent between 1929 and 1939, and hourly real wage rates for unskilled labor increased an astounding 51 percent.[72] This occurred during a period in which real per capita gross national product grew by only 2 percent. A strong argument can be made that there was a redistribution of income from one sector of the labor force to another during the 1930s. More importantly, it appears that money wage levels did matter, and that the widespread belief that they did not had a traumatic impact on the U.S. economy and, ultimately, on the character of economic thinking.[73]

Table 9
Deviation of Money Wage Rate from Equilibrium,
United States, 1929–41

	Annual	Hourly
1929	0.0%	0.0%
1930	6.7	5.0
1931	11.4	9.7
1932	18.5	10.8
1933	17.0	19.6
1934	13.2	25.2
1935	8.1	22.4
1936	1.0	16.6
1937	5.1	28.3
1938	4.5	30.1
1939	4.0	28.9
1940	2.6	28.0
1941	4.1	28.5

Note: The equilibrium wage is viewed as the wage that would maintain the 1929 relationships between money wages, productivity, and prices.

Historical Example (3): The Great Depression in Britain

The Great Drepression was by most measures nearly as severe in Europe as in the United States. Is the von Misesian framework useful in explaining the European experience? The answer is clearly "Yes," and is confirmed by econometric testing. A large portion of the fluctuations in unemployment in a dozen European nations for which data are available can be explained by a model incorporating measures of changes in wages, prices, and productivity. Of special interest in this regard is the British experience, particularly since the economic environment of Great Britain at this time fostered the intellectual development of the Keynesian macroeconomic orthodoxy that in turn led to the neo-Keynesian or modern progressive view that "wages do not matter."

While ultimately the rising unemployment in Britain stemmed from the same labor market disequilibrium conditions that afflicted the United States, the scenario unfolded somewhat differently. To begin, Britain after 1920 was subject to very high unemployment, with the rate falling below 10 percent only in one year, 1927.[74] Yet for all the unemployment, real output rose over the decade at a rate that compared rather favorably with past British historical experience.[75] As Daniel Benjamin and Louis Kolchin have demonstrated, however, the opportunity cost of being unemployed was sharply reduced by extremely generous unemployment insurance payments enacted during this period.[76] Our own statistical analysis leads us to concur with Benjamin and Kolchin's endorsement of the views of Edwin Cannan, Lionel Robbins, Jacques Rueff, and

William Beveridge: namely, that the dole caused the unemployment problem, rather than exchange rate policies, deficiencies in British entrepreneurship, or other factors (as argued by Keynes and others).[77] In addition, however, Benjamin Anderson argues cogently that high wages imposed by postwar union militancy aggravated unemployment; our statistical findings are consistent with that viewpoint.[78]

While the Benjamin and Kolchin evidence convincingly explains why unemployment in the late 1920s typically exceeded 10 percent rather than perhaps 3 percent as was the case before 1913, their evidence does not explain why the unemployment rate doubled to more than 20 percent by 1932. The dole was not made more generous; indeed it was reduced as the Depression proceeded. Nor can one explain the rise in the unemployment rate in terms of evidence of underconsumption. It is interesting to note that between 1927 and 1932, when unemployment more than doubled, real consumption expenditures per capita actually *rose*.[79]

The von Misesian framework, by contrast, does explain most of the rise in unemployment. As table 10 indicates, however, the proximate causes of the labor market disequilibrium were rather different in Britain. While Hoover and other progressives delayed the adjustment of money wages in the United States, at least a partial wage adjustment eventually occurred that prevented the Depression from being far worse. In Britain, however, money wages were indeed inflexible downward, even in 1932 (explaining the emphasis on wage inflexibility in Keynes's work). Prices, however, were more flexible, falling significantly. Thus, real wages rose sharply, causing unemployment.

Table 10
Wages, Prices, and Productivity, United States and Britain, 1929–38

	Money Wages	Prices	Real Wages	Productivity	Adjusted Real Wages[a]
United States[b]					
1929	100	100	100	100	100
1933	73	75	97	83	117
1938	86	82	104	99	105
Great Britain					
1929	100	100	100	100	100
1933	95	85	112	111	101
1938	106	100	106	116	91

Sources: For the United States, see text. Britain: E.H. Phelps Brown and Margaret Browne, *A Century of Pay* (London: Macmillan, 1968); B.R. Mitchell, *Abstract of British Historical Statistics* (Cambridge: Cambridge University Press, 1976).

Note: 1929 = 100.

[a]Real wages divided by productivity.

[b]The annual wage data referred to in text are used.

Britain's comparative wage rigidity no doubt reflected the fact that it (unlike the United States at this time) had strong anticompetitive elements in labor markets, notably large and militant labor unions which only a few years earlier (1926) had called a general strike. Britain's deflation probably reflected a failure to allow normal increases in the stock of money, which, in turn, was likely the result of a futile attempt by the central bank to deflate, in order to maintain gold convertibility at $4.86 per pound. In light of even greater deflation in the United States, this British attempt was probably doomed, but the resultant unanticipated real wage increases contributed to higher unemployment.

To compare the United States and Britain during the downturn in the early 1930s, in both nations unexpected declines in prices contributed to an enhancement in real wages that aggravated the unemployment problem. In the United States, money wages were strictly downward for an inordinate period owing to the exhortations of Hoover and some members of the industrial elite, but belatedly money wage adjustments occurred. In Britain, however, these adjustments never occurred to any major extent, contributing significantly to the Depression. In Britain, labor productivity rose, in contrast to the United States and in contrast to the commonly accepted notion that downturns inevitably lead to a decline in aggregate demand which in turn causes a decline in productivity as labor adjustments lag output changes.

It is interesting that real output per person rose in Britain in most years in the thirties. Indeed, measured by output changes, there was no real Great Depression in Britain at all. The Depression was largely confined to the labor market. Unlike the United States, Great Britain did not stand completely still with respect to real output growth in the thirties.[80] Unemployment was high in Britain not because of demand deficiencies, but rather because monopoly elements in labor markets combined with inappropriate public policies (deflationary monetary policies and excessive unemployment compensation payments) to cause labor market disequilibrium.

Recovery came quicker and more robustly in Britain than in the United States. Whereas unemployment in Britain by 1937 had returned to the natural or normal rate of the 1920s, in the United States, unemployment was still more than three times the normal rate of the twenties.[81] The reason is comparatively simple: money wages rose much faster in the United States, especially for industrial workers, than in Britain. Indeed, real wages fell in Britain as the same comparative money wage rigidity combined with prices that rose to the levels prevailing in the twenties. In the United States, widespread new forms of government labor market intervention and growing anticompetitive institutional arrangements (labor unions) caused the real wage increase. Britain either already had these institutions and interventions established or did not institute them on a widespread scale as part of a progressive reform of the economy. As a consequence, Britain had returned to normalcy fully a year before Hitler invaded Poland.

Historical Example (4): The 1960s

Move forward roughly two decades in time. A.W. Phillips has observed his "loops," Richard Lipsey has refined them empirically, and Paul Samuelson and Robert Solow have given the relationship their blessing.[82] The Phillips curve lives and neo-Keynesianism is in its prime as a new U.S. political administration assumes the reins of power in 1961. What follows has often been interpreted, erroneously, as the finest example of "progressive" economic policy formulation at work. In reality, the period 1961–70 is a classic instance of the von Misesian-classical model in operation. Beginning in 1961, the sum of the rates of change in productivity and prices exceeds the rate of change in money wage rates as unanticipated price inflation is introduced into the economy in a systematic fashion. By today's standards, the amount of inflation in the 1960s seems minor. However, the important thing is its unanticipated character. Between 1961 and 1965, the consumer price level rises by about 5 percent and the sum of the rates of change in productivity and prices consistently exceeds the rate of change in money wage rates. By 1965, the productivity-adjusted real wage rate has drifted downward from its 1961 level by 3.3 percent. The decline in the adjusted real wage rate creates a profit wedge in favor of business and produces a 23 percent rise in the corporate profit share of national income.[83]

All this occurred because of the operation of a money illusion effect in labor markets. The real wage rate paid to labor rose less rapidly than did labor's average productivity, redistributing income from employees to employers. The result was an expansion of employment opportunities and a fall in the unemployment rate, with a lag of about one year.[84]

After 1965, though, the money illusion disappeared and the long-run labor market adjustment mechanism took hold. The rate of change in money wage rates then exceeded the sum of the rates of changes in prices and productivity, despite an escalation of the rate of price inflation to almost 5 percent a year. In 1969, the productivity-adjusted real wage rate surged back to its 1961 level, the corporate profit share of national income fell sharply; in 1970, a year later, the unemployment rate averaged 4.9 percent, 1.4 percentage points higher than in 1969. A graphic representation of these changes is shown in figure 5.

The 1961–69 experience is instructive. It illustrates how a mild burst of unanticipated inflation (about 5 percent between 1961 and 1965) can be used to push the unemployment rate temporarily below its equilibrium level by redistributing real income from workers to employers. However, the reduced unemployment is only temporary. As the longer-term labor market adjustment begins to operate, the income redistribution is reversed and the unemployment rate returns to a level that is more capable of being maintained on a permanent basis, that is, toward the equilibrium, or natural, rate of unemployment.

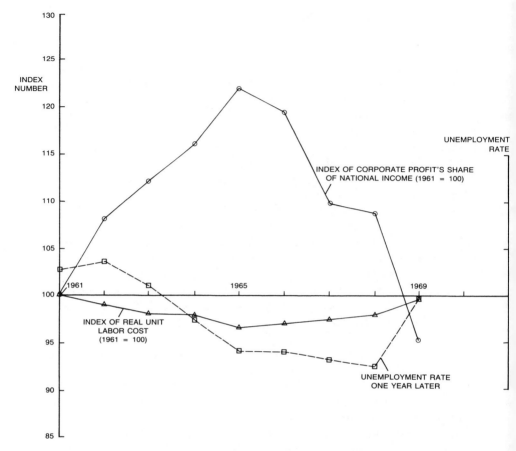

Figure 5. The Economics of the 1960s

Historical Example (5): Stagflation in the 1970s and 1980s

As the United States entered the decade of the 1970s, the phenomenon of stagflation emerged, a state of affairs in which, despite persistent amounts of price inflation, the unemployment rate remained at levels substantially greater than those occurring in the halcyon days of the mid-1960s, contradicting the predictions of neo-Keynesian macroeconomic thinking.[85] However, the events of this period are thoroughly compatible with the von Misesian-classical conception of economic affairs. The formal statistical analysis based on this framework explains the behavior of the unemployment rate in both the 1960s and 1970s quite well in figure 6. More specifically, unemployment rose in 1970 (4.9 percent) and 1971 (5.9 percent) in the face of an upward movement in

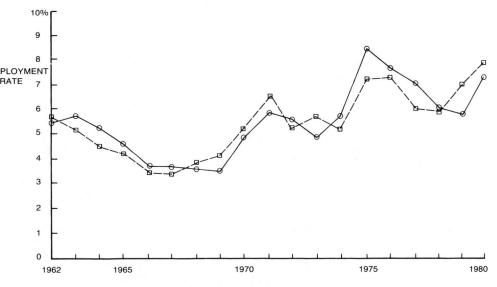

Figure 6. Unemployment, 1962–80

prices, measured by the implicit price deflator for gross national product (4.5 percent in 1970 and 4.4 percent in 1971). The source of the increase in unemployment was a quickening of the pace of money wage rate increases as inflationary expectations became pervasive in the economy.

Ordinarily, increases in unemployment produce a marked slowing of the rate of increase in money wage rates, but not in the early 1970s. Between 1969 and 1973, money wage rates advanced at an average of 7.1 percent a year, with a minimum of 6.5 percent in 1972, and a maximum of 8.0 percent in 1973. The steady escalation of the rate of price inflation during the 1960s was by then being reflected in the labor market in the form of pronounced inflationary expectations. All through the 1970s, the rate of increase in money wage rates showed a general upward trend until, at the end of the decade, it exceeded 10 percent. Further, the rate of increase in money wage rates began to diverge rather systematically from the sum of the rates of change in productivity and prices. Table 11 shows the data for the 1960–69, 1969–73, and 1973–79 business cycles, measuring from peak to peak. These data suggest an upward drift in the equilibrium real wage rate and a corresponding increase in the equilibrium, or natural, rate of unemployment, similar to the shift introduced in the 1930s.[86]

A rather likely explanation for the rise in the equilibrium unemployment rate is that workers' labor supply responses were changing in a fashion that affected the intensity of their job search effort, once they became unemployed, as well

Table 11

Rates of Change in Money Wage Rates, Prices, and Productivity, United States, 1960–79

	Mean Annual Rate of Change in	
	Money Wage Rates	Prices plus Productivity
1960–69	5.3%	5.3%
1969–73	7.1	6.9
1973–79	9.0	8.6

as their reservation wage (the wage rate below which they will not accept employment but will prolong the search process). A major factor in this regard is the existence of substantial unemployment compensation programs. The evidence is clear that the availability of unemployment compensation programs is positively related to the level of unemployment.[87] Also, there is a sizable body of research substantiating the premise that there is a predictable work incentive response at the level of the population as a whole to the availability of transfer payment income. Carl Brehm and Thomas Saving demonstrate this with respect to general assistance payments, as does Hirschel Kasper.[88] Further, in a more specific sense, the work of Benjamin and Kolchin, dealing with Britain between the two World Wars, is particularly supportive of this argument.[89] The critical concept is that accessibility to unemployment compensation benefits in the United States has been rising. Over the course of the 1961–69 business cycle, about two-thirds of the civilian labor force was in employment covered by unemployment compensation systems. Contrast this with the almost 80 percent in covered employment in the years 1974–79.[90]

In addition to unemployment compensation benefits, there are other social transfer payment systems to consider. The food stamp program did not exist in the 1960s. By the end of the 1970s, payments under this program amounted to over $6 billion annually.[91] Vendor medical payments more than quadrupled during the 1970s. All told, social welfare expenditures in the United States rose from being about 13 percent of personal income in 1960 to almost one-fourth of personal income at the end of the 1970s.[92] Such a growth in the relative importance of "safety-net" expenditures alters people's attitudes with respect to what is an acceptable job, producing an upward drift in the equilibrium unemployment rate.

Historical Example (6): Fourth Quarter 1982

Beginning in the second quarter of 1981, the rate of price inflation in the United States showed signs of declining. From mid-1981 to mid-1982, the annual inflation rate measured by the implicit price deflator for gross national product was 5.5 percent, compared to 9.5 percent in the previous year.[93] The drop was particularly acute in the first quarter of 1982, when the inflation rate fell to 3.8 percent. In this quarter, the rate of change in money wage rates was 7.3 percent, down somewhat from the previous year, but not by as much as the fall in the rate of price inflation. Since the productivity change in this quarter was −1.0 percent, the productivity-adjusted real wage rate rose sharply, portending a future rise in unemployment. Experimentation reveals that the lag between changes in the productivity-adjusted real wage rate and changes in unemployment is about three quarters. Thus, the behavior of money wages, prices, and productivity in the first quarter 1982, interpreted in the von Misesian-classical framework, predicted a significant rise in unemployment in the fourth quarter of 1982. The reality? The unemployment rate for all civilian workers rose from an average of 10.0 percent in the third quarter to 10.7 percent in the fourth quarter of 1982.[94]

What happened in 1982 is simple. An unanticipated decline in the rate of price inflation produced an upward movement in the productivity-adjusted real wage rate, just as the unanticipated decline in the price level between 1929 and 1930 produced a similar rise. Subsequent to this, labor market adjustment began to occur and the rate of change in money wage rates slowed from 7.3 percent to 5.6 percent by the fourth quarter of 1982. Accompanied by significant improvements in productivity, this had the effect of actually reducing the productivity-adjusted real wage rate, suggesting a decline in unemployment beginning in the first half of 1983.

Conclusion: Wage Rates Do Matter

The primary theme of this extended article is straightforward: "The level of money wage rates is a vital factor in macroeconomic affairs." This is not a new discovery. At one time, it was the prevailing orthodoxy. Alfred Marshall, Irving Fisher (at times), A.C. Pigou, Lionel Robbins, Jacob Viner, Alvin Hansen rather early on, and even William H. Beveridge, among others, expounded it.[95] But, it fell out of favor in the 1930s and, in the years since, has had little popularity within the mainstream of the economics profession, whose leaders espoused what von Mises called the "progressive" view in his 1953 remarks cited earlier. The view that wages do not matter spread far beyond the economics profession proper. It is a convenient attitude for political figures who do not wish to alienate the labor union establishment; it is one of those intuitively appealing propositions for many intellectuals with little training in economics. Popularity, though, is no substitute for logic and evidence. Evaluated in terms of the latter, the popular view that wages do not matter fares badly and, more importantly, the von Misesian-classical hypotheses appear to offer meaningful and profound insights into the nature of a wide variety of historical incidents in the United States during the twentieth century. It is unfortunate that these insights have largely been ignored, beginning with the 1930s.[96] Much mischief has been done by a failure to appreciate what the von Misesian-classical framework has to contribute, which takes us to a secondary theme of this article.

In recent remarks on the occasion of the Keynes Centenary published in *The Economist,* John R. Hicks makes the remarkable statement, "The ship needs continual steering."[97] This is a classic remark, especially from one who earlier in his career appeared to feel otherwise, in that it embodies quintessentially the refusal by many intellectuals to recognize the existence of a definable equilibrium or natural rate of unemployment to which the economy continually tends. The existence of this blind spot has had serious consequences. In the United States, it has contributed to the growth of the idea that the U.S. economy can be managed or fine-tuned with great precision in the short run. That philosophy had been confidently extolled at the start of the 1960s and it was clearly the prevailing mood all through that decade and the next.

However, looking back on this era from the perspective of the early 1980s, it is easy to question whether the optimism of the early 1960s was warranted. Compare 1980 to 1961. The unemployment rate in 1961 was 6.7 percent, to that time the highest rate for the post-World War II period. In 1980, it was 7.1 percent and rising, but still lower than it had been in 1975 and 1976. As for inflation, in 1961, the rate of price inflation was 1.0 percent. In 1980, it was 11.1 percent and had been as high as 13.0 percent in 1979. Real economic growth was adequate, but not spectacular by historical standards, running at 3.55 percent per year, just slightly less than the long-term historical average of about 3.6 percent a year. Even the interval of greatest economic growth in this period, 1961–69, showed only a rate of growth of 4.7 percent, compared, for example, to the 6.0 percent that marked a similar period, 1921–29. Or, take the period 1921–41, embracing the Great Depression of the 1930s. The real growth rate in that interval was slightly greater (3.60 percent) than it was in the two decades under discussion here.[98]

The rather mixed record of success in "managing" the U.S. economy between 1961 and 1980 raises the issue of whether, given the existence of an equilibrium rate of unemployment, short-term manipulation and control of economic variables have much to offer from the standpoint of improving economic performance. Perhaps, it may be postulated, the economy would do just as well, or even better, if national economic policy focused more on providing conditions that are conducive to long-term economic growth, rather than emphasizing the control of short-term economic conditions. To explore that possibility, the actual performance of the U.S. economy in the period 1961–80 can be compared with the results of a simulation of the economy that assumes no attempt at managing it in the short run, except for a 2 percent fixed rate of growth in the monetary base.[99]

Table 12

Comparison of Actual Performance of Economy with Simulation Assuming 2 Percent Rate of Growth in Monetary Base, United States, 1961–80

Performance Component	Actual Performance	Simulated Performance
Real growth rate	3.55%	3.57%
Average unemployment rate	5.22	5.38
Average rate of price inflation	4.73	0.78

A comparison of the results of the simulation with the actual performance of the economy is shown in table 12. The only substantial difference is in the rate of price inflation. Two decades of attempts at short-term management of the U.S. economy produced about 4 percent a year more price inflation with no appreciable effect on unemployment or the real growth rate, the latter two being determined by the underlying structural realities of the economy, that is, the forces that determine the natural rate of unemployment within the context of the von Misesian-classical theoretical framework. With a zero rate of growth in the monetary base, the comparison would be even more striking. Productivity gains would have been reflected in the form of falling prices and there would have been an era of price deflation (over 1 percent a year) rather than price inflation with, of course, little difference in the real level of economic performance.

Lest the foregoing remarks suggest that the rate of price inflation is totally irrelevant to the time path of the real economic magnitudes of a society, it should be emphasized that the simulations that have been reported assume no feedback between the price level and the processes of capital accumulation and technological change. What is evaluated is the usefulness of short-term attempts at managing the economy, given the level of labor productivity in the system. In the longer run, persistent price rises, especially an increasing rate of price inflation, are likely to have negative impacts on levels of saving and, ultimately, investment, thereby shifting a society to a lower economic growth path. For example, it is probably no accident that over the period 1973–82, productivity in the nonfarm business sector of the U.S. economy increased by less than 5 percent. And, for the last five years of that period, it actually declined very slighty.[100]

One last concluding remark. Von Mises, and others like him, were correct in rejecting the "progressive" view that the level of money wage rates does not matter. Not only is it important but, in conjunction with the levels of prices and productivity, it is the key to understanding patterns of variation in aggregate levels of employment and output. With the aid of the von Misesian-classical analysis, such disparate phenomena as high unemployment rates, low unemployment rates, high unemployment accompanied by inflation (stagflation), low unemployment in unison with inflation, swift economic recoveries, and aborted economic recoveries can be understood in an intelligent fashion. No special economics are needed for each situation. What other theoretical apparatus can make the same claim?

Statistical Appendix

The Unemployment Relationship

The unemployment rate (U) is explained in terms of variations in the levels of money wage rates, prices, and productivity—the factors that determine the productivity-adjusted real wage rate (w_r^*). For the period 1901–41, the following relationship has been estimated using multiple regression analysis:

$$U = 4.07 + \underset{(0.08)}{0.73} \; (w_r{}^*_{t-1})_A + \underset{(0.04)}{0.33} \; (w_r{}^*_{t-1})_H + \underset{(0.17)}{0.07} \; (\dot{W}_t)_A$$

$$+ \underset{(0.10)}{0.28} \; (\dot{W}_t)_H - \underset{(0.18)}{0.62} \; (\dot{\pi}_t)_A - \underset{(0.18)}{0.03} \; (\dot{\pi}_t)_H - \underset{(0.17)}{0.88} \; (\dot{P}_t),$$

$$R^2 = 0.92, \quad \overline{R}^2 = 0.91, \quad \text{D-W} = 1.25 \tag{1}$$

where $\dot{W}$ denotes the rate of change in money wage rates, $\dot{\pi}$ the rate of change in average labor productivity, and $\dot{P}$ the rate of change in the price level. The subscripts A and H denote, respectively, annual and hourly measures of wages and productivity.[101] The consumer price index is used as the measure of price level changes. The values in parentheses beneath the regression coefficients are the standard errors associated with the coefficients.

For the years 1949–80, a unified data set containing all the necessary information is available from the Bureau of Labor Statistics. Using it, the following regression equation has been estimated:

$$U = 4.79 + \underset{(0.12)}{0.72} \; (w_r{}^*_{t-2}) + \underset{(0.18)}{0.39} \; (\dot{W}_{t-1}) - \underset{(0.11)}{0.46} \; (\dot{\pi}_{t-1})$$

$$- \underset{(0.16)}{0.32} \; (\dot{P}_{t-1})$$

$$R^2 = 0.72, \quad \overline{R}^2 = 0.68, \quad \text{D-W} = 1.57 \tag{2}$$

In both regressions, w_r^* is expressed as a deviation from the mean value of its index number. In equation 2, all independent variables are lagged one year.

The Money Wage Adjustment Relationship, 1901–41

The von Misesian-classical framework implies that changes in money wage rates will reflect exactly changes in prices and productivity over time. A multiple regression equation embodying these relationships and a variable measuring the fraction of the labor force that is unionized has been estimated for the annual and hourly wage series used in the 1901–41 employment model for those same years. The results are:

$$W^H = 0.0114 + 0.622\ \dot{\pi}_H + 0.628\ \dot{p} + 0.132\ U^*$$
$$(0.157) \qquad (0.059) \qquad (0.043)$$

$$R^2 = .82, \quad \overline{R}^2 = .80, \quad \text{D-W} = 1.66 \tag{3}$$

and

$$W^A = 0.0157 + 0.381\ \dot{\pi}_A + 0.431\ \dot{p} + 0.113\ U^*$$
$$(0.189) \qquad (0.071) \qquad (0.052)$$

$$R^2 = .61, \quad \overline{R}^2 = .58, \quad \text{D-W} = 0.97 \tag{4}$$

where W denotes the level of money wage rates, $\dot{\pi}$ is the rate of change in the average productivity of labor, $\dot{p}$ is the rate of change in the wholesale price index, U^* is the fraction of the labor force that is unionized, and the subscripts H and A indicate, respectively, hourly and annual measures of wages and productivity.[102]

Notes

1. *Historical Statistics of the United States,* part 1 (Washington, D.C.: 1975), series D-86 for unemployment rates and series F-32 for gross national product. Throughout this article, the standard data series for unemployment rates are used, with recognition that there has been a challenge to the validity of those data during the Great Depression years. See Michael R. Darby, "Three-and-a-Half Million U.S. Employees Have been Mislaid: Or An Explanation of Unemployment, 1934–1941," *Journal of Political Economy* 84, 1976.

2. A.C. Pigou, *Industrial Fluctuations,* 1st ed. (London: Macmillan, 1927), p. 176.

3. A.C. Pigou, *Theory of Unemployment* (London: Macmillan, 1933), p. 252. Pigou makes his arguments in a variety of other places. For example, see his "Real and Money Wage Rates in Relation to Unemployment," *Economic Journal* 47, 1937, and "Money Wages in Relation to Unemployment," *Economic Journal* 48, 1938.

4. It is perhaps something of an exaggeration to ascribe this position entirely to Pigou. A number of other economists espoused similar views. Recognizing that the list is incomplete, we cite a few, beginning with Jacob Viner, *Balanced Deflation, Inflation, or more Depression* (Minneapolis, Minn.: University of Minnesota Press, 1933), especially pp. 12–13. See also W.H. Beveridge, *Causes and Cures of Unemployment* (London: Longmans, Green and Co., 1931), p. 25, and *Unemployment, A Problem of Industry* (London: Longmans, Green and Co., 1930), chapter 16; Wilford I. King, *The Causes of Economic Flucations* (New York: Ronald Press Co., 1938), chapter 8; and Lionel Robbins, *The Great Depression* (New York: Macmillan, 1934).

5. John A. Hobson, *The Economics of Unemployment* (New York: Macmillan, 1923), p. 84.

6. W.T. Foster and W. Catchings, *Profits* (Boston: Houghton Mifflin, 1925) and *Business Without a Buyer* (Boston: Houghton Mifflin, 1927); and C.H. Douglas, *Credit-Power and Democracy* (London: C. Palmer, 1920) and *Warning Democracy* (London: C.M. Grieve, 1931). A more recent interpretation of the Great Depression with underconsumptionist overtones in John Kenneth Galbraith, *The Great Crash, 1929* (Boston: Houghton Mifflin, 1976).

7. Murray N. Rothbard, *America's Great Depression* (Princeton, N.J.: Van Nostrand, 1963), p. 45.

8. Henry Ford, The *New York Times,* November 22, 1929, p. 2.

9. The *New York Times,* November 22, 1929, p. 1. It is interesting to note that Hoover's inclinations toward underconsumptionism were recognized and, of course, approved, by trade unionists. Witness a statement by the AFL's John P. Frey in 1929 relating to a public works scheme of Hoover's. In effect, Frey argued that the president was in agreement with the AFL's position that depressions were the result of underconsumption and low wages. See Joseph Dorfman, *The Economic Mind in American Civilization* (New York: Viking Press, 1959), vol. 4, pp. 349–50. See also Ronald Radosh, "The Development of the Corporate Ideology of American Labor Leaders, 1914–1933" (doctoral dissertation in history, University of Wisconsin, 1967).

10. Rothbard, *America's Great Depression,* chapter 8. Not to be ignored is the fact that ideas such as those that enamored Hoover were not as unorthodox among professional economists as sometimes claimed. See J. Ronnie Davis, *The New Economists and the Old Economists* (Ames, Iowa: Iowa State University Press, 1971).

Davis presents an interesting array of statements by economists and other academics relating to the issue of the impact of wage reductions on the economy (pp. 94–99).

11. John M. Keynes, *The General Theory of Employment, Interest and Money* (London: Macmillan, 1936).

12. Abba P. Lerner, "Mr. Keynes' 'General Theory of Employment, Interest and Money,'" *International Labor Review* 34, 1936. See also W.B. Reddaway, "The General Theory of Employment, Interest and Money," *Economic Record* 12, 1936. A systematic description of the though of this time is contained in Lawrence R. Klein, *The Keynesian Revolution* (New York: Macmillian, 1947). For a taxonomic description of the various views of the aggregate demand schedule for labor, see Sidney Weintraub, "A Macroeconomic Approach to the Theory of Wages," *American Economic Review* 46, 1956.

13. Paul M. Sweezy, personal letter to John B. Shelley, dated February 11, 1977, cited in Dana C. Hewins and John B. Shelley, "Sweezy's Kink: Macro Foundations of a Micro Theory," *Economic Inquiry* 17, 1979.

14. For a description of the various dimensions of the Keynesian critique of classical economics, see Alvin H. Hansen, *A Guide to Keynes* (New York: McGraw-Hill, 1953). More recent appraisals and restatements of the total thrust of Keynesianism are Abba P. Lerner, "From 'The Treatise on Money' to 'The General Theory,'" *Journal of Economic Literature* 12, 1974; and Hyman P. Minsky, *John Maynard Keynes* (New York: Columbia University Press, 1975).

15. Peter Temin, *Did Monetary Forces Cause the Great Depression?* (New York: Norton, 1976), p. 140. Temin also attempts to demonstrate that the Great Depression was brought on by an autonomous shift in the consumption function. That view has been challenged (successfully, we think) by Thomas Mayer, "Consumption in the Great Depression," *Journal of Political Economy* 86, 1978.

16. Keynes, *The General Theory*. In chapter 2, Keynes is very explicit. In reference to the principle that real wages and employment are systematically related, he says, "I am not disputing this vital fact which the classical economists have (rightly) asserted as indefeasible."

17. Ludwig von Mises, *The Theory of Money and Credit* (New Haven, Conn.: Yale University Press, 1953). Permission granted by Mrs. Margit von Mises. Quotes from 1981 *Liberty Classics,* Indianapolis, edition.

18. Milton Friedman, "The Role of Monetary Policy," *American Economic Review* 58, 1968.

19. In particular, see Jerome Stein, *Monetarist, Keynesian, and New Classical Economics* (Cambridge, United Kingdom: B. Blackwell, 1982).

20. The key assumptions are constant returns to scale and neutral disembodied technical progress.

21. The underlying statistical models are moderately complex. They are described briefly in the statistical appendix. The logic and structure of the models are more fully developed in Lowell Gallaway and Richard Vedder, *The "Natural" Rate of Unemployment,* staff study, Subcommittee on Monetary and Fiscal Policy, Joint Economic Committee, Congress of the United States (Washington, D.C.: 1982).

22. *Federal Reserve Bulletin,* various issues.

23. *Historical Statistics,* series D-86.

24. The productivity-adjusted real wage rate on a quarterly basis is calculated by dividing the manufacturing wage bill by the product of Federal Reserve Board

(not the wage bill) and the index of average labor productivity (not total output) should be used. However, converting the wage bill and the index of industrial production to wage rate and productivity measures involves dividing both of them by the same quantity of labor *(L)*. Since *L* appears in both the numerator and denominator of the expression for the adjusted real wage rate, it cancels out and can be ignored.

25. As calculated from *Historical Statistics,* series D-688.

26. lbid,, series D-683 and D-688.

27. lbid., series D-724 and Paul A. David and Peter Solar, "A Bicentenary Contribution to the History of the Cost of Living in America" in Paul Uselding, ed., *Research in Economic History,* vol. 2 (Greenwich, Conn.: JAI Press, 1977), pp. 59–60.

28. Broadus Mitchell, *Depression Decade,* vol. 9, *The Economic History of the United States* (New York: Rinehart, 1947), p. 84; and Arthur Schlesinger, Jr., *The Age of Roosevelt: The Crisis of the Old Order, 1919–1933* (Boston: Houghton Mifflin, 1957), p. 249. Interestingly, though, some observers of the period disagree with this assessment. For example, Leo Wolman, *Wages in Relation to Economic Recovery* (Chicago: 1931) notes, "[I]t is indeed impossible to recall any past depression of similar intensity and duration in which the wages of prosperity were maintained as long as they have been during the depression of 1930–1931." Similarly, Don Lescohier, "Working Conditions," vol. 3, *History of Labor in the United States, 1896–1932,* John R. Commons and Associates, eds. (New York: Macmillan, 1935) states:

> The first impact of the depression of the "thirties" did not affect the wage structure. . . . In 1921 wage cuts were advocated early in the depression to liquidate labor costs. In 1930–31 they were apposed both by government and by leading employers, in the hope that the maintenance of wage earners' incomes would furnish a market for products and help business recovery. In 1921 they were inaugurated long before business had reached a dangerous position; in 1931 they became common only after a large number of businesses had taken heavy losses. Realization of the reluctance of a large number of employers to cut wages caused wage earners and the public to accept them calmly when they did come, perhaps too calmly (p. 92).

29. *Historic Statistics,* series D-802, D-813, D-818, and D-824, respectively.

30. Robbins, *The Great Depression,* p. 224.

31. Geoffrey H. Moore, ed., *Business Cycle Indicators,* vol. 2, *Basic Data on Cyclical Indicators* (Princeton: Princeton University Press, 1961), p. 129.

32. Benjamin M. Anderson, *Economics and the Public Welfare* (New York: Van Nostrand, 1949), p. 72.

33. *Historical Statistics,* series D-839.

34. Anderson, *Economics,* p. 220.

35. Without the productivity adjustment, real wages in manufacturing (in 1923 prices) rose from 58.9 cents an hour in December 1929 to 62.5 cents an hour in December 1930. After that, they continued to rise to 66.3 cents an hour in January 1932. Wilford I. King, *Causes of Fluctuations,* pp. 182–83. See also Sol Shaviro, "Wages and Payroll in the Depression, 1929–1933" (unpublished M.A. essay, Columbia University, 1947).

36. Milton Friedman and Anna J. Schwartz, *A Monetary History of the United States, 1867–1960* (Princeton, N.J.: Princeton University Press, 1963).

37. U.S. Bureau of the Census, *National Income and Product Accounts of the United States, 1929–1976* (Washington, D.C., Department of Commerce, Bureau of Economic Analysis, 1981), p. 308.

38. Moore, *Business Cycle Indicators*, p. 106.

39. Harold Barger, *Outlay and Income in the United States, 1921–1938* (New York: National Bureau of Economic Research, 1942), appendix B, table 28. A smaller profit decline is reported in a less comprehensive survey conducted by the Federal Reserve Bank of New York. See Irving Fisher, *Booms and Depressions: Some First Principles* (New York: Adelphi, 1932), p. 98.

40. Robbins, *The Great Depression*, p. 205. The data were originally published in *Commercial and Financial Chronicle*.

41. This is based on the Standard and Poor's index, which fell 32.9 percent from September to November 1929. The second decline actually began in April 1930. A similar pattern is observed using the Dow-Jones index, which fell 39.7 percent from April to December 1930, compared to 37.0 percent from September to November 1929. The recovery in stock prices after November 1929 was robust; the April 1930 Dow-Jones index was the eleventh highest recorded in history, exceeded only in the first ten months of 1929. See Moore, *Cyclical Indicators*, pp.108–9

42. Ben Bernanke, "Nonmonetary Effects of the Financial Crisis in the Propagation of the Great Depression," *American Economic Review*, June 1983, p. 261.

43. Ibid., p. 262

44. Federal debt declined about $700 million in both 1929 and 1930, but rose more than $600 million in 1931. See *Historical Statistics*, series Y-493.

45. If one uses the consumer price index to measure price changes, real interest rates on bank loans in 1929 averaged about 6 percent, rising to about 7.7 percent in 1930, and to about 13 percent in 1931. This is based solely on current year price changes. A real interest rate model using weighted averages of past price chages would show a smaller rise. Interest rate data are based on Federal Reserve System reports. See Moore, *Cyclical Indicators*, p. 154.

46. *Historical Statistics*, series F-54.

47. Friedman and Schwartz, *A Monetary History*, table A-1, pp. 712–13.

48. Ibid., table B-3, p. 803.

49. Ibid. The deposit/currency ratio fell from 11.57 in October 1929, to 4.44 in March 1933, a decline of 7.13 points, with 3.87 points (54 percent) of that decline occurring between October 1930 and October 1931.

50. IBID., pp.308–13.

51. The price would fall to $750 only for a consol, a bond with no maturity. Short-term bonds would sell at a small discount from face value because the owner of the bond would receive the face value at maturity.

52. *Historic Statistics*, series X-581.

53. Capital accounts were $10,372 million. Ibid., series X-587.

54. Most nominal interest rate series show little change in the early years of the Great Depression, and, indeed, many show some decline. This masks two phenomena, however. First, declining commodity prices during the period led to rising real interest rates over time. Second, most interest rate series report actual transactions, probably ignoring a growing number of customers who were crowded out because of sharply rising risk premiums. It is possible that interest rates demanded of some average potential borrower rose, even though actual interest rates reflected in transactions did not rise.

55. Data from U.S. Bureau of Economic Analysis, *Fixed Residential Business Capital in the United States, 1929–1973* (Washington, D.C.: Department of Commerce,

1974), reported in *Historical Statistics*. The exact data series employed is F-484 for producers' equipment valued at 1958 prices. This series falls from a 1929 level of $74.1 billion to $59.2 billion in 1933. Simon Kuznets, *Capital in the American Economy* (Princeton, N.J.: Princeton University Press, 1961), table R-5, p. 492, concludes that net capital formation was almost zero in 1931, and decidedly negative in the years 1932–34.

56. Use of the consumer price index yields lower-bound measures of the extent of wage disequilibrium. This index fell substantially less than did the wholesale price index during the Great Depression. Consumer prices (*Historical Statistics*, series E-135) fell 24.3 percent, while wholesale prices (Ibid., series E-23) declined by 30.8 percent.

57. The codes in question were the blanket codes introduced pending the development of the specific industry codes. See David A. Shannon, *Between the Wars: America, 1919–1941* (Boston: Houghton Mifflin, 1965), pp. 154–55. See also Michael M. Weinstein, "Some Macroeconomic Impacts of the National Industrial Recovery Act, 1933–1935," chapter 14, pp. 262–81, in Karl Brunner, ed., *The Great Depression Revisited* (Boston: Kluwer/Nijhoff, 1981) and *Recovery and Redistribution under the NIRA* (Amsterdam: North-Holland Publication Company, 1980).

58. *Historical Statistics*, series D-802.

59. Section 7(a) of the National Industrial Recovery Act was added to allay the fears of labor leaders that industry would act cooperatively against labor. It required that every industry code developed under the act include provisions guaranteeing the right of employees to organize and bargain collectively and that employees could not be required as a condition of employment to either join a company union or refrain from joining a union of their choice.

60. After the National Industrial Recovery Act was declared unconstitutional by the Supreme Court, the provisions of section 7(a) were reenacted in a more detailed fashion, including the establishment of an administrative machinery to police the law, in the National Labor Relations Act of 1935.

61. Probably the best known study of this question is H. Gregg Lewis, *Unionism and Relative Wages in the United States* (Chicago: University of Chicago Press, 1963). Also worth noting are John Maher, "Union, Non-Union Wage Differentials," *American Economic Review* 46, 1956; and Adrian W. Throop, "The Union–Non-Union Wage Differential and Cost-Push Inflation," *American Economic Review* 58, 1968.

62. The basic data employed in these calculations are taken from Lowell E. Gallaway, "Trade Unionism, Inflation, and Unemployment" in George Horwich, ed., *Monetary Process and Policy: A Symposium* (Homewood, Ill.: R.D. Irwin, 1967), pp. 60–66. At first blush, the indication of a significant change in what we call the union/nonunion wage differential appears to conflict with Lewis's findings in *Unionism and Relative Wages*, which suggest a stable union/nonunion differential over time. However, we have defined our differential in terms of traditionally organized industries compared to traditionally unorganized ones. Actually, there are substantial numbers of nonunion members in the work force of what we have called the unionized industries. For example, in 1920, when trade union membership peaked at over five million, only about one-forth of the work force in our unionized industries were union members. See Leo Wolman, *Ebb and Flow in Trade Unionism* (New York: National Bureau of Economic Research, 1936). They made up about 90 percent of union membership, though. By contrast, on the eve of World War II, when union membership had recovered to over ten million (compared to its 1933 low of less than three million), union workers

were approaching accounting for one-half the work force in our unionized industries. In fact, what our wage differential measure attempts to capture is the impact of the changing volume of unionism on the interindustry wage structure and, ultimately, on the average wage rate. Actually, we feel that we may have underestimated the union impact by employing a relative wage differential measure rather than focusing on the absolute differential (in real terms) between the unionized and nonunionized areas. For a theoretical discussion of why the relative wage criterion may not be appropriate, see Gallaway, "Trade Unionism." If we had used the absolute differential for purposes of this evaluation, the effect of increases in union membership on the interindustry wage structure would have been even more dramatic.

63. The detailed statistical analysis is described in the statistical appendix to this article.

64. This is done by estimating the impact of growth in union membership on wage levels and then translating the unionization-induced wage shifts into changes in unemployment.

65. Total supplements are from *Historical Statistics,* series D-893. Average annual earnings from ibid., series D-722. See also Albert Rees, *New Measures of Wage-Earner Compensation in Manufacturing, 1914–1957,* occasional paper 75 (Princeton, N.J.: National Bureau of Economic Research, 1960).

66. Detailed supplement data are from *Historical Statistics,* series D-907 and D-908. The percent increase in the total wage bill attributable to the increase in a particular supplement is calculated and the impact of such an increase on unemployment is estimated using the statistical relationships reported in the statistical appendix to this article.

67. The strongest proponents of a monetary explanation for the recession of 1937–38 are Friedman and Schwartz, *A Monetary History.*

68. There is an abundance of literature that suggests a fiscal policy explanation for the downturn in 1938. See E. Cary Brown, "Fiscal Policy in the 'Thirties': A Reappraisal," *American Economic Review* 46, 1956; Alvin H. Hansen, *Fiscal Policy and Business Cycles* (New York: W.W. Norton, 1941); Arthur Smithies, "The American Economy in the Thirties," *American Economic Review* 36, 1946; and Kenneth D. Roose, "The Role of Net Government Contribution to Income in the Recession and Revival of 1937–1938." *Journal of Finance,* 6, 1951. Roose's views are also stated in his *Economics of Recession and Revival* (New Haven, Conn.: Yale University Press, 1954).

69. Interestingly, Roose, *Economics of Recession,* also expresses views that are consistent with our findings. He comments, "Most important of all, however, was the reduced profitability of investment, beginning in the first quarter or 1937. This resulted from increases in costs, in which labor played a prominent part." (pp. 238–39).

70. This estimate is based on calculations made using the statistical model of unemployment cited earlier.

71. It is interesting to note that the statistical model of unemployment that we present systematically underpredicts the level of unemployment during the period in which the growth in wage supplements is most pronounced, namely 1936–38. Since the supplements are not included in the wage measure used to predict unemployment, this may account for the underpredictions in these years.

72. King, *Causes of Fluctuations,* pp. 80–81, noted this phenomenon rather early, remarking that, "all through the depression, those who were fortunate enough to have jobs were, on the average, earning more money per hour than they were in 1929."

73. The total dismissal of the importance of the money wage rate adjustment mechanism became complete during World War II. In Britain, for example, Sir William Beveridge, cited earlier as supporting the classical view of the world, swung full circle and embraced the aggregate demand notions, especially the idea that government spending could produce full employment. In his "The Government's Employment Policy," *Economic Journal,* June–September 1944, pp. 161–62 (a commentary on the government's White Paper of May 26, 1944), he refers to a statement from Winston Churchill's 1929 budget speech as chancellor of the exchequer, to wit: "It is the orthodox Treasury dogma steadfastly held that, whatever might be the political and social advantages, very little additional employment and no permanent additional employment can, in fact, and as a general rule, be created by State borrowing and State expenditure," by commenting, "By the renewed experience of full employment the dogma has been consumed by the fires of war, and the White Paper may be regarded as a ceremonial scattering of its ashes."

Also worth noting is the dialog among Keynes, Hayek, and Frank Graham centering on the usefulness of a commodity standard of money to replace the now defunct gold standard. It begins with Hayek, "A Commodity Reserve Currency," *Economic Journal,* June–September 1943, pp. 176–84, and Keynes's remarks, "The Objective of International Price Stability," ibid., pp. 185–87. Keynes takes the position that the level of money wage rates must be taken as given and everything else adjusted to it. Frank Graham, "Keynes vs. Hayek on a Commodity Reserve Currency," *Economic Journal,* December 1944, pp. 422–29, takes up the issue again and Keynes's view is restated in "A Note by Lord Keynes," ibid., pp. 429–30.

In the United States, one of the classic statements of the "new" economics is Franco Modigliani, "Liquidity Preference and the Theory of Interest and Money," *Econometrica,* January 1944, pp. 45–88. Also, Alvin Hansen has reversed his position and is on his way to becoming the great interpreter of Keynes for a generation of graduate students via his *A Guide to Keynes.* Of course, it could be argued that the weight of the empirical evidence was on the side of Keynes in this issue. Not so. John Dunlap, "The Movement of Real and Money Wage Rates," *Economic Journal,* September 1938, pp. 413–34, reports evidence inconsistent with the Keynesian position that changes in real wages rate cannot be produced by changes in money wage rates. Admittedly, Dunlop attempts to explain away the data as somehow reflecting other things. However, Lorie Tarshis, "Changes in Real and Money Wages," *Economic Journal,* March 1939, pp. 150–54, reports even stronger evidence along these lines. By the end of World War II, though, Keynesianism was sufficiently in the ascendancy to permit the summary disregarding of this evidence. Lawrence Klein, *The Keynesian Revolution,* in reflecting on Tarshis's article, ponders whether "Keynes was backing the wrong horse" (p. 107). However, he resolved his dilemma by rather cavalierly stating in the very next sentence, "Our main concern . . . . is not with the empirical problem but with the theoretical relation of wage cuts to unemployment.

74. The rate was 9.7 percent in 1927, while the median annual rate for the years 1921–29 was 11.05 percent. On unemployment statistics, see Department of Employment and Productivity, *British Labour Statistics: Historical Abstract 1886–1968* (London: H.M. Stationery Off., 1971).

75. Real output rose 2.75 percent a year from 1921 to 1929, and even 1.66 percent annually from the boom year of 1920 to relatively depressed 1930; by contrast,

real growth per annum from 1900 to 1913 was only 1.65 percent. These calculations are derived from C.H. Feinstein, *National Income, Expenditure and Output of the United Kingdom, 1855–1965* (Cambridge, U.K.: Cambridge, University Press, 1972).

76. Daniel K. Benjamin and Levis A. Kolchin, "Searching for an Explanation of Unemployment in Interwar Britain," *Journal of Political Economy,* June 1979.

77. See Edwin Cannan, "The Problem of Unemployment," *Economic Journal,* March 1930; Robbins, *The Great Depression;* Jacques Rueff, "Ces variations du chomage en Angleterre," *Revue politique et parliamentaire,* December 10, 1925; William Beveridge, *The Causes and Cures* and *Unemployment, A Problem.* This list is by no means exhaustive. These persons and others recognized that not only did unemployment insurance payments raise the opportunity cost of working, but they inspired union militancy and, accordingly, produced higher money wage rates. Among the other writers, see, especially, A.C. Pigou, "Wage Policy and Unemployment," *Economic Journal,* September 1927, and John R. Hicks, *The Theory of Wages* (London: Macmillan, 1932). A prominent politician who believed unemployment compensation raised unemployment was Winston Churchill. See his article, "The Dole," *Saturday Evening Post,* March 29, 1930.

On the view of Keynes and other economists, see Keith J. Hancock, "Unemployment and the Economists in the 1920's," *Economica,* November 1930. See also Keynes, "Some Comsequences of the Economic Report," *New Statesman and Nation,* August 15, 1931.

78. Anderson, *Economics.* Like the authors in the previous footnote, Anderson argued that unemployment insurance payments raised wages.

79. On consumption spending, see Feinstein, *National Income;* Richard Stone, et al., *The Measurement of Consumers' Expenditures and Behaviour in the United Kingdom, 1920–1938,* two volumes (Cambridge, U.K.: Cambridge University Press, 1954). For statistics dealing with a variety of economic variables in this period, including consumption, see B.R. Mitchell, *Abstract of British Historical Statistics* (Cambridge, U.K.: Cambridge University Press, 1976).

80. That is actually an understatement. Output in 1939 was more than 21 percent higher that in 1929, with the per annum growth rate of 1.94 percent being high by historical standards. Real gross national product fell only 6 percent from 1929 to the trough in 1932. See Feinstein, *National Income.*

81. The 1937 British unemployment rate of 10.8 percent was actually slightly below the median rate of the 1920s. See Department of Employment and Productivity, *British Labour Statistics.* The U.S. unemployment rate of 14.3 percent in 1937 compares with a median rate for the 1920's of 3.75 percent. See *Historical Statistics,* series D-86.

82. A.W. Phillips, "The Relation between Unemployment and the Rate of Change of Money Wage Rates in the United Kingdom, 1861–1957," *Economica,* N.S., vol. 25, 1958; Richard G. Lipsey, "The Relation between Unemployment and the Rate of Change in Money Wage Rates in the United Kingdom, 1862–1957: A Further Analysis," *Economica,* N.S. vol. 27, 1960; and Paul A. Samuelson and Robert M. Solow, "Analytical Aspects of Anti-inflationary Policy," *American Economic Review* 50, 1960.

83. The corporate profit share of national income rose from 11.33 percent in 1961 to 13.98 percent in 1965. *Historical Statistics,* series F-163 and F-179.

84. The choice of a one-year lag produces the best explanation for unemployment variations in the post-World War II period. The logic of some type of lag is appealing. Employers may well respond to increasing productivity-adjusted real wage rates by searching for alternatives other than the laying off of a labor force that is experienced in its tasks. Also, once it becomes obvious that labor force reductions are necessary, it is tempting to accomplish them through a process of attrition, by simply not replacing workers who quit, die, or retire. The concept of a lag is certainly consistent with the arguments presented in Walter Oi, "Labor as a Quasi-Fixed Factor," *Journal of Political Economy* 70, 1962.

85. Fortunately for the defenders of the neo-Keynesian paradigm, the inflation of the period could be explained away as a phenomenon associated with the movements of specific commodity prices, especially oil. However, these are movements in *relative* prices and not in the overall price level.

86. Estimates reported in Gallaway and Vedder, *"Natural" Rate*, indicate that the equilibrium rate of unemployment was about 4.4 percent in the 1960s and 5.7 percent in the early 1970s, standing at 6.6 percent by the end of that decade.

87. Some of the representative studies of this subject are the early work of Gene Chapin, "Unemployment Insurance, Job Search, and the Demand for Leisure," *Western Economic Journal* 9, 1971; and, later, Martin Feldstein, "Unemployment Compensation: Adverse Incentives and Distributional Anomalies," *National Tax Journal* 27, 1974.

88. C.T. Brehm and T.R. Saving, "The Demand for General Assistance Payments," *American Economic Review*, December 1964, pp. 1002–18; and Hirschel Kasper, "Welfare Payments and Work Incentives: Some Determinants of the Rates of General Assistance Payments," *Journal of Human Resources*, 1968. See also Robert E. Hall, "Effects of the Experimental Negative Income Tax on Labor Supply" in Joseph A. Pechman and Michael Timpane, eds., *Work Incentives and Income Guarantees: The New Jersey Negative Income Tax Experiment* (Washington, D.C.: 1975); and Lowell E. Gallaway, "Negative Income Tax Rates and the Elimination of Poverty," *National Tax Journal*, September 1966, pp. 298–307, for further evidence dealing with the question of work incentives.

89. Benjamin and Kolchin, "Unemployment in Interwar Britain."

90. U.S. Employment and Training Administration.

91. U.S. Social Security Administration.

92. Total social welfare expenditure data are from the Social Security Administration. Personal income data are from the Department of Commerce.

93. Joint Economic Committee of the Congress of the United States, *Economic Indicators* (Washington, D.C.: March 1983), p. 16.

94. Ibid., p. 12.

95. Alfred Marshall, *Principles of Economics* (London: Macmillan, 1920); Irving Fisher, *Booms and Depressions*; A.C. Pigou, *Theory of Unemployment*; Lionel Robbins, *The Great Depression*; Jacob Viner, *Balanced Deflation*; A.H. Hansen, *Business Cycle Theories* (Boston: 1927); and W.H. Beveridge, *Unemployment, A Problem*. For a thorough discussion of the thinking about business cycles prior to, during, and immediately after the Great Depression, see Gottfried von Haberler, *Prosperity and Depression* (Cambridge, Mass.: Harvard University Press, 1958).

96. Not everyone has ignored these notions. In addition to von Mises, it should be noted that Friedrich Hayek, *Unemployment and Monetary Policy* (San Francisco: Cato Institute, 1979) and W.H. Hutt, *The Keynesian Episode: A Reassessment* (Indianapolis: Liberty Press, 1979) have continued to propound what we have called the von Misesian-classical view of macroeconomics. We especially call attention to Hutt's views on the general subject of the underconsumptionist position, which are well summarized in his "Illustration of Keynesianism" taken from his *Politically Impossible* (London: Institute of Economic Affairs, 1971). His specific view on Hoover and wage reductions was related to the authors in private dinner conversation.

97. John R. Hicks, "A Sceptical Follower," *The Economist*, June 18, 1983, p. 19.

98. The growth rates are calculated from the real gross national product statistics reported by the U.S. Department of Commerce, Bureau of Economic Analysis.

99. The magnitude employed is the adjusted monetary base which consists of (1) reserve accounts of financial institutions at Federal Reserve Banks, (2) currency in circulation (currency held by the public and in the vaults of all depository institutions), and (3) an adjustment for reserve requirement rate changes. A detailed description of the simulation can be found in Gallaway and Vedder, *"Natural" Rate*.

100. *Economic Indicators*, p. 16.

101. The data sources are *Historical Statistics*, series D-683, D-688, and D-724, and David and Solar, ibid.

102. The data source for the trade union membership variable is *Historical Statistics*, series D-948.

A Critique of Monetarist and Austrian Doctrines on the Utility and Value of Money

Richard H. Timberlake, Jr.

> From the first, the Austrians entertained a wish . . . to apply their marginal utility theory to the case of money—which both the enemies of this theory and some of its foremost sponsors . . . declared to be impossible.
> —Joseph A. Schumpeter[1]

The current epoch of inflation over much of the world has emphasized yet again the acute relationship between the quantity of national moneys and domestic price levels. Inflation has also underscored the inadequacy of the Keynesian model in dealing with money–price level relationships. Keynes for the most part disposed of price level movements by assuming prices constant. His focus was on employment and interest rates (Keynes, 1936). Keynesianism swept the economics profession at a time when inflation was not a problem. Therefore, economists who embraced Keynesian doctrine as a *general* theory have had a less-than-satisfactory framework for treating price level changes.

Keynes's great intellectual victory in the middle half of the twentieth century has obscured at least two major doctrines that dealt specifically and directly with the quantity of money and prices. One was early monetarist theory, then known as the quantity theory of money. This doctrine was developed by Irving Fisher, E.W. Kemmerer, and others in the United States. In Britain, similar analysis resulted from the works of Edwin Cannan, A.C. Pigou, and economists of the Cambridge school, who were beneficiaries of the earlier classical works of John Stuart Mill, Henry Thornton, and David Ricardo. The other development was the Austrian theory of money initiated by Karl Menger, and continued and enlarged upon by Ludwig von Mises, Friedrich Hayek, Murray Rothbard, and other economists in the Austro-German tradition. These two

I am grateful for helpful suggestions from Will Mason, Nancy Wulwick, and my wife, Hildegard.

doctrines shared important similarities and registered some differences, but both were fundamentally distinct from the Keynesian theory that has eclipsed them. Neglect of these doctrines has left economics less rich than it otherwise would be, and the doctrines themselves have had less impact on current theory and policy than they would have had if they had focused their attention on points of agreement and come to terms with their differences.

This article explores the fundamental operational concepts in monetarist and Austrian theories that bear on the utility and value of money, in order to determine where they are compatible and to assess the logic and significance of their differences.

Money evolved from commodities that were not money. Self-sufficient households, when they began to specialize, first bartered goods and services directly. They then learned to barter indirectly for items they did not want, but which they knew they could use subsequently in other exchanges for things they did want. These indirect bartering devices became media of exchange.

Primitive commodity moneys were varied and innovative (Jevons, 1898, 20–28). The more widely a given commodity money circulated, the more utility it had as a money and the more valuable it tended to become in terms of other goods. Carl Menger observed that, "Money commodities came to have utility as money beyond their utilities as commodities because they brought people closer to their ultimate goals of getting the goods and services they wanted" (1981, 262). This evolution is so inferentially logical that it hardly needs empirical substantiation. If it had not occurred, any historian could have invented it.

In the course of time, however, even the most refined commodity moneys gave way to token representations in order to economize their costs as media of exchange; and finally—if "finally" is now—the commodity itself has faded from the scene. Economics systems have been left with only paper and book-keeping representations that are initiated and accepted under the coercive authority of the state.

The concept of subjective utility in economic analysis was introduced by Carl Menger, and, contemporaneously, by the English economist William Stanley Jevons and the French economist Leon Walras in the great triple coincidence of economic thought (Schumpeter, 1954, 825–29, 1055, passim). Menger developed a table showing assumed cardinal values for the declining marginal utilities of ten economic goods as envisioned by some economic man. However, he did not defend the simplifying assumption of cardinality for the utility schedule, nor did he include either an income constraint or a utility schedule for money (Menger, 1981, 125–28).

The inability to discriminate conceptually between commodity utility and monetary utility is evident in all the works on money in this period. Jevons, for example, wrote correctly:

Since money has to be exchanged for valuable goods, it should itself possess value, and it must therefore have utility as the basis of value. Money . . . is only received to be passed on. The utility of the substance for other purposes must have been the prior condition for its employment as money. . . . It is doubtful whether the most powerful government could oblige its subjects to accept and circulate as money a worthless substance which they had no other motive for receiving (1898, 31).

Jevons's statement shows how difficult it was to penetrate the veil of the commodity in order to perceive the special utility of money. This analytic difficulty often led to the observation: "Money itself has no marginal utility, since it is not intended for consumption" (Wicksell, 1935, 20).

Ludwig von Mises came closer than any other economist of the time to a valid interpretation of the utility of money. He first wrote: "The subjective value [utility] of money is conditioned by its objective *exchange* value (emphasis added)." So far so good. However, he then restated the conventional error:

Money has no utility other than that arising from the possibility of obtaining other economic goods for it. . . . This peculiarity of the value of money can also be expressed by saying that, as far as the individual is concerned, money has no use-value [utility] at all, but only subjective exchange value (1980, 118, 130).

Von Mises's statement acknowledged the necessity for money to have utility—that it is an economic item to be brought into the panorama of market evaluation. But since its perceived utility was locked into its purchasing power for buying other things, the contradiction followed that money has no utility of its own.

Three factors probably contributed to this widely accepted view. First, at the time this issue came into economists' thinking, almost all money was commodity money, or pretended to be. Since some commodity first gave monetary life to any commodity money, the supposition followed that money without its redemptive commodity could not have value of its own and certainly could not have utility. Second, the awareness that the nominal quantity of money units could change without changing the real value of the total stock of money seemed to discourage the notion that the total stock is real capital, regardless of the fact that the size of the nominal stock is irrelevant to the value of the real stock. Third, since money "only" existed to be exchanged for something else, its utilty had to be something akin to an imaginary number. It was derived from the utilities of the things it could buy. To their everlasting credit, the Austrians insisted on bringing money into the general theory of value by emphasizing a demand function for money, but they lacked a utility theory of money *qua* money with which to complete the analysis.

Schumpeter correctly interpreted the Austrian view to mean that the exchange value of money—what it will buy—must be known before the individual can assign any utility to a unit of money: "It is therefore impossible to do in the case of money what can be done in every other case, namely, to deduce its exchange value from . . . schedules of marginal utility: to attempt to do so seems to spell circular reasoning" (1954, 1090). Indeed, this "problem" came to be known as the "Austrian circle" (Rothbard, 1976, 167).

Von Mises recognized and accepted the sequence of thought that led into the Austrian circle, and he tried to break out of it with his "regression theorem." He argued that money's value and utility today could be traced back incrementally day-by-day, year-by-year, decade-by-decade "in temporal regression" to the time when the money was a commodity money; then, as summarized by Murray Rothbard, "to the last day of barter, at which point the temporal element in the demand for the money commodity disappears, and the causal forces in the current demand and purchasing power of money are fully and completely explained."[2] Rothbard claims that this theorem "fully explains the *current* demand for money and integrates the theory of money with the theory of marginal utility" (Rothbard, 1976, 167–69, emphasis added; von Mises, 1980, 131–36).

Don Patinkin rejected the circularity argument by noting that it does not distinguish between "demand" as a schedule of alternative quantities, and "demand" as an amount demanded:

> It is true that the amount demanded of money [by an individual or by all individuals]—as well as of any other good—depends upon prices. Nevertheless, it is also true that the equilibrium prices depend upon the demand functions. The "circularity charge" is simply a denial of this elementary distinction (1965, 116).[3]

Patinkin's observation does not quite hit the mark. Von Mises did not confuse "demand" and "quantity demanded." Nonetheless, this paradox is an illusion and the regression theorem is an awkward and useless contrivance which does nothing more than reargue the origin of commodity money. All these "problems" result from not recognizing money's utility *as money*, and from a confusion of utility and value. Money does not have utility "only" to buy other things. It has the utility of being the exclusive vehicle for allocating expenditures of income over time. This role should be analyzed as one factor contributing to the terms on which money is exchanged for goods and services (that is, its value). If fiat paper money were dumped into a primitive barter economy and forced into acceptance by the impress of legal tender, its price would be established in terms of other things because of the monetary function it fulfilled and because its quantity was limited. Note that the coercive authority that would force acceptance of the money by means of the legal tender power cannot fix the terms on which the money is exchanged. The price level and the corresponding "price" of money—expressed by the inversion of the price level—are determined by the number of money units imposed on the economy, the efficacy of the payments system as a means of metering payments over time (that is, on the monetary utility of money), the stability of the economic environment, the productivity of enterprise, *et hoc genus omne.*

A memorable article that dealt definitively with this issue was written by W.H. Hutt in 1954. Hutt first reviewed the state of utility theory with respect to money and found it wanting, even though he, too, thought von Mises had come the closest to a correct interpretation. Money has utility, Hutt explained, because it is a "wealth-unit *ready* to be activated." It also has the property of being the most easily adjusted asset in case as excess quantity accumulates. It yields service, and therefore an implicit rate of return to its owners. Adam Smith, Hutt observed, had written that money was unproductive because it was like a highway (Hutt, 1954, 217). "But Mises," Hutt declared, "would insist that a highway *is* productive" (von Mises, 1980, 170). He cited a passage from von Mises that is notable both for its insight and also because it contradicts von Mises's previous assertion that "money has no use-value at all (Hutt, 1954, 218)." Wrote von Mises:

> It must be recognized that from the economic point of view there is no such thing as money being idle. All money, whether in reserves or literally in circulation, . . . is devoted in exactly the same way to the performance of a monetary function. . . . All money . . . lies in some individual's stock ready for eventual use. . . . What is called storing money is a way of using wealth (von Mises, 1980, 170).

Hutt contributed important details to the utility argument. Money does *not* do its work by circulating, he stated.

> If the work of money is circulation, then money is always "idle" because transactions are quasi-instantaneous. . . . The transfer [of money] itself occupies a mere moment whilst the services which flow from the possession of money are continuous over time. The essence of all these services is *availability.*

Real money units are thus like a real piano, which has utility because it is ready to be played even when it is silent. Money assets, Hutt emphasized, are "subject to the same laws of value as other scarce things [and] are equally productive in all intelligible senses (1954, 218–20).

Irving Fisher was as ambivalent as von Mises with respect to the utility of money. In *The Purchasing Power of Money,* published just the year before von Mises's *Theory of Money and Credit,* Fisher wrote that marginal utilities, unlike prices, are "not only impossible to measure, but are unequal and vary unequally among individuals." He recognized that money has marginal utility, which would vary directly with the purchasing power of money "*if* all prices and *all money incomes* change in the same ratio" (1911, 220).

Fisher, similar to von Mises, fell into the error of not allowing money to have its own utility because he (of all people) neglected money's real value when analyzing its utility. "The quantity theory of money . . . rests," he wrote, ". . . upon the fundamental peculiarity which money alone of all goods possesses—the fact that it has no power to satisfy human wants except a power to purchase things which do have such power" (1911, 32).

What Fisher, von Mises, and others did not recognize explicitly was that this "exception" to money's "uselessness" was all important. It can be brought into focus most meaningfully by changing the statement, "Money can only be used to buy other things," to, "Money is the exclusive means for buying other things." These statements are similar; but one describes money's function with the demeaning adverb "only," while the other uses the elite adjective "exclusive."

In his *Rate of Interest* written in 1907, Fisher offered a view of money's utility very similar to von Mises's more profound expression:

> The most salable of all properties is, of course, money and as Karl Menger pointed out, it is precisely this salability which makes it money. The *convenience* of surely being able, without any previous preparation, to dispose of it for any exchange . . . is itself a sufficient return upon the capital which a man seems to keep idle in money form. This liquidity of our cash balance takes the place of any rate of interest in the ordinary sense of the word (1907, 212; also cited in Patinkin, 1965, 580; emphasis added).

Fisher's notion of an implicit return on money held is identical to Hutt's "yield." Patinkin noted the ambiguity in the two passages from Fisher and the fact that Fisher wrote the meaningful interpretation of monetary utility in 1907, and the conventionally incorrect view four years later in 1911.

All this emphasis on the utility of money in the late nineteenth and early twentieth centuries should have culminated in an epic work on the subject. However, if the "culmination" of monetary economics was Keynes's *General Theory*, the marginal utility of money is conspicuous by its absence. It appeared in only one paragraph in which Keynes treated the general properties of money. Beside the fact that the supply of money is completely inelastic under a fiat paper money system, Keynes wrote, the demand for money has an elasticity of substitution of zero,

> which means that as the exchange value of money rises [the price level falls] there is no tendency to substitute some other factor for it. . . . This [inelasticity] follows from the peculiarity of money that its utility is solely derived from its exchange-value, so that the two rise and fall *pari passu*, with the result that as the exchange-value of money rises there is no motive or tendency . . . to substitute some other factor for it (1936, 231).

This treatment has money held in a portfolio of interest-earning assets, and *not* as an exchange medium appreciating to the point where it would be too valuable to be held any longer and would be "sold."

The fallacy in Keynes's argument lies in the clause, "its utility is solely *derived* from its purchasing power" (emphasis added). The utility *schedule* of money is indeed proportional to money's purchasing power. However, money does not "derive" its utility from its purchasing power. Its utility is derived from its effectiveness as a rationing device for household and business income over time—as Keynes himself recognized at one point. "One reason for holding cash," he observed without any particular emphasis, "is to bridge the interval between the receipt of income and its disbursement" (1936, 195).

Keynes did not redeem himself with another passage in which he explicitly recognized the utility of money held, as did Fisher and von Mises. While he saw that the marginal utility schedule of money was geared to the exchange-value of the money unit, he did not notice that this linkage would permit money to be entered into a marginal utility calculus for establishing spending equilibrium between money and other economic wealth. (See appendix.) In Keynes's world, a falling price level that increased the exchange-value of the money unit generated no behavioral reaction that would stabilize general dis-equilibrium conditions, but only further acquisitions of the wealth-item that was appreciating. This oversight is consistent with his inability to derive a real balance effect that would get the economy into "full employment" equilibrium.

A resolution of the value-utility argument over money requires some reassessment of money. Much of the confusion and error in characterizing money has resulted from concentrating on the nominal quantity rather than on the real quantity. In the absence of expectations, the real quantity is largely independent of the nominal quantity. A nominal unit of money loses utility during an inflation in proportion to the rise in prices. But a real unit of money— the nominal unit adjusted for changes in the value of the money unit—loses no utility until it no longer performs in its usual way as a disburser of income between payment periods. As in all other determinations of real value, money's utility is a feature that contributes to its demand, and the real income of money users is a second conventional determinant. However, the quantity of nominal money units is as irrelevant to the real value of the money stock as is the calibration of apples in bushels or pounds to the real value of apples.

Utility and value are not on the same plane. Utility precedes value and is parallel to scarcity. To label the utility of money "subjective value" as von Mises did is to foster a contradiction in terms. Money has subjective *utility* and objective *value*, regardless of whether a price index (inverted) measures its value accurately or not.

This correction does not deny the principle that consumption guides production. Nonetheless, the scarcity of resources used in getting the supply of anything to market is essential for setting the terms on which the demand is satisfied.

Both Fisher and von Mises emphasized the impossibility of measuring subjective utilities. Both saw utility as a force operating in markets, and also as a force whose magnitude marginally declines. To Fisher, its unmeasurability was a reason to use an objective measure—a price index—as a guide to "corrections in a monetary standard" (Fisher, 1911, 22). He did not mean to throw out the gold standard. He simply recommended periodic modifications to the fixed official price of gold because the production of gold was so great at the time that he feared a gold inflation (!) (Fisher, 1911, 248–50).

His prescription in practice called for only an occasional change in the mint price of gold to adjust for severe changes in its real price that were associated with a chronically rising or falling level of money prices. "Our ideal, he wrote "is not primarily *constancy* of the dollar but rather *dependability*. Fluctuations which can be foreseen and allowed for are not evils. . . . [No one] should expect the monetary unit to insure him against every wind that blows" (1911, 223; emphasis added).

Fisher's mathematical and statistical training undoubtedly led to his confidence in the use of a price index as a vehicle to measure the value of the money unit. Without such a construction, the common general confusion between relative prices and the price level could never be resolved, so changes in money prices were not likely to be distinguished from changes in real prices. "Individual prices," he wrote, "cannot be fully determined by supply and demand, money cost of production, etc., without surreptitiously introducing the price level itself" (1911, 175). He recognized that the price level when inverted is the only conceptual means for expressing the price of money, and that a price index is the only practical means for estimating the price level.

Von Mises argued that since money prices ("objective exchange values") were the result of subjective utilities, their general level was not explicitly measurable. Money prices he saw as indispensable means for valuing economic goods and services, but, paradoxically, the value of money itself was unquantifiable (von Mises, 1980, 62).

Von Mises here derived what can be labeled the Austrian principle of money: "Every variation in the quantity of money introduces a dynamic factor into the static economic system" (von Mises, 1980, 168). When the stock of money—even if money is gold—changes, the circumstances of the change (where and how the money comes into the system, and who first gets it) inevitably result in relative price changes. In addition, the distribution of wealth and income also change (von Mises, 1978, 81). Thus far, von Mises's analysis and Fisher's had much in common: Money in practice is not neutral in the short run.

Statistically speaking, von Mises noted, these changes in relative prices and real incomes change the "scaling factors" that weight the prices computed in any index. Statistical doctrine cannot provide an accurate means for weight changes. Therefore, "the idea that change in the purchasing power of money may be measured is scientifically untenable" (von Mises, 1978, 99). On the other hand, "any index method is good enough to make a rough statement about the extremely severe depreciation of the value of a monetary unit. [but it] is not necessarily either scientifically correct or applicable in practice" (von Mises, 1978, 89; also 1980, 216–22). Since monetary changes alter relative prices, von Mises argued, a policy to stabilize the price level would have to fix all relative prices and would result in severe distortions to the economic allocation of resources.

The difference between the two schools over this issue is both conceptual and practical. Both recognized that the purchasing power of money is a reflection of money prices inverted. Von Mises even stated that the "fictitious" concept of a "price level" enables the observer "to distinguish and determine whether changes in exchange relationship between money and other commodities arise on the money side or the commodity side. . . . This distinction is urgently needed" (1978, 85). Fisher developed much the same argument (Fisher, 1911, 174–79). However, Fisher also believed that the price index, with all of its imperfections, was statistically valid and operationally useful. Since money prices are measurable data, a price index is "an ascertainable magnitude with a meaning common to all men" (Fisher, 1911, 220).

The conceptual validity of a price index seems logical. Imagine an economy in which the purchase and sale of one commodity dominates all exchanges. The market price of that commodity in terms of the money unit when inverted would also be the market price of the money unit in terms of that commodity. If the number of commodities exchanged for money were to increase, the conceptual means of evaluating the money unit would not change. It would still be the value of the money unit in terms of some aggregate of goods. Indeed, the value of the money unit cannot be measured in any other way. The validity of the concept cannot be denied because of the imperfection of the method used to measure it.

The propriety of using index numbers to measure prices, and hence the value of the money unit, is another story. It depends ultimately on the statistical reliability of the method for deriving the index, and is essentially an empirical issue. For example, given two periods, one of reasonably stable prices and one of pronounced inflation, do relative prices change significantly more in the inflationary period than they do in the stable period? If so, von Mises's rejection of indexes would have some practical weight.

The Austrian view of the value of money, as set out by von Mises, argued correctly that money must be analyzed in a general theory of value. The value of money is determined in all markets where money is exchanged, he wrote. "To explain its determination is the task of the theory of the value of money" (von Mises, 1980, 141). Very properly, he applied an implicit real balance effect to show how an adjustment of prices resulted from a change in the quantity of money:

An increase in a community's stock of money [alters] the ratio between the demand for money and the stock of it . . .; [people] have a relative superfluity of money and a relative shortage of other economic goods. The immediate consequence of both circumstances is that the marginal utility to them of the monetary unit diminishes. This necessarily influences their behavior in the market. They are in a stronger position as buyers. . . . They are able to offer more money for the commodities that they wish to acquire. It will be the obvious result of the [circumstances] that the prices of the goods concerned will rise. . . . Thus the increase of prices continues, having a diminishing effect until all commodities . . . are reached by it (von Mises, 1980, 160–61).

No quantity theorist or monetarist could describe the adjustment to an excess supply of money more effectively. Following this passage, however, von Mises made a substantive criticism of the "mechanical version" of the quantity theory of money: "A thorough comprehension of the means by which money changes prices makes [the quantity theorists'] point of view untenable" (1980, 161). Consequently, "no fixed relationship can be established between the changes in the quantity of money and those of the [money] unit's purchasing power" (von Mises, 1978, 91).

To von Mises, Fisher's manipulations with "neutral" money seemed impossibly mechanistic. The quantity theory assumes an exogenous quantity of money and employs a velocity of circulation and a total output of goods and services—variables outside the decision-making volition of human beings. In his view, therefore, it could not reflect subjective valuations of individuals, (von Mises, 1980, 153–54).

This charge is understandable and has long been a criticism of the quantity theory. Another criticism of some moment is that the quantity theory sublimates the real balance effect implicit in its workings, and hides the utility of money. Von Mises's use of the real balance effect, and his simultaneous criticism of the quantity theory, imply that he, too, saw the quantity theory in this light. He recognized Fisher as one who "takes his stand upon the subjective theory of value," but who is "unable to show the way subjective valuations are affected by variations in the ratio between the stock of money and the demand for money" (von Mises, 1980, 158).[4]

If Fisher oversold his price index thesis because of his faith in statistical measurement, von Mises's arguments were often whimsical. He had the habit of acknowledging that economic concepts have magnitudes, and he would use these devices analytically; but then he would argue that assigning any precise values to these variables by statistical measurement was improper.

All index-number systems are based upon the idea of measuring the utility of a certain quantity of money.[5] . . . Their purpose is the determination of the subjective significance of the quantity of money in question. For this, recourse must be had to the quite nebulous and illegitimate fiction of an eternal human with invariable valuations (von Mises, 1980, 221).

Recognition of the quantity theory's defects as an engine of analysis was expressed by A.C. Pigou when he wrote that he favored the form of the cash balance (or "Cambridge") equation to the quantity theory because the cash balance approach

> focuses attention on the proportion of their resources that people choose to keep in the form of [money] instead of focusing it on "velocity of circulation." . . . [The cash balance method] brings us at once into relation with volition—an ultimate cause of demand—instead of something that seems at first sight accidental and arbitrary (1951, 174).

D.H. Robertson made a similar distinction. The cash balance equation, he wrote, "is the more useful for enabling us to understand the underlying forces determining the value of money; while the [quantity theory] is the more useful for equipping us to watch with understanding the actual processes by which in real life the prices of goods and services change" (1948, 38–39). The cash balance equation thus lent itself to the construction of a demand for money that answered von Mises's criticisms of the quantity theory and, as well, provided a vehicle for understanding the true utility of money.

In most important respects, Austrian and monetarist monetary doctrines employ similar constructions and similar methods to analyze money's impact on the economy. Both imply an awareness of the utility of money as money. Both develop demands for money that are methodologically consistent with demand constructions for all other goods and services. Both emphasize the necessity and importance of markets for specifying prices as guides to economic decision making. Both see the value of money in its classical garb as an inversion of money prices. Both make use of the real balance effect. Both deny the short-run neutrality of money; and both deplore the misbehavior of "managed" monetary systems. Wherein then lie their differences?

Most of the disagreements are either methodological misunderstandings or questions of empirical fact. One lingering difference between the two, in contrast to their many common principles, is in the validity each assigns to the statistical measurement of prices. Austrians incongruously deny validity of indexes yet continuously make use of the concept. In this day and age of statistical refinement—never mind the many misuses of statistics—this intellectual position is untenable. Just because a device is not perfect does not mean that it is useless. It should be used, however, with caution and with an understanding of its frailties. The Austrian criticism is a well-considered caveat if it limits itself to this point.

Fisher seems to have leaned too far in the other direction by assigning too deterministic a role to index numbers and by emphasizing too literally the influence of money on prices. Schumpeter hazards the guess that Fisher's vested interest in a "piece of social engineering"—the compensated-dollar plan—"pushed aside all other considerations" (Schumpeter, 1954, 1103).

Another methodological issue is the Austrian contentiousness for insisting that utility can only be measured ordinally and not cardinally. Utility is a force that has magnitude and direction, as the Austrians know better than anyone else. Therefore, it can be treated *as if* its values are specific (as, indeed, Menger did). In fact, the only necessary condition for determining market equilibrium between money and goods is that all marginal utility schedules decline (Patinkin, 1965, 95). When people then give up money to get other wealth, they run themselves up the utility schedules of money and down the utility schedules of other wealth, until they reach a new equilibrium. (See appendix.)

Austrian doctrine also objects to the assumption of fixed utility schedules for other wealth when only a change in money disturbs some previous equilibrium. This issue is also methodological rather than substantive. Since the nonneutrality of money and the heterogeneity of individuals' utility schedules do not violate in any way the conclusion that changes in the quantity of money significantly affect prices, the assumption of monetary neutrality and the specification of cardinal utilities are simplifications that clarify the analysis by showing it unadorned. The argument, in short, is not over a question of fact but over the efficacy of method.

Austrian doctrine on price indexes and utilities has some substantive basis, and is very useful in limiting enthusiasm for authoritarian tampering with the monetary system. However, the concept of circularity in the utility, value, and demand for money is an illusion, and the regression theorem therefore is a pointless contrivance. If a paradox is imaginary, the "solution" to it is worthless.

All professional specialists tend to culture their intellectual rent factors or vested interests, and economists are not exceptions. When this practice is carried on so intensively over minor details that it produces what appear to be ideological differences, it becomes counterproductive to the momentum of valid first principles. All of which is to say that, as allies, monetarists and Austrians both would better serve their common interests.

Appendix:
The Equilibrium Value for the
Marginal Utility of Money

Assume declining marginal utility schedules for money, M, and all other goods and services, R. Money exchanges for these goods and services at market prices until a typical individual maximizes his utilities for money and goods relative to their prices. That is, in equilibrium (ephemeral as it might be) the marginal utility of money relative to the price of money equals the marginal utility of goods relative to the price of goods.

$$\frac{MU_M}{p_M} = \frac{MU_M}{P_R} \tag{1}$$

The price of goods, P_R, is some construction of the general price level, and the price of money, p_M, is $\frac{1}{P_r}$. Therefore, equation 1 can be reduced to three terms:

$$\frac{MU_M}{\left(\dfrac{1}{P_R}\right)} = \frac{MU_R}{P_R} \tag{2}$$

and

$$MU_M = \frac{MU_R}{P_R^2} \tag{3}$$

This last equation states that the marginal utility of the nth money unit in equilibrium is equal to the marginal utility of goods divided by the price level *squared*.

To visualize this explanation, let the original equilibrium in equation 1 occur when P_R and p_M are both 1. In this case, MU_M would aldo equal MU_R. Now let a monetary inflation, say, triple the price level by a threefold increase in the stock of money. The new equilibrium, assuming no expectations of further price change, occurs when

$$\frac{MU_M}{\left(\dfrac{1}{3}\right)} = \frac{MU_R}{3}, \text{ and}$$

(4)

the new equilibrium marginal utility of money is

$$MU_M = \frac{MU_R}{9}$$

(5)

When the money stock and the price level triple, the marginal utility of the nth dollar in equilibrium is one-ninth what it was originally. This value is explained by nothing that the whole schedule of monetary utility for nominal money units must be scaled down to one-third of its former value, and in addition everyone must hold three times the former number of money units. Equilibrium, therefore, occurs on a utility schedule that has been reduced by a factor of 3 at a point three times as far out on the money axis.

Notes

1. Schumpeter, 1954, 1089.
2. Cf. Jevons's statement earlier in this article.
3. While Patinkin rejects the Austrian circle and, therefore, von Mises's regression theorem, he nonetheless gives full credit to von Mises's contribution.
4. By the "demand for money," von Mises indicated that he meant "volume of transactions [divided by] velocity of circulation." Using the algebra of the equation of exchange,

$$\frac{T}{V} = \frac{M}{P}, \text{ and } \frac{M}{M}$$

in contemporary parlance is the real value of the total stock of money (von Mises, 1980, 158).
5. Not "utility," but value. And not "subjective significance" in the next sentence but objective value as registered by markets.

References

Cannan, Edwin. *Money*, 8th ed. London: Staples Press, 1946.

Fisher, Irving. *The Purchasing Power of Money*. New York: Macmillan, 1911.

_____. *The Rate of Interest*. New York: Macmillan, 1907.

Hutt, William H. "The Yield from Money Held," in *Individual Freedom: Selected Works of William H. Hutt*. Pejovich and Klingaman, eds. Westport Conn.: Greenwood, 1975.

Jevons, William Stanley. *Money and the Mechanism of Exchange*. New York: Appleton, 1898.

Keynes, John M. *The General Theory of Employment, Interest and Money*. New York: Harcourt Brace, 1936.

Menger, Carl. *Principles of Economics*. Translated by James Dingwall and Bert Hoselitz. New York: New York University Press, 1981.

Patinkin, Don. *Money, Interest and Prices*, 2d ed. New York: Harper & Row, 1965.

Pigou, A.C. "The Value of Money," *Quarterly Journal of Economics* 32 (1917–18): 38–65. Reprinted in *Readings in Monetary Theory*. Lutz and Mints, eds. New York: Blakinston, 1951, pp. 162–83. References are to this latter source.

Robertson, Dennis H. *Money*. New York: Pitman, 1948.

Rothbard, Murray. "The Austrian Theory of Money," in *The Foundations of Modern Austrian Economics*. Edwin G. Dolan, ed. Kansas City, Mo.: Sheed and Ward, 1976.

Schumpeter, Joseph A. *History of Economic Analysis*. New York: Oxford University, 1954.

Von Mises, Ludwig. *On the Manipulation of Money and Credit*. Essays originally written between 1923 and 1946. Translated by Bettina Bien Graves. Dobbs Ferry, N.Y.: Free Market Books, 1978. Reprinted with the permission of the publisher, Free Market Books.

_____. *The Theory of Money and Credit*. Originally written in 1912. Translated by H.E. Baston, 1934. Indianapolis: Liberty Classics, 1981.

Walras, Leon. *Elements of Pure Economics*. Translated by William Jaffe. Homewood, Ill.: Irwin, 1954.

Wicksell, Knut. *Lecture on Political Economy, Vol. II: Money*. Translated by E. Classer, and edited with an introduction by Lionel Robbins. New York: Macmillan, 1935.

Breaking Out of the Walrasian Box: The Cases of Schumpeter and Hansen

Murray N. Rothbard

S ince World War II, mainstream neoclassical economics has followed the general equilibrium paradigm of Swiss economist Leon Walras (1834–1910).[1] Economic analysis now consists of the exegesis and elaboration of the Walrasian concept of general equilibrium, in which the economy pursues an endless and unchanging round of activity—what the Walrasian Joseph Schumpeter aptly referred to as "the circular flow." Since the equilibrium economy is by definition a changeless and unending round of robotic behavior, everyone on the market has perfect knowledge of the present and the future, and the pervasive uncertainty of the real world drops totally out of the picture. Since there is no more uncertainty, profits and losses disappear, and every business firm finds that its selling price exactly equals its cost of production.

It is surely no accident that the rise to dominance of Walrasian economics has coincided with the virtual mathematization of the social sciences. Mathematics enjoys the prestige of being truly "scientific," but it is difficult to mathematize the messy and fuzzy uncertainties and inevitable errors of real world entrepreneurship and human actions. Once one expunges such actions and uncertainties, however, it is easy to employ algebra and the tangencies of geometry in analyzing this unrealistic but readily mathematical equilibrium state.

Most mainstream economic theorists are content to spend their time elaborating on the general equilibrium state, and simply to assume that this state is an accurate presentation of real world activity. But some economists have not been content with contemplating general equilibrium; they have been eager to apply this theory to the real world of dynamic change. For change clearly exists, and for some Walrasians it has not sufficed to simply translate general equilibrium analysis to the real world and to let the chips fall where they may.

The author learned the basic insights of this article many years ago from lectures of Professor Arthur F. Burns at Columbia University.

As someone who has proclaimed that Leon Walras was the greatest economist who ever lived, Joseph A. Schumpeter (1883–1950) faced this very problem. As a Walrasian, Schumpeter believed that general equilibrium is an overriding reality; and yet, since change, entrepreneurship, profits, and losses clearly exist in the real world, Schumpeter set himself the problem of integrating a theoretical explanation of such change into the Walrasian system. It was a formidable problem indeed, since Schumpeter, unlike the Austrians, could not dismiss general equilibrium as a long-run tendency that is never reached in the real world. For Schumpeter, general equilibrium had to be the overriding reality: the realistic starting point as well as the end point of his attempt to explain economic change.[2]

To set forth a theory of economic change from a Walrasian perspective, Schumpeter had to begin with the economy in a real state of general equilibrium. He then had to explain change, but that change always had to *return* to a state of equilibrium, for without such a return, Walrasian equilibrium would only be real at *one single point* of past time and would not be a recurring reality. But Walrasian equilibrium is a world of unending statis; specifically, it depicts the consequences of a fixed and unchanging set of individual tastes, techniques, and resources in the economy. Schumpeter began, then, with the economy in a Walrasian box; the only way for any change to occur is through a change in one or more of these static givens.

Furthermore, Schumpeter created even more problems for himself. In the Walrasian model, profits and losses were zero, but a rate of interest continued to be earned by capitalists, in accordance with the alleged marginal productivity of capital. An interest charge became incorporated into costs. But Schumpeter was too much of a student of Böhm-Bawerk to accept a crude productivity explanation of interest. The Austrian approach was to explain interest by a social rate of time preference, of the market's preference for present goods over future goods. But Schumpeter rejected the concept of time-preference as well, and so he concluded that in a state of general equilibrium, the rate of interest as well as profits and losses are all zero.

Schumpeter acknowledged that time-preference, and hence interest, exist on consumption loans, but he was interested in the production structure. Here he stressed, as against the crude productivity theory of interest, the Austrian concept of imputation, in which the values of products are imputed back to productive factors, leaving, in equilibrium, no net return. Also, in the Austrian manner, Schumpeter showed that capital goods can be broken down ultimately into the two original factors of production, land and labor.[3] But what Schumpeter overlooked, or rather rejected, is the crucial Böhm-Bawerkian concept of time and time-preference in the process of production. Capital goods are not *only* embodied land and labor; they are embodied land, labor, and *time*, while interest becomes a payment for "time." In a productive loan, the creditor of course exchanges a "present good" (money that can be used now) for a "future good" (money that will only be available in the future). And the primordial fact of time-preference dictates that every one will prefer to have wants satisfied now than at some point in the future, so that a present good will always be worth more than the *present prospect* of the equivalent future good. Hence, at any given time, future goods are discounted on the market by the social rate of time-preference.

It is clear how this process works in a loan, in an exchange between creditor and debtor. But Böhm-Bawerk's analysis of time-preference and interest went far deeper, and far beyond the loan market for he showed that time-preference and hence interest return exist apart from or even in the absence of any lending at all. For the capitalist who purchases or hires land and labor factors and employs them in production is buying these factors with money (present good) in the expectation that they will yield a future return of output, of either capital goods or consumer goods. In short, these original factors, land and labor, are future goods to the capitalist. Or, put another way, land and labor produce goods that will only be sold and hence yield a monetary return at some point *in the future*; yet they are paid wages or rents by the capitalist now, in the present.

Therefore, in the Böhm-Bawerkian or Austrian insight, factors of production, hence workers or landowners, do *not* earn, as in neoclassical analysis, their marginal value product in equilibrium. They earn their marginal value product discounted by the rate of time-preference or rate of interest. And the capitalist, for his service of supplying factors with present goods and waiting for future returns, is paid the discount.[4] Hence, time-preference and interest income exist in the state of equilibrium, and not simply as a charge on loans but as a return earned by every investing capitalist.

Schumpeter can deny time-preference because he can somehow deny the role of time in production altogether. For Schumpeter, production apparently takes no time in equilibrium, because production and consumption are "synchronized."[5] Time is erased from the picture, even to the extent of assuming away accumulated stocks of capital goods, and therefore of any age structure of distribution of such goods.[6] Since production is magically "synchronized," there is then no necessity for land and labor to receive any advances from capitalists. As Schumpeter writes:

> There is no necessity [for workers or landowners] to apply for any "advances" of present consumption goods. . . . The individual need not look beyond the current period. . . . The mechanism of the economic process sees to it that he also provides for the future at the same time. . . . Hence every question of the accumulation of such stocks [of consumer goods to pay laborers] disappears.

From this bizarre set of assumptions, "it follows", notes Schumpeter, "that everywhere, even in a trading economy, produced means of production are nothing but transitory items. Nowhere do we find a stock of them fulfilling any functions." In denying, further, that there is any "accumulated stock of consumer goods" ready to pay laborers and landowners, Schumpeter is also denying the patent fact that wages and rents are always paid out of the accumulated savings of capitalists, savings which could have been spent on consumer goods but which laborers and landowners will instead spend with their current incomes.

How can Schumpeter come to this conclusion? One reason is that when workers and landowners exchange their services for present money, he denies that these involve "advances" of consumer goods, because "It is simply a matter of exchange, and not of credit transactions. The element of time plays no part." What Schumpeter overlooks here is the profound Böhm-Bawerkian insight that the time market is not merely the *credit* market. For when workers and landowners earn money *now* for products that will only reap a return to capitalists in the future, they *are* receiving advances on production paid for out of capitalist saving, advances for which they in effect pay the capitalists a discount in the form of an interest return.[7]

In most conceptions of final equilibrium, net savings are zero, but interest is high enough to induce *gross* saving by capitalists to just replace capital equipment. But in Schumpeter's equilibrium, interest is zero, and this means that *gross* saving is zero as well. There appear to be neither an incentive for capitalists to maintain their capital equipment in Schumpeterian equilibrium nor the means for them to do so. The Schumpeterian equilibrium is therefore internally inconsistent and cannot be maintained.[8]

Lionel Robbins puts the case in his usual pellucid prose:

> If there were no yield to the use of capital . . . there would be no reason to refrain from consuming it. If produced means of production are not productive of a net product, why devote resources to maintaining them when these resources might be devoted to providing present enjoyment? One would not have one's cake rather than eat it, if there were no gain to be derived from having it. It is, in short, *an* interest rate, which, other things being given, keeps the stationary state—the rate at which it does not pay to turn income into capital or capital into income. If interest were to disappear the stationary state would cease to be stationary. Schumpeter can argue that no *ac*cumulation will be made once stationary equilibrium has been attained. But he is not entitled to argue that there will be no *de*cumulation unless he admits the existence of interest.[9] (emphasis added)

To return to Schumpeter's main problem, if the economy begins in a Walrasian general equilibrium modified by a zero rate of interest, how can any economic change, and specifically how can economic development, take place? In the Austrian–Böhm-Bawerkian view, economic development takes place through greater investment in more roundabout processes of production, and that investment is the result of greater net savings brought about by a general fall in rates of time-preference. Upon such a fall, people are more willing to abstain from consumption and to save a greater proportion of their incomes, and thereby invest in more capital and longer processes of production. In the Walrasian schema, change can only occur through alterations in tastes, techniques, or resources. A change in time-preference would qualify as a very important aspect of a change in consumer "tastes" or values.

But for Schumpeter, *there is no* time-preference, and no savings in equilibrium. Consumer tastes are therefore irrelevant to increasing investment, and besides there are *no savings* or interest income out of which such investment can take place. A change in tastes or time-preferences cannot be an engine for economic change, and neither can investment in change emerge out of savings, profit, or interest.

As for consumer values or tastes apart from time-preference, Schumpeter was convinced that consumers were passive creatures and he could not envision them as active agents for economic change.[10] And even if consumer tastes change actively, how can a mere shift of demand from one product to another bring about economic development?

Resources for Schumpeter are in no better shape as engines of economic development than are tastes. In the first place, the supplies of land and labor never change very rapidly over time, and furthermore they cannot account for the necessary investment that spurs and embodies economic growth.

With tastes and resources disposed of, there is only one logically possible instrument of change or development left in Schumpeter's equilibrium system: technique. "Innovation" (a change in embodied technical knowledge or production functions) is for Schumpeter the only logically possible avenue of economic development. To admire Schumpeter, as many economists have done, for his alleged realistic insight into economic history in seeing technological innovation as the source of development and the business cycle, is to miss the point entirely. For this conclusion is not an empirical insight on Schumpeter's part; it is logically the only way that he can escape from the Walrasian (or neo-Walrasian) box of his own making; it is the only way for any economic change to take place in his system.

But if innovation is the only way out of the Schumpeterian box, how is this innovation to be financed? For there are no savings, no profits, and no interest returns in Schumpeterian equilibrium. Schumpeter is stuck: for there is no way within his own system for innovation to be financed, and therefore for the economy to get out of his own particularly restrictive variant of the Walrasian box. Hence, Schumpeter has to invent a *deus ex machina*, an exogenous variable from outside his system that will lift the economy out of the box and serve as the only possible engine of economic change. And that *deus ex machina* is inflationary bank credit. Banks must be postulated that expand the money supply through fractional reserve credit, and furthermore, that lend that new money exclusively to innovators—to new entrepreneurs who are willing and able to invest in new techniques, new processes, new industries. But they cannot do so because, by definition, there are no savings available for them to invest or borrow.

Hence, the conclusion that innovation is the instrument of economic change and development, and that the innnovations are financed by inflationary bank credit, is *not* a perceptive empirical generalization discovered by Joseph Schumpeter. It is not an empirical generalization at all; indeed it has *no* genuine referent to reality. Suggestive though his conclusion may seem, it is solely the logical result of Schumpeter's fallacious assumptions and his closed system, and the only logical way of breaking out of his Walrasian box.

One sees, too, why for Schumpeter the entrepreneur is always a disturber of the peace, a disruptive force *away* from equilibrium, whereas in the Austrian tradition of von Mises and Kirzner, the entrepreneur harmoniously adjusts the economy in the direction of equilibrium. For in the Austrian view the entrepreneur is the main bearer of uncertainty in the real world, and successful entrepreneurs reap profits by bringing resources, costs, and prices further in the direction of equilibrium. But Schumpeter starts, not in the real world, but in the never-never land of general equilibrium which he insists is the fundamental reality. But in the equilibrium world of stasis and certainty there are no entrepreneurs and no profit. The *only* role for entrepreneurship, by logical deduction, is to innovate, to disrupt a preexisting equilibrium. The entrepreneur cannot adjust, because everything has already been adjusted. In a world of certainty, there is no room for the entrepreneur; only inflationary bank credit and innovation enable him to exist. His only prescribed role, therefore, is to be disruptive and innovative.

The entrepreneur, then, pays interest to the banks, interest for Schumpeter being a strictly monetary phenomenon. But where does the entrepreneur-innovator get the money to pay interest? Out of profits, profits that he will reap when the fruits of his innovation reach the market, and the new processes or products reap revenue from the consumers. Profits, therefore, are *only* the consequence of successful innovation, and interest is only a payment to inflationary banks out of profit.

Inflationary bank credit means, of course, a rise in prices, and also a redirection of resources toward the investment in innovation. Prices rise, followed by increases in the prices of factors, such as wages and land rents. Schumpeter has managed, though not very convincingly, to break out of the Walrasian box. But he has not finished his problem. For it is not enough for him to break out of his box; he must also get back in. As a dedicated Walrasian, he must return the economy to *another* general equilibrium state, for after all, by definition a real equilibrium is a state to which variables tend to return once they are replaced. How does the return take place?

For the economy to return to equilibrium, profits and interest must be evanescent. And innovation of course must also come to an end. How can this take place? For one thing, innovations must be discontinuous; they must only appear in discrete clusters. For if innovation were *continuous*, the economy would never return to the equilibrium state. Given this assumption of discontinuous clusters, Schumpeter found a way: When the innovations are "completed" and the new processes or new products enter the market, they outcompete the old processes and products, thereby reaping the profits out of which interest is paid. But these profits are made at the expense of severe losses for the old, now inefficient, firms or industries, which are driven to the wall. After a while, the innovations are completed, and the inexorable imputation process destroys all profits and therefore all interest, while the sudden losses to the old firms are also ended. The economy returns to the unchanging circular flow, and stays there until another cluster of innovations appears, whereupon the cycle starts all over again.

"Cycle" is here the operative term, for in working out the logical process of breakout and return, Schumpeter has at the same time seemingly developed a unique theory of the business cycle. Phase I, the breakout, looks very much like the typical boom phase of the business cycle: inflationary bank credit, rise in prices and wages, general euphoria, and redirection of resources to more investment. Then, the events succeeding the "completion" of the innovation look very much like the typical recession or depression: sudden severe losses for the old firms, retrenchment. And finally, the disappearance of both innovation and euphoria, and eventually of losses and disruption—in short, a return to a placid period which can be made to seem like the state of stationary equilibrium.

But Schumpeter's doctrine only *seems* like a challenging business cycle theory worthy of profound investigation. For it is not really a cycle theory at all. It is simply the only logical way that Schumpeter can break out and then return to the Walrasian box. As such, it is certainly an ingenious formulation, but it has no genuine connection with reality at all.

Even within his own theory, indeed, there are grave flaws. In the Walrasian world of perfect certainty (an assumption which is not relaxed with the coming of the innovator), how is it that the old firms wait until the "completion" of the innovation to find suddenly that they are suffering severe losses? In a world of perfect knowledge and expectations, the old firms would know of their fate from the very beginning, and early take steps to adjust to it. In a world of perfect expectations, therefore, there would be no losses, and therefore no recession or depression phase. There would be no cycle as economists know it.

Finally, Schumpeter's constrained model can only work if innovations come in clusters, and the empirical evidence for such clusters is virtually nil.[11] In the real world, innovations occur all the time. Therefore, there is no reason to postulate any return to an equilibrium, even if it had ever existed in the past.

In conclusion, Schumpeter's theory of development and of business cycles has impressed many economists with his suggestive and seemingly meaningful discussions of innovation, bank credit, and the entrepreneur. He has seemed to offer far more than static Walrasian equilibrium analysis and to provide an economic dynamic, a theoretical explanation of cycles and of economic growth. In fact, however, Schumpeter's seemingly impressive system has no relation to the real world at all. He has not provided an economic dynamic; he has only found an ingenious but fallacious way of trying to break out of the static Walrasian box. His theory is a mere exercise in equilibrium logic leading nowhere.

It is undoubtedly at least a partial realization of this unhappy fact that prompted Schumpeter to expand his business cycle theory from his open-cycle model of the *Theory of Economic Development* of 1912 to his three-cycle schema in his two-volume *Business Cycles* nearly three decades later.[12] More specifically, Schumpeter saw that one of the problems in applying his model to reality was that if the length of the boom period is determined by the length of time required to "complete" the innovation and bring it to market, then how could his model apply to real life, where simultaneous innovations occur, each of which requires a different time for its completion? His later three-cycle theory is a desperate attempt to encompass such real-life problems. Specifically, Schumpeter has now postulated that the economy, instead of unitarily breaking out and returning to equilibrium, consists of three separate hermetically sealed, strictly periodic cycles—the "*Kitchin*", the "*Juglar*," and the "*Kondratieff*"—each with the same innovation-inflation-depression characteristics. This conjuring up of allegedly separate underlying cycles, each cut off from the other, but all adding to each other to yield the observable results of the real world, can only be considered a desperate lapse into mysticism in order to shore up his original model.

In the first place, there are far more than three innovations going on at one time in the economy, and there is no reason to assume strict periodicity of each set of disparate changes. Indeed, there is no such clustering of innovations as would be required by the theory. Secondly, in the market economy, all prices and activities interact; there therefore can never be any hermetically sealed cycles. The multicycle scheme is an unnecessary and heedless multiplication of entities in flagrant violation of Occam's Razor. In an attempt to save the theory, it asserts propositions that cannot be falsifiable, since another cycle can always be conjured up to explain away anomalies.[13] In an attempt to salvage his original model, Schumpeter only succeeded in adding new and greater fallacies to the old.

In the years before and during World War II, the most popular dynamic theory of economic change was the gloomy doctrine of "secular stagnation" (or "economic maturity") advanced by Professor Alvin H. Hansen.[14] The explanation of the Great Depression of the 1930s, for Hansen, was that the United States had become mired in permanent stagnation, from which it could not be lifted by free market capitalism. A year or two after the publication of Keynes's *General Theory*, Hansen had leaped on the New Economics to become the leading American Keynesian; but secular stagnation, while giving Keynesianism a left-flavor, was unrelated to Keynesian theory. For Keynes, the key to prosperity or depression was private investment: flourishing private investment means prosperity; weak and fitful investment leads to depression. But Keynes was an agnostic on the investment question, whereas Hansen supplied his own gnosis. Private investment in the United States was doomed to permanent frailty, Hansen opined, because (1) the frontier was now closed; (2) population growth was declining rapidly; and (3) there would be hardly any further inventions, and what few there were would be of the capital-saving rather than labor-saving variety, so that total investment could not increase.

George Terborgh, in his well-known reputation of the stagnation thesis, *The Bogey of Economic Maturity*, concentrated on a statistical critique.[15] If the frontier had been "closed" since the turn of the century, why then had there been a boom for virtually three decades until the 1930s? Population growth too, had been declining for many decades. It was easy, also, to demolish the rather odd and audacious prediction that few or no further inventions, at least of the labor-saving variety, would ever more be discovered. Predictions of the cessation of invention, which have occurred from time to time through history, are easy targets for ridicule.

But Terborgh never penetrated to the fundamentals of the Hansen thesis. In an age beset by the constant clamor of population doomsayers and zero-population-growth enthusiasts, it is difficult to conjure up an intellectual climate when it seemed to make sense to worry about the *slowing* of population growth. But why, indeed, should Hansen have considered population growth as *ipso facto* a positive factor for the spurring of investment? And why would a slowing down of such growth be an impetus to decay? Schumpeter, in his own critique of the Hansen thesis, sensibly pointed out that population growth could easily lead to a fall in real income per capita.[16]

Ironically, however, Schumpeter did not recognize that Hansen, too, in his own way, was trying to break out of the Walrasian box. Hansen began implicitly (not explicitly like Schumpeter) with the circular flow and general equilibrium, and then considered the various possible factors that might change—or, more specifically, might increase. And these were the familiar Walrasian triad: land, labor, and technique. As Terborgh noted, Hansen had a static view of "investment opportunities." He treated them as if they were a limited physical entity, like a sponge. They were a fixed amount, and when that maximum amount was reached, investment opportunities were "saturated" and disappeared. The implicit Hansen assumption is that these opportunities could be generated only by increases in land, labor, and improved techniques (which Hansen limited to *inventions* rather than Schumpeterian innovations). And so the closing of the frontier meant the drying up of "land-investment opportunities", as one might call them, the slowing of population growth, the end of "labor-investment opportunities," leading to a situation where innovation could not carry the remaining burden.

And so Hansen's curious view of the economic effects of diminishing population growth, as gloomily empirical as it might seem, was not really an empirical generalization at all. Indeed, it said nothing about dynamic change or about the real world at all. The allegedly favorable effect of high population growth was merely the logical spinning out of Hansen's own unsuccessful variant of trying to escape from the Walrasian box.

Notes

1. Before World War II, the dominant paradigm, at least in Anglo-American economics, was the neo-Ricardian partial equilibrium theory of Alfred Marshall. In that era, Walras and his followers, the earliest being the Italian Vilfredo Pareto, were referred to as "the Lausanne school." With the Walrasian conquest of the mainstream, what was once a mere school has now been transformed into "microeconomics."

2. In maintaining that Schumpeter was more influenced by the Austrians than by Walras, Mohammed Khan overlooks the fact that Schumpeter's first book, and the only one still untranslated into English, *Das Wesen und der Hauptinhalt der Theoretischen Nationalekonomie* (The Essence and Principal Contents of Economic Theory) (Leipzig, 1908), written while he was still a student of Böhm-Bawerk, was an aggressively Walrasian work. Not only is *Das Wesen* a nonmathematical apologia for the mathematical method, but it is also a study in Walrasian general equilibrium that depicts economic events as the result of mechanistic quantitative interactions of physical entities, rather than as consequences of purposeful human action—the Austrian approach. Thus, Fritz Machlup writes that

> Schumpeter's emphasis on the character of economics as a quantitative science, as an equilibrium system whose elements are "quantities of goods," led him to regard it as unnecessary, and, hence, as methodologically mistaken for economics to deal with "economic conduct" and with "the motives of human conduct" (Fritz Machlup, "Schumpeter's Economic Methodology," *Review of Economics and Statistics* 33 (May 1951: 146–47).

Cf. Mohammed Shabbir Khan, *Schumpeter's Theory of Capitalist Development* (Aligarh, India: Muslim University of India, 1957).

On *Das Wesen*, see Erich Schneider, *Joseph Schumpeter: Life and Work of a Great Social Scientist* (Lincoln, Neb.: University of Nebraska Bureau of Business Research, 1975), pp. 5–8. On Schumpeter as Walrasian, also see Schneider, "Schumpeter's Early German Work, 1906–17," *Review of Economics and statistics* (May 1951): 1–4; and Arthur W. Marget, "The Monetary Aspects of the Schumpeterian System," ibid. p. 112ff. On Schumpeter as not being an "Austrian," also see "Haberler on Schumpeter," in Henry W. Spiegel, ed., *The Development of Economic Thought* (New York: John Wiley and Sons, 1952), pp. 742–43.

3. Thus, Schumpeter wrote that

> in the normal circular flow the whole value product must be imputed to the original productive factors, that is to the services of labor and land; hence the whole receipts from production must be divided between workers and landowners and there can be no permanent net income other than wages and rent. Competition on the one hand

and imputation on the other must annihilate any surplus of receipts over outlays, any excess of the value of the product over the value of the services of labor and land embodied in it. The value of the original means of production must attach itself with the faithfulness of a shadow to the value of the product, and could not allow the slightest permanent gap between the two to exist. . . . To be sure, produced means of production have the capacity of serving in the production of goods. . . . And these goods also have a higher value than those which could be produced with the produced means of production. But this higher value must also lead to a higher value of the services of labor and land employed. No element of surplus value can remain permanently attached to these intermediate means of production (Joseph A. Schumpeter, *The Theory of Economic Development: An Inquiry Into Profits, Capital, Credit, Interest, and the Business Cycle.* New York: Oxford University Press, 1961, pp. 160, 162).

4. See the attack on this Austrian view from a Knightian neoclassical perspective in Earl Rolph, "The Discounted Marginal Productivity Doctrine," in W. Fellner and B. Haley, eds., *Readings in the Theory of Income Distribution* (Philadelphia: Blakiston, 1946), pp 278–93. For a rebuttal, see Murray N. Rothbard, *Man, Economy, and State* vol. I (Los Angeles: Nash Publishing Co., 1970), 431–33.

5. On this alleged synchronization, see Khan, *Schumpeter's Theory*, pp. 51, 53. The concept of synchronization of production is a most un-Austrian one that Schumpeter took from John Bates Clark, which in turn led to the famous battle in the 1930s between the Clark-Knight concept of capital and the Austrian views of Hayek, Machlup, and Boulding. See ibid., p. 6n. Also see F.A. Hayek, "The Mythology of Capital," in Fellner and Haley, *Readings*, pp. 355–83.

6. In Khan's words, for Schumpeter "capital cannot have any age structure and perishes in the very process of its function of having command over the means of production" (Khan, *Schumpeter's Theory*, p. 48). Schumpeter achieves this feat by sundering capital completely from its embodiment in capital goods, and limiting the concept to only a money fund used to purchase those goods. For Schumpeter, then, capital (like interest) becomes a purely monetary phenomenon, not rooted in real goods or real transactions. See Schumpeter, *Economic Development*, pp. 116–17.

7. See Schumpeter, *Economic Development*, pp. 43–44.

8. Clemence and Doody attempt to refute this charge, but do so by assuming a zero rate of time-preference. Capitalists would then be interested in maximizing their utility returns over time without regard for when they would be reaped. Hence, capital goods would be maintained indefinitely. But for those who believe that everyone has a positive rate of time-preference, and hence positively discounts future returns, a zero rate of return would quickly cause the depletion of capital and certainly the collapse of stationary equilibrium. Richard V. Clemence and Francis S. Doody, *The Schumpeterian System* (Cambridge, Mass: Addison-Wesley, 1950), pp. 28–30.

9. In the excellent critique of Schumpeter's zero-interest equilibrium by Lionel Robbins, "On a Certain Ambiguity in the Conception of Stationary Equilibrium," *Economic Journal* 40 (June 1930): pp. 211–14. Also see Gottfried Haberler, "Schumpeter's Theory of Interest," *Review of Economics and Statistics* (May 1951): 122ff.

10. Thus, Schumpeter wrote: "It is not the large mass of consumers which induces production. On the contrary, the crowd *is mastered and led by the key personalities in production*" (italics are Schumpeter's) in "Die neuere Wirtschaftstheorie in den Vereinigten Staaten" ("Recent Economic Theory in the United States") *Schmollers Jahrbuch* (1910), cited in Schneider, *Joseph A. Schumpeter*, p. 13.

11. See Simon S. Kuznets, "Schumpeter's Business Cycles," *American Economic Review* (June 1940).

12. Joseph A. Schumpeter, *Business Cycles: A Theoretical, Historical, and Statistical Analysis of the Capitalist Process*, 2 vols. (New York: McGraw-Hill, 1939).

13. This does not mean that *all* propositions must be falsifiable; they can be self-evident or deduced from self-evident axioms. But no one can claim that the alleged *Kitchin, Juglar,* and *Kondratieff* cycles are in any sense self-evident.

14. See Alvin H. Hansen, *Fiscal Policy and Business Cycles* (New York: W.W. Norton, 1941). For a clear summary statement of his position, see Hansen, "Economic Progress and Declining Population Growth," in G. Haberler, ed., *Readings in Business Cycle Theory* (Philadelphia: Blakiston, 1944), pp. 366–84.

15. George Terborgh, *The Bogey of Economic Maturity* (Chicago: Machinery and Allied Products Institute, 1945).

16. Schumpeter, *Business Cycles*, p. 74.

Two Forgotten Articles by Ludwig von Mises on the Rationality of Socialist Economic Calculation

William Keizer

In the past few years, there has been a remarkable revival of academic interest in the Austrian economist Ludwig von Mises's pioneering and incisive critique of the rationality of economic calculation under socialism. An entire issue of the *Journal of Libertarian Studies* was devoted to the subject. Other journals have included articles by Karen I. Vaughn and Peter Murrell.[1] Less well known to American readers will be articles by the German economists R. Neck and S.G. Schoppe.[2] From the late 1940s onward until this recent spate of publications, it was commonly held in western academic circles that von Mises's original critique had been convincingly refuted by:

1.   The Polish economist Oskar Lange's 1936 model of "market socialism" (also known as the "competitive solution"), as was expressed in A. Bergson's comprehensive survey of the debate of 1948.[3]

2.   The evident viability and high growth rates of the socialist economies of Eastern Europe, where the problems raised by von Mises were simply ignored or bypassed as irrelevant—an attitude theoretically underpinned and academically sanctioned by western "centralist" socialists such as M. Dobb and Paul Sweezy.[4]

3.   The rapid rise in the early 1960s of cybernetic optimal planning models using high-powered computer technology, as was later believed by Lange himself.[5]

Most commentators on this famous "socialist controversy" held the view that von Hayek's later arguments against the rationality of socialist economic calculation were a step back from the strict "impossible" charged by von Mises, to a more modest and weaker "impractical" or even "less efficient than capitalism."[6] With that, the original charge lost much of its force and it appeared as if the socialists had won the debate.

Starting in the early 1970s, these same factors caused a gradual change in this prevalent western view of the debate.

- Lange's neoclassical solution came under serious attack, not only from von Hayek and other neoliberals, but also from the centralist socialists such as Dobb and Sweezy (and implicitly the Soviet theoreticians, who never even acknowledged its existence). In 1971, P.C. Roberts convincingly showed that Lange's market socialism could not be called "socialism" as traditionally defined by Marxists. What Lange did was vindicate market relationships, not refute von Mises's criticism.[7] In this line of reasoning Lange actually proved von Mises to be right: without real market relationships and real competition between the "socialist" firms, there can be no rational calculation. This is exactly what von Mises had averred, but he had extended the argument beyond the line Lange implicitly drew, by stating that there could be no independent firms under socialism, as they could not freely dispose over their means of production. Without decentralized property rights, there are no independent firms, no real competition, and no real market relations— and hence no rational calculation. Von Mises had stated (and in the two articles under discussion reiterated) that by "socialism" he understood a *centrally* planned economy, without independent firms acting as if they were the owners of their means of production. In his reply to arguments brought forward by Karl Polanyi and Heimann (to be discussed later) von Mises conceded that rational calculation is possible under *syndicalism*, where the workers or the managers either own the means of production or else behave as if they own them. His challenge was directed at centrally and imperatively planned *state socialism*, which he understood Marxists to want, not at syndicalism or workers' self-management. His quarrel was with Marx, not with Proudhon or the other "associative" socialists! Syndicalist or other market-based systems of socialism are no answer to his critique.

- The slowing down and ultimate stagnation of the growth rates of the Soviet and Eastern European economies, their inability to provide their citizens with a high standard of living, and the many instances of waste and inefficiency cited by Soviet economists themselves cast doubts on the rebuttal of von Mises's critique by the praxis of existing socialism.

- By the early 1970s, it was evident that the "computopian" ideals of a decade earlier had been unfounded. The mathematical planning models were incapable of reforming the practice of the Soviet planning system.

- New interest in the debate was also aroused by the burgeoning literature on the theory of property rights, which was seen to be the essence of von Mises's critique.[8]

The Central European Debate of the 1920s

All presentations of von Mises's critique refer only to his original 1920 article published in the *Archiv für Sozialwissenschaft und Sozialpolitik*. It was translated into English and republished by Hayek in his 1935 reader on the subject.[9] Occasional reference is made to his major work on socialism, *Die Gemeinwirtschaft* of 1922.[10] In the light of the subsequent controversy over what von Mises precisely wrote and meant, it is necessary to go back to the original German texts. There has been considerable misrepresentation of his actual arguments and many authors quote them only from secondary sources. It is, of course, easy to refute an argument if one starts by misrepresenting it. Von Mises then becomes a kind of straw man, which not only does injustice to his intellectual stature and critique, but also lulls his opponents into a false sense of security. One does not improve the economic theory of socialism by caricaturing the most fundamental criticism of it.

With the publication of "Die Gemeinwitschaft," the matter seemed to rest as far as von Mises own contributions to the debate were concerned. In the 1930s, Hayek took over some of his arguments in an Anglo-Saxon continuation of the debate, with new proponents of socialism (such as Dobb, Sweezy, H.D. Dickenson, A.P. Lerner, and Lange) on the opposite side. For most English-speaking scholars on the subject, *this* was the real "socialist controversy," which was then believed to have terminated with Bergson's aforementioned article. Unknown to most commentators, however, there was an extensive controversy about the rationality of socialist economics in the German journals of the 1920s, with many eminent German and Austrian economists as participants. This controversy was never satisfactorily settled, but rather was overtaken by political events, such as the National Socialist take-over of power and the suppression of socialism. Some original contributors to this debate emigrated to the United States, where they did not continue this Central European part of the debate (with the exception of Hayek, who had not taken part in the discussion of the 1920s).

Not only then are there a number of interesting contributions to the debate by various continental European authors, but there also exist two more articles written by von Mises himself on this subject in 1924 and 1928. In these he discusses and rebuts the counterarguments made by several German and Austrian proponents of socialism in response to his original critique. In doing so, he clarifies and extends his earlier arguments against the rationality of socialist economic calculation. Although they appeared in the same journal as his first article, only an excerpt of the 1924 paper has been translated into English and is therefore available to non–German-speaking readers. It is somewhat obscurely tucked away as part of the appendix to his book *Socialism* and has hardly been noticed by later authors.[11] To my knowledge there is no English translation of the whole article, nor of the 1928 article. In view of the later misunderstandings over what von Mises really meant, it is worth taking notice of these two articles as further evidence of what he really wrote. Here now is a synopsis of these two articles, with a commentary in the light of more recent research. In translating I have tried to stay as close as possible to von Mises's own wording.

"New Contributions to the Problem of Socialist Economic Calculation"

Von Mises opens his second article, "Neue Beiträge zum Problem der sozialistischen Wirtschaffsrechnung ' ("New Contributions to the Problem of Socialist Economic Calculation," henceforth "N.B."), which appeared in the "Archiv für Sozialwissenschaft" in 1924, with the statement: "The problem of economic calculation is the major and fundamental problem of socialism."[12] That this had not been realized until then was due to two reasons. First, for the adherents of the objective theory of value, there was no problem at all. If value was objectively determinable and calculable, then economic calculation would not present any problem, even in a socialist society. If they had, however, but visualized the actual construction of a socialist economy, the contradictions of the objective theory of value would soon have become apparent. One cannot solve the problem of value by means of the classical theory of value. Second, all preoccupation with the (future) problems of a socialist society and economic system were strictly prohibited by Marxism. "One was allowed to praise socialism, but not to think about it" (N.B., p. 488).

Von Mises states that it is now no longer possible to evade the problem. He has demonstrated that a socialist society is totally incapable of performing economic calculation, so that economizing ("wirtschaften") or rational economic action is impossible under socialism. He then proceeds to refute the arguments of a number of socialist authors who sought to disprove his original case.

He first discusses the Ph.D. thesis of A.W. Cohn, "Kann das Geld abgeschaft werden?" ("Can Money be Abolished?," University of Jena, 1920). Cohn quotes von Mises's original article extensively and appears to agree with its conclusions. But he then states that the problem had already been solved long ago by A. Schäffle's "social tax."[13] Schäffle had suggested that representatives of the trade unions and the consumers should periodically meet to set differentiated "taxes" (which might be negative) on the labor costs of the consumer goods produced. The "Central Office for Production Accounting" is presumed to know the (homogenous) labor time embodied in the various products. If the volume and intensity of demand exceeds the available supply, then the social tax should be higher than the average labor costs of the product, and vice versa. Thus there arise market-clearing prices on the basis of the labor theory of value. The idea is commonly found in the mid-1870s, as in Marx's own distinctions between "labour values," "*Produktionspreise*," and the daily fluctuating actual market prices.

Von Mises considers this proposal as good as any other for clearing the market for consumer goods, but *only* for this specific purpose.

> For a socialist society can arrange the distribution of (consumer) goods according to whatever principle it pleases, but if it wishes to make them exchangeable against each other, then it is bound to those relationships that arise out of the solely-permitted exchange of consumer goods for each other.

That is to say, if the socialist planning authorities wish to allow "consumer freedom of choice," they must set their selling prices according to the demand and supply relationships existing on the market for consumer goods.[14] This is the only kind of market permitted under socialism—there can be no market for producer goods. The usefulness of this social tax for the purpose of economic calculation is an entirely different matter, for here it must fail completely. According to von Mises, Schäffle's basic error lies in believing that under collectivist production, "social labor" would be a concrete and calculable reality, which could be used as a measure of value. As erroneous is Shäffle's implicit conviction that rational prices for producer and investment goods can be derived from a set of market-clearing prices for consumer goods. Schäffle and Cohn see the problem solely in terms of finding market-clearing prices for consumer goods. As von Mises was to state in his reply to the arguments of Heimann, that is *not* the core of his problem, which is economic calculation involving investment goods, requiring subjective estimates of an uncertain future. Here market-clearing prices for present goods are but one element of a large set of required data, and insufficient by themselves.

The second author discussed is Karl Polanyi.[15] He admits that von Mises's problem is "the key problem of the socialist economy" and believes it to be insoluble in a centrally administered economy—which is precisely what von Mises, quoting the Marxist classics, defines the socialist economy to be₁ Polanyi's attempt at a solution is to propose a "functionally-organised socialist transition economy," which von Mises interprets as the kind of social order the English Guild Socialists had in mind. He finds Polanyi's concept of such a system as nebulous as that of the Guild Socialists. The "body politic" is to be the "owner" of the means of production, but it does not have the right of use ("usus") over them. That is reserved for the producers' "association," chosen by the workers on a sectoral basis. This ownership arrangement resembles the Yugoslav property system.

Von Mises considers the basic flaw of this construction to be the vagueness by which it seeks to evade a crucial question: Is the system supposed to be *socialist* or *syndicalist*? Polanyi first assigns the means of production to society as a whole, the "commune," and thus seeks to absolve himself from the charge of "syndicalism" (which must have been quite a crime among Austrian Marxists in the early 1920s₁) But von Mises states, "Property is the right of use, and if that is assigned to the production associations, then these are the owners and then we are dealing with a syndicalist society" (N.B., p. 491). A choice must be made: there can be no reconciliation between socialism and syndicalism. This strict distinction between the two (which von Mises had in common with all Marxist socialists of the time—and perhaps of today), he made on the basis of a theory of property rights. Property rights over the means of production must be assigned to some concrete body: if neither the "commune" nor the production associations have the final say in their allocation, then the system is not viable. If final decision-making power rests with the commune (the *political* organization of the community), then one is dealing with a "zentrale Verwaltungswirtschaft," a centrally administered economy such as Soviet Russia's. Polanyi agrees that rational economic calculation is impossible here. If the final power rests with the production associations, then there exists a syndicalist commonwealth.

Polanyi's confusion on this point make him suggest a pseudosolution to von Mises's problem. His associations engage in mutual exchange relations, they give and receive as if they were the owners of the goods, and thus a market and market prices are created Polanyi does not notice that this is irreconcilable with the essence of *socialism*.[17] von Mises agrees that rational economic calculation is possible under syndicalism or under any other producer cooperative-based system where the cooperative bodies are the owners of the means of production. Thus, there is some kind of group-collective *private* ownership, what the Maoists during the Chinese cultural revolution used to criticise as Yugoslav group-capitalism. Group-capitalism is also capitalism and allows rational calculation. But von Mises reiterates his contention that this is impossible under a centrally planned administrative socialist system and says that Polanyi concedes this. All Guild Socialists make the same mistake: they confuse their particular brand of syndicalism with socialism, properly so called. The debate with Polanyi shows that von Mises's original challenge was directed against a centrally administered socialist economy, as was then, during "war communism," and later again in the Stalinist epoch, being constructed in the Soviet Union. It was explicitly not aimed at syndicalism, guild socialism, or some sort of market socialism with independent firms. He readily concedes the rationality of economic calculation in any system in which the enterprises, cooperatives, associations, or whatever have full property rights and are the owners of the means of production. If property rights are dispersed over several decision makers who must interact with one another, then markets (also for producer goods) exist and rational exchange relationships and prices can be established.

The third author discussed is the well-known Marxist E. Heimann.[18] He follows Max Weber in rejecting the concept of a moneyless socialist society, so that his socialism is characterised by monetary calculation. He also suggests separate "production groups," but again does not specify their exact relationship to society as a whole, that is, to the state and its supreme planning organ. Thus he speaks of market exchange relations between the production units, without realizing that the "planned economy," properly so called, is without market exchange. What here could be called "selling" and "buying" is in its nature something very different. Heimann lapses into this error because he sees the defining characteristic of a planned economy as the monopolistic concentration of the individual branches of production, rather than as the dependence of all production on the uniform will of a central social organ. Von Mises finds this misconception all the more surprising as already the name "planned economy" and all of Heimann's arguments stress the monolithism of the guidance of the economy. "Here, and nowhere else, lies the dividing line between sociaism and capitalism" (N.B., p. 493).

Von Mises defines "pure socialism" as the "strictly centrally-organised commonweal" and the "fully-implemented planned economy" (N.B., p. 493). The possibility that superficially independent departments may have been delegated the task of administering the individual branches of industry, under the monolithic leadership of a central bureau, does not alter the fact that only this bureau has all the authority. The relationships between the separate departments are not established on a market through the competition of buyers and sellers, but by government order. The problem is, that this government intervention lacks any measure to make calculation possible as the government cannot orient itself on exchange relationships formed on the market. The government can, of course, base its calculations on exchange relationships that it establishes *itself*, but such a determination is arbitrary. It is not based upon the subjective evaluations of the economic subjects, which have been carried over to the producer goods through the interaction of all citizens in the processes of production and exchange. Therefore, they cannot form the basis of rational economic calculation (N.B., p. 494).

These last sentences show that von Mises (as well as everybody else in those daysı) envisaged socialism as operating under consumer sovereignty.[19] He explicitly excludes "planners' sovereignty"—the authoritarian determination of the output assortment and hence the scarcity relations between all goods and services on the basis of the "planners' " (the political rulers') *own* subjective preferences. The task of the socialist economy was to maximize social welfare on the basis of the individual citizens' own preferences. It was this that he found socialist calculation incapable of doing.

Heimann suggests that economic calculation should be based on the average costs of production, including wages. This argument is circular, even when one defines "costs" as "utility forgone." In a socialist state, the second-best opportunity can only be determined by the state, and the problem is, whether the state can calculate at all what this net-best opportunity isı In every conceivable form of socialist society, the competition between entrepreneurs (who, in a system based on private property, strive to allocate goods and services to their most profitable use) is replaced by the planned actions of the state. But it is only this competition between entrepreneurs (who mutually seek to wrest capital goods and labor away from each other) that forms pricesı Where production and economic activity occur on a planned basis (by order of a central bureau that everything is subservient to), the basis of profitability accounting disappears and only accounting in physical terms remains. As in Lange's "competitive solution," Heimann believes that as soon as there is real competition on the markets for consumer goods, the price relationships established there will be transmitted to all the stages of production. One must only apply the pricing rule properly, independent of the constitution of the parties on the markets for producer goods. Von Mises states that this will only occur if *real* competition exists. Heimann visualizes socialist society as the association of a number of "monopolies" (the production departments of the whole socialist organism), with each assigned a delimited sector of production to supply. When these monopolies buy on the producer goods "markets," this cannot be called competition, as the government has previously assigned to them the field in which they must operate and which they may not leave. Competition only exists when each firm produces those goods that appear to offer it the highest profitability. These conditions are only met under private ownership of the means of production (N.B., p. 495).

Heimann's description of a socialist economy only deals with the current production of consumer goods with the aid of raw materials. Thus he gives the impression as if the separate departments of the socialist economy were capable of acting on their own. But far more important than this is the replacement of existing capital stock and investment in new capital goods. The crux of rational economic calculation lies in deciding on these matters, not on disposing existing capital, which to a certain degree has already been predetermined by these decisions. These replacement and investment decisions, which bind for decades to come, cannot be made dependent on the momentary demand for consumer goods. They must be oriented upon the future; they must be "speculative." Heimann's system of having the expansion or contraction of production follow more or less automatically from the state of demand for consumer goods fails utterly here. Solving the valuation problem by reducing it to costs is theoretically only possible in an empirically nonexistent static state. In statics prices and costs coincide, but in dynamics this is not the case (N.B., p. 495).

Von Mises briefly refers to the writings of a number of Soviet economists such as Tchaianov, Strumilin, Bucharin, and Varga, as were known to him through publications of Leichter and Varga.[20] Tchaianov sought to establish some kind of input–output relationships in physical terms between the various sectors of the economy, whereas Strumilin attempted to construct labor values, as did Varga. None of these attempts tried to cope with the crux of von Mises's problem, which is that of *economic* calculation.

The fifth author von Mises discusses is Karl Kautsky, whose rejection of the labor theory of value as the basis for economic calculation under socialism ("the hopeless task of measuring running water with a sieve") he notes with satisfaction.[21] Instead of labor values, Kautsky suggests that the new socialist society should at first employ what it finds readily available: the historical prices, expressed in gold currency, as established under the previous capitalist regime. These outdated prices are the result of a long historical process and are imprecise and imperfect, but they are the sole basis for a smooth continuation of the circulation process under socialism. These prices are at first left unchanged.[22] But whenever social interest demands it, the prices of individual goods are altered from the historical levels set by capitalism. Kautsky assumes this to be an easier task than to determine labor values for all goods. "Of course this must not be done in an arbitrary way."[23] Von Mises comments that unfortunately Kautsky fails to indicate how this could be done in any other way than arbitrarily. Kautsky's suggestions are not worth further elucidation. Historical prices cannot be used in the long run, and Kautsky does not indicate *how* the necessary corrections should be made (N.B., p. 497).

Von Mises finally discusses Leichter, who rigorously adheres to the labor theory of value.[24] Von Mises repeats the arguments he made against this theory in his 1922 book *Die Gemeinwirtschaft*. The labor theory of value is useless for economic calculation because it is incapable of converting labor of different qualities to a single standard (the so-called "reduction problem") and because it does not take into account the natural factors of production. Leichter believes that the importance of the various labor tasks can be compared with each other. Von Mises says that such comparisons can of course be made, but that they will lead to different results, depending on the subjective valuations of the person who made them. And what does "importance" mean in this context? Does it refer to the importance of being on the job, of producing better work, or the arduousness of the work, and so forth? Each of these comparisons yields a different result, but only one can be the basis of the reduction factor. Leichter's contention that practice daily solves this problem by establishing wages (which was also Marx's solution to this problem)[25] is wholly erroneous. Wage rates are established in market exchange on the basis of subjective valuations, and the problem is precisely whether it is possible to reduce the various kinds of labor to a single standard in a society without market exchange. Leichter attempts his way out of this circular reasoning by stressing that modern wage negotiations have "nearly" nothing to do with "market haggling" in the normal sense of the word—supply and demand play "nearly" no role in determining the wage differentials. Von Mises notes that the double insertion of the word "nearly" robs these arguments of their basis.

The origin of Leichter's (and Marx's) error lies in an inadequate and unclear comprehension of the nature of the market mechanism and market price creation. To Leichter, the essence of the market seems to be "haggling" and reference to supply and demand. Von Mises states, however, that "haggling" may even be absent altogether. Even where "fixed" prices that "allow of no reduction" exist, the market mechanism acts in its usual way, except that the state of the market does not so much influence the price through the actual negotiations of the market parties, but through their behavior, such as the absence or queuing of buyers and the corresponding behavior of the sellers.

Von Mises's other argument against the labor theory of value is that economic calculation should not only comprise labor, but also the material means of production, such as those provided by Nature. Leichter does not demonstrate how the problem of socialist economic calculation can be solved regarding these scarce goods, on which no labor has been spent. He does remark that "society" will set higher prices for these scarce goods. Von Mises argues that the problem is not whether society sets higher or lower prices, but whether it will be able to do so on the basis of the results of economic calculation. "It was never doubted that society can dispose: I maintain that it cannot do so rationally, i.e. on the basis of a calculation" (N.B., p. 500). Orthodox Marxists have been as incapable as others in finding a useful system of economic calculation for a socialist society.

"New Papers on the Problem of Socialist Economic Calculation"

In volume 60 (1928) of the *Archiv*, von Mises once again returned to the problem of discussing the contributions of a number of new authors in a piece titled "Neue Schriften zum Problem des sozialistische Wirtschaftsrechnung" ("New Papers on the Problem of Socialist Economic Calculation," henceforth "N.S.").[26] In the same number of the *Archiv* that his second article appeared, J. Marschak attempted to refute his original argument by showing that there is no rational economic calculation under capitalism either.[27] (See also the arguments of Lange and Dobb against the rationality of economic calculation under capitalism). Von Mises asks himself whether "a criticism of economic calculation under capitalism yields anything as proof of the possibility of economic calculation under socialism. [Marschak] simply follows the example of all other socialist authors: speak as little as possible of socialism and as much as possible of the inadequacies of the capitalist system" (N.S., p. 187). Marschak then seeks to demonstrate that economic calculation is possible under syndicalism. "That has never been disputed, least of all by me. But the scientific problem to be debated is economic calculation in a socialist, not in a sydicalist commonwealth. Marschak evades this, the real, question" (N.S., p. 187).

He next disposes of O. Neurath's new proposal for calculation in physical terms, on account of its inability to add up different goods.[28] There follows a discussion of a book by the exiled Russian economist Boris Brutzkus, who extensively treats the problem of economic calculation under Soviet socialism.[29] Brutzkus concurs with von Mises that without economic calculation, rational economic action under whatever kind of economic system is impossible. He also is of the opinion that the fact that production requires the combination of three factors (land, labor, and capital) retains its validity and importance under socialism. Therefore, a calculation solely in terms of labor values is incapable of providing an indication of the greater or lesser profitability of enterprises. With that the drafting of a uniform plan, the essence of Marxism, becomes impossible. Von Mises quotes Brutzkus to the effect that:

With this the socialist commonwealth, even with the entire instrumentarium of scientific theory and a gigantic statistical apparatus, is incapable of measuring the needs of its citizens and of evaluating them and is therefore not in a position to give the necessary directives to the producing units (N.S., p. 189).

Von Mises finds Brutzkus's book the first one that deals with the problem of the Soviet Union in a scientific way. All other works are of a descriptive nature and the presentation of the facts either suffers from an uncritical hatred of the Soviet Union (from which he therefore obviously wished to dissociate himself) or from its uncritical adulation.

By way of a final judgment on the decade's literature on the subject (which arose out of that undeniable political triumph of uncompromising socialism, the Russian revolution), von Mises quotes the prosocialist author Cassau as saying:

All experiences of the past decade have bypassed the ideology of "proletarian socialism" without influencing it. Hardly ever before has this ideology had so many possibilities of extension, and has it been so barren, as during this heyday of the debates on the socialisation of the economy (N.S., p. 189).

Conclusion

On the basis of von Mises's replies to his socialist critics in the two articles discussed here, the following conclusions may be drawn as to what von Mises really meant, especially as to what kind of socialist system his original critique was addressed.

1. On the basis of a theory of property rights, von Mises draws a clear distinction between Marxian socialism, properly so called, and syndicalism.

2. A socialist system under which property rights reside with decision makers *within* the separate firms, such as associations or workers' councils, he calls "syndicalism." Here the firms are independent; real competition exists between them. His critique is not aimed at syndicalism; rational economic calculation is possible here.

3. By socialism properly so called, von Mises understands a centrally planned and administered system, what is now often termed "state socialism." All firms here are subordinate to a central political authority. All production takes place according to an imperative, all-encompassing central plan. There are no independent firms and there is no real market or real competition between them. His critique is aimed at this variety of socialism, which he understood Marxists to want and to be in the process of establishing in the Soviet Union at that time.

4. All sorts of market socialist systems can be classified as either syndicalist or socialist according to their property rights structures. If they are syndicalist, they dress up the market in the terminology of socialist planning (in the words of P.C. Roberts). Several authors aver that this applies to Lange's "competitive solution." Such systems are no answer to von Mises's challenge. If they are de facto state socialist, they dress up socialism in pseudo–market terminology. His critique is also aimed at such systems.

5. The goal of socialism is postulated as the maximization of the individuals' welfare (and, by aggregation, social welfare), as defined by the individuals' *own* subjective preferences. Socialism operates under consumer sovereignty (or under citizen and consumer sovereignty, if one admits collective and merit goods). It expressly excludes the state of "planners' sovereignty." This must not be interpreted as a normative judgment on the part of von Mises. Writing before the advent of Stalinist totalitarianism, he (as well as his socialist opponents) conceived of socialism as seeking to maximize its citizens' welfare as they saw it themselves.

6. In the light of the above qualifications, his critique may be reformulated as follows: "Socialism, properly so called, is incapable of maximizing individual and social welfare based on individual preferences."

Notes

1. *The Journal of Libertarian Studies* 5, no. 1 (Winter 1981), with articles by R. Bradley, D. Lavoie, and D. Steele. K.I. Vaughn, "Economic Calculation under Socialism: the Austrian Contribution," *Economic Inquiry* 18 (1980). P. Murrell, "Did the Theory of Market Socialism Answer the Challenge of Ludwig von Mises? A Reinterpretation of the Socialist Controversy," *History of Political Economy* 15, no. 1 (1983).

2. R. Neck, "Die 'Sozialismusdebatte' in Lichte ausgewählter neuerer Entwicklungen der ökonomischen Theorie," and S.G. Schoppe, "Das Problem der Wirtschaftsrechnung in einer Zentralverwaltungswirtschaft aus neuer bürokratietheoretischer Sicht," both in *Jahrbuch für Sozialwissenschaft*, vol. 33 (1982).

3. A. Bergson, "Socialist Economics," in H.S. Ellis, ed., *A Survey of Contemporary Economics* (Philadelphia: Blakiston Co., 1948), p. 446. Two decades later, Bergson was less convinced of the efficiency of the "competitive solution." See A. Bergson, "Market Socialism Revisited," *Journal of Political Economy* 75, no. 5 (1967), pp. 657–8 and 671–72.

4. See, for instance, M. Dobb, "Welfare Economics and the Economics of Socialism," in part II, *A Socialist Economy* (Cambridge: Cambridge University Press, 1969); and P.M. Sweezy, *Socialism* (New York: McGraw-Hill, 1949).

5. O. Lange, "The Computer and the Market," in C. Feinstein, ed., *Socialism, Capitalism and Economic Growth: Essays Presented to M. Dobb* (Cambridge: Cambridge University Press, 1967). On this point see also G.R. Feiwel, "On the Economic Theory of Socialism: Some Reflections on Lange's Contributions," *Kyklos* 25 (1972): 614–16.

6. F.A. Hayek, "The Present State of the Debate," in F.A. Hayek, ed., *Collectivist Economic Planning* (London: Routledge, 1935); also his "Socialist Calculation III: The 'Competitive Solution,'" *Economica*, no. 26 (1940). See also O. Lange, "On the Economic Theory of Socialism," in B.E. Lippincott, ed., *On the Economic Theory of Socialism* (New York: 1964), pp. 63–64.

7. P.C. Roberts, "Oskar Lange's Theory of Socialist Planning," *Journal of Political Economy* 79 (1971).

8. G. Warren Nutter, "Markets without Property: A Grand Illusion," in E.G. Furubotn and S. Pejovich, eds., *The Economics of Property Rights* (Cambridge, Mass.: 1974).

9. L. von Mises, "Die Wirtschaftsrechnung im sozialistischen Gemeinwesen," *Archiv für Sozialwissenschaft und Sozialpolitik* 47 (1920), translated into English by S. Adler and published in Hayek, *Collective Economic Planning*.

10. L. von Mises, *Die Gemeinwirtschaft*, Jena (1922), translated by J. Kahane under the title *Socialism* (London: 1936).

11. See L. von Mises, *Socialism* (reprint of the 1951 edition) (London: Jonathan Cape, 1974) pp. 516–21. His appendix, with the excerpt of the 1924 article, was added to the revised second German edition of 1932, which was used for J. Kahane's English translation of 1936. The excerpt comprises 5-1/2 of the original's thirteen pages (pp. 490–95 of pp. 488–500) and deals with only two (Polanyi's and Heimann's) of the original six counterproposals.

12. L. von Mises, "Neue Beiträge zum Problem der sozialistischen Wirtschaftsrechnung," in *Archiv für Sozialwissenschaft und Sozialpolitik* 51 (1924).

13. A. Schäffle, *Bau und Leben des sozialen Körpers*, vol. 3 (Tübingen: 1878).

14. "Consumer freedom of choice" means that the central planners authoritatively determine the volume, assortment, and quality of the consumer goods, but the consumers are free to spend their money income as they please. See also P.J.D. Wiles, *The Political Economy of Communism* (Oxford: 1962), pp. 35, 96–97.

15. K. Polanyi, "Die funktionelle Theorie der Gesellschaft und das Problem der sozialistischen Rechnungslegung," in *Archiv für Sozialwissenschaft und Sozialpolitik* 52 (1924).

16. See K.C. Thalheim, "Formen und Bedeutung des Eugentums an Produktionsmitteln in marktsozialistischen Systemen," in C. Watrin, ed., *Studien zum Marktsozialismus* (Berlin: 1976), pp. 66–68.

17. See on this point P.C. Roberts, "Oskar Lange's Theory."

18. E. Heimann, *Mehrwert und Gemeinwirtschaft* (Berlin: 1922).

19. This should actually be called "consumer-and-worker sovereignty" or, in Rothbard's words, "individual self-sovereignty in the market" (M.N. Rothbard, *Man, Economy and State*, vol. 2. Princeton, N.J: 1962, p. 562). For the sake of simplicity I abstract here from collective and merit goods.

20. For an interesting review of the various attempts to solve the problem of socialist economic calculation in the Soviet Union in 1919–20, see A. Nove, "Marx, the Market and 'Feasible Socialism,'" in U. Gärtner and J. Kosta, eds., *Wirtschaft und Gesellschaft. Festgabe für O. Sik* (Berlin: Dunker und Humblot, 1979).

21. K. Kautsky, *Die proletarische Revolution und ihr Programm* (Berlin: Dietz Nachfolger, 1922).

22. O. Lange also suggested taking the historical prices inherited from capitalism as a starting point. See O. Lange, "On the Economic Theory of Socialism," p. 86.

23. K. Kautsky, *Proletarische Revolution*, p. 322.

24. O. Leichter, *Die Wirtschaftsrechnung in der socialistische Gesellschaft* (Vienna: Verlag der Wiener Volksbuchhandlung, 1923).

25. See K. Marx, *Das Kapital*, Erster Band (Berlin: 1975), p. 59.

26. L. von Mises, "Neue Schriften zum Problem der sozialistische Wirtschaftsrechnung," *Archiv für Sozialwissenschaft und Sozialpolitik* 60 (1928).

27. J. Marschak, "Wirtschaftsrechnung und Gemeinwirtschaft," *Archiv für Sozialwissenschaft und Sozialpolitik* 51 (1924).

28. O. Neurath, *Wirtschaftsplan und Naturalrechnung* (Berlin: E. Laub, 1925). Neurath was the prime exponent of a moneyless socialist economy and of planning in physical terms.

29. B. Brutzkus, *Die Lehren des Marxismus im Lichte der russischen Revolution* (Berlin: H. Sack, 1928).

Rent Seeking: Some Conceptual Problems and Implications

E.C. Pasour, Jr.

There is increasing use of the concept of rent seeking to describe resource-wasting activities of individuals and groups seeking wealth transfers.[1] A wide range of activities are presumably of this type including agricultural price supports, occupational licensing, labor unions, import and export quotas, and education subsidies. The term *rent seeking* is used to describe attempts both to obtain and to maintain wealth transfers. Although the terminology of rent seeking is quite recent, the behavior that it describes "has been with us always" (Buchanan, 1980, p. 3). Moreover, rent-seeking behavior has become more important as institutional changes have created opportunities that did not exist when there was general agreement that the state should play a more limited role. Mancur Olson (1982) contends that the increase in specialized pressure groups is a key factor in the declining economic growth rate of nations—adding to the criticism of this widespread phenomenon in which organized groups use the power of the state to further their own economic ends.

There is an implicit assumption in the literature that rent-seeking behavior can be objectively identified and that waste due to rent seeking can, at least in principle, be measured (Posner, 1975; Tullock, 1967). The problem of identifying rent-seeking activity under real world conditions is shown in this article to be similar to that of determining monopoly waste and other market inefficiencies.[2] It follows that rent-seeking waste can only be identified by substituting the observer's own standard of value. Moreover, if an activity is a legitimate function of the state, it is held that the lobbying associated with instituting and maintaining the activity is not necessarily wasteful. Consequently, since the appropriate role of the state is normative, identifying a particular activity as wasteful must necessarily be based on norms that lie outside of economic theory.

This article was presented as a paper at a New York University-Liberty Fund Research seminar in Austrian economics, August 7–11, 1983. The author wishes to thank members of the seminar and Terry Anderson, Marc Johnson, Dwight Lee, Jim Leiby, Rolf Mueller, and Ray Palmquist for helpful comments and suggestions.

The procedure of this article is as follows. Shortcomings of the conventional long-run equilibrium approach used in identifying monopoly waste are first described. The problem of groups attempting to achieve income transfers through the power of the state—nonmarket rent seeking—is then discussed. The lack of an appropriate benchmark in identifying inefficiency and waste under real world conditions of uncertainty (which renders information costly and is a major source of "government failure") is emphasized throughout the analysis. Despite the fact that rent-seeking theory provides no objective means of separating beneficial from wasteful government activities, it is argued that such waste exists because of imperfect coordination in political markets. There is increasing concern about the effects of activities by individuals and groups on the economic and political order and a growing perception that redistribution is the explanation for many government activities ostensibly justified on the basis of the "public interest." Implications of the increase in redistributive activities are discussed in the last section of the article. Although economic education is identified as a necessary precondition in reducing the scope for rent-seeking behavior, it is argued that ethical considerations are inherent in the use of state power to stifle competition where individuals are assumed to have the right to engage in mutually beneficial exchange.

Downward-Sloping Demand Curves and Resource Misallocation

There is a close relationship between rent-seeking theory and conventional measurements of monopoly waste. Monopoly is traditionally defined as a situation where demand is not perfectly elastic (Friedman, 1976, p. 126). In analyses of the resource (or "welfare") cost of monopoly by A.C. Harberger, Richard Posner, Gordon Tullock and others, long-run equilibrium is taken as the point of reference, and real world markets are compared with the perfectly competitive equilibrium. If the economy were perfectly competitive, there would be no profits or losses. Consequently, in this long-run competitive equilibrium framework, all profits are due to monopoly, are considered to be permanent, and imply a welfare loss (Littlechild, 1981).

The alternative to considering monopoly as a market situation where demand is not perfectly elastic is to view market competition as a *process* (Hayek, 1948; Kirzner, 1973, 1979). In the analysis of firms facing downward-sloping demand curves, the market process approach stresses the necessity of using a model that allows above-average rates of return due to entrepreneurship. While there is no role for entrepreneurial activity in competitive equilibrium where all decisions by market participants are perfectly coordinated, there are often profit opportunities for alert entrepreneurs under real world conditions where markets are seldom (if ever) in equilibrium.

Consider the example of an entrepreneur who develops a product before other potential producers and, consequently, faces a downward-sloping demand curve. The seller charges the monopoly price, OP (figure 1). In the conventional long-run equilibrium approach, the rectangle (T) is considered to be monopoly profit and the triangle (W.C.) a deadweight resource cost.[3] In this approach, all traces of monopoly power represented by less than perfectly elastic demand involve a "welfare cost" and are branded as socially harmful. However, the relevant alternative to output oq_1, for the time being at least, is not OQ_2, but rather no output at all. Under these conditions, it is inappropriate to depict the producer's action as socially harmful and generating a deadweight loss (W.C.). Instead, using the same analytical tool, the action of the decision maker can be said to generate a social gain given by his own entrepreneurial profit (T) plus the consumer surplus (C.S.) (Littlechild, 1981, p. 358).

The long-run equilibrium approach overlooks or discounts the importance of entrepreneurial activity to cope with change and the returns necessary to induce the decision maker to perform that function. In the words of Buchanan (1980, p. 5): "By seeking always to find new opportunities . . . and to exploit more fully existing opportunities, profit-seeking entrepreneurs generate a dynamic process of continuous resource reallocation that ensures economic growth and development." In marked contrast, there is no scope for beneficial profits in the conventional approach to economic analysis. The extra income earned by successful entrepreneurs is taken to be a measure of welfare loss rather than the return necessary to evoke beneficial entrepreneurial activity. This

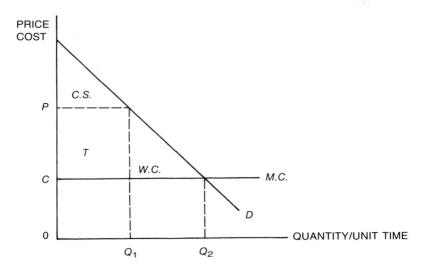

Figure 1. Monopoly Waste—Conventional Approach

approach fails to recognize that profits and losses are the signals that direct economic activity in a market economy. In the words of von Mises (1974, p. 119): "Profits are never normal. They appear only where there is a maladjustment. . . . The greater the preceding maladjustments, the greater the profit earned by their removal." For economic decision makers who are risk averters, it may be necessary to have even higher expected returns to remove maladjustments in resource use. Thus it is necessary to consider a long-run view of the market process in understanding the importance of entrepreneurial returns.[4]

The long-run equilibrium framework used in identifying the welfare cost of monopoly is inappropriate under real world conditions where returns include short-run disequilibrium profits due to entrepreneurial alertness. The entrepreneurial profits which may appear to be "rents" from a short-run perspective are, in fact, the driving force of the market system.[5] Moreover, since the amount of entrepreneurial activity hinges on the expected returns, a social policy which arbitrarily confiscates the returns due to entrepreneurial alertness will inevitably discourage such alertness in the future (Kirzner, 1973). In summary, by considering all downward-sloping firm demand curves to be socially wasteful, conventional analyses of monopoly fail to take into account the nature and role of profits in the market process.

The long-run equilibrium framework used by Tullock, Posner, and others in analyzing rent-seeking waste associated with monopoly is also inappropriate. Although rent seeking mainly focuses on transfers obtained through the aegis of the state, the term is also used to describe activities motivated by lure of profits when the monopolies are not rooted in government power.[6] Specifically, it is held that rent-seeking resource waste in the market situation shown in figure 1 consists not only of the traditional deadweight loss (*W.C.*), but also of some or all of the transfer (*T*) which, it is argued, is dissipated in attempts to obtain or maintain monopoly profits. As suggested, however, the description of these areas as resource waste ignores the benefits of entrepreneurial activity. Although the competitive entrepreneurial process (if successful) generates profits, the cost inherent in the uncertainty and innovation associated with attempts to obtain such profits should not be regarded as waste since effective resource use "will continue to require resources devoted to coping with and initiating changes" (Worcester, 1982, p. 86). Thus, entrepreneurial activity, reflected in downward-sloping demand curves, results in the creation of added value rather than rent-seeking waste. Moreover, except when monopoly is defined in terms of government restrictions on entry, there is no way to distinguish downward-sloping demand curves due to entrepreneurial foresight from other cases of "monopoly." Consequently, in the case of downward-sloping demand curves, there is no way to distinguish rent-seeking activity from the profit seeking of the market process except where competition is restricted through state power.

Nonmarket Rent Seeking

Rent seeking, as suggested, is mainly used to describe the effects of attempts by groups to achieve profits through government restrictions on entry (Buchanan, 1980, p. 9).[7] So long as the functions of government are restricted to those of the classical minimal state, there are relatively few opportunities to obtain income transfers in this way. As the functions of government have increased, however, there has been a concomitant increase in attempts by individuals and groups to create income opportunities through political activity. Lee (1983, pp. 15–16) describes the increase in rent-seeking activities in the United States:

> For over a century most government activity, as measured by revenue raised and spent, took place at the state and local level where intergovernmental competition imposed restraint. . . . In the environment established by this government restraint there was little to gain from political enterprise, or transfer activity, but much to gain from market enterprise, or productive activity. . . . But the existence of political power, even when restrained, establishes potential opportunities for some to benefit at the expense of others that will never be completely ignored. . . . There can be no reasonable doubt that there has been a dramatic expansion in the range of activities that have been subjected to government control over the last century.

Consider, as an example of rent seeking, the case of agricultural price supports where product prices and producer incomes are increased by restricting output through the use of production allotments. Traditionally it has been assumed that producers initially assigned allotment rights receive windfall gains. Posner (1975, p. 809), assuming that supply is perfectly elastic, however, shows that, "at the margin, the cost of obtaining a monopoly is exactly equal to the expected profit." If this is correct, the cartel gains would be completely dissipated through competitive rent-seeking activity. The forgone consumer surplus would not be converted into monopoly profit but would instead be dissipated in the form of real resource expenditures including lobbying and other activities required to obtain (and maintain) the favorable legislation (figure 2).

In figure 2, as cost increases from MC to MC_9, the entire value of the expected returns is exhausted through rent-seeking activity. This rent-seeing model then is similar to the theory of the firm in the conventional equilibrium approach of neoclassical theory. In market equilibrium, all decisions perfectly mesh, all profit opportunities are exhausted, and since competition is no longer an active force, there is no scope for entrepreneurship. Similarly, there is no scope for rent-seeking activity in the equilibrium depicted in figure 2. Stated differently, the equilibrium condition depicted implies the cessation of rent seeking since all opportunities to secure income transfers through political means have been exhausted and there is no further potential for gain.

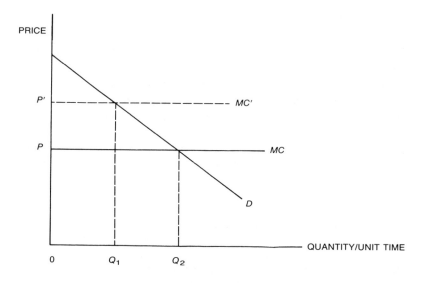

Figure 2. Rent Seeking—Constant Costs and Competitive Conditions

Noncompetitive Rent Seeking

Tullock argues that the rent-seeking incentive remains "even if we can find an equilibrium" (1980b, p. 98). He contends that costs are likely to be increasing rather than constant (as in figure 2) so that "the supply curve slants up and to the right from its very beginning" (ibid). Using an experimental game with some special assumptions about individual knowledge, Tullock examines the properties and outcomes of strategy games. In the specific game analyzed, a fixed prize is offered and participants are asked to make sealed bids for the prize. It is assumed that "if there is a correct solution for individual strategy, then each player will assume that the other parties can also figure out what the correct solution is" (ibid., p. 99). Marginal adjustments in bids are allowed and players are considered to be able to compare marginal costs and marginal returns. Tullock finds situations in which individual players will make contributions larger than the expected prize (overbidding) and cases in which the sum of players' bids is less than the value of the prize (underbidding). Since both underbidding and overbidding are observed, there appears to be no general tendency toward exact dissipation of the prize. Thus, it is argued, the competitive model where the expected return is exactly wasted cannot be taken as *the* general rent-seeking model (Tollison, 1982, p. 586).

It is not clear, however, that games that assume that individuals can figure out the correct strategy by comparing marginal costs and returns provide any useful information about rent-seeking activity under real world conditions of uncertainty. In rent seeking through the political process, there is uncertainty both about the size of the prize (value of the advantage secured through political means) and the probability of success in achieving it. Under these conditions, one might expect each rent-seeking group to invest in political activity so long as the expected benefits exceed the expected costs. As in the case of market entrepreneurship, however, there is no reason to think that returns would be exactly dissipated where choices are always shrouded in uncertainty. The decision maker faces similar information problems whether the wealth-seeking activity is directed toward the market process or the political arena. In either case, neither the alternative outcomes nor the probabilities of their occurrences can be fully known at the time of choice—raising questions as to the usefulness of probability theory in analyzing choice.[8]

Although individual interpretations and expectations will differ where real world conditions are constantly changing, there are opportunities for individuals and groups to engage in rent seeking through the political process just as there are opportunities for alert entrepreneurs in markets for goods and services. It is ironic that while profit maximization in both conventional neoclassical theory and rent-seeking theory is developed within an equilibrium framework, the emphasis placed on wealth-seeking behavior is quite different. In the conventional theory of the firm, the focus is on equilibrium conditions and entrepreneurship is largely neglected (Kirzner, 1973, 1979; Schultz, 1980). In the case of rent seeking, in contrast, the focus is on lobbying and other activity of groups attempting to use the political process for economic gain.

Problems in Identifying Rent-Seeking Waste

Since rent seeking is but one form of economic waste or inefficiency, first consider the general problem of identifying inefficiency in economic activity. Economic efficiency studies in conventional welfare economics typically use the benchmark of perfect competition which assumes price-taking behavior and perfect markets requiring perfect communication, instantaneous equilibrium, and costless transactions (Hirshleifer, 1980, p. 232). Since no real world market can match these conditions, *all* real world markets are inefficient on the basis of this criterion.[9] Consider, for example, conventional monopoly theory which evaluates the extent of monopoly waste by comparing market conditions against the perfectly competitive norm (Armentano, 1982). Resource waste (as just shown) will appear to be an important problem on the basis of this criterion even when the extra income earned in any period is due to entrepreneurship. Moreover, market failure in the form of advertising, incomplete information, and externalities (as well as monopoly) will inevitably appear to be pervasive when real world markets are compared against the competitive norm (Pasour, 1981).

Demsetz (1969) has labeled this procedure of comparing existing "imperfect" arrangements with an unattainable ideal "the nirvana approach." Although it is clearly inappropriate to use a model that assumes away problems facing the entrepreneur in assessing entrepreneurial efficiency, no one has discovered an appropriate benchmark for evaluating the efficiency of real world choices made under conditions of uncertainty and costly information. Efficiency inevitably involves valuation; to be meaningful in a choice sense, any efficiency measurement must be based on the costs and returns confronting the decision maker. It is opportunity cost that influences individual choice, however, and the value of the sacrificed alternative to the decision maker cannot be determined by an outside observer. Moreover, the ultimate end of action is always the satisfaction of desires of the acting individual and "no man is qualified to declare what would make another man happier" (von Mises, 1966, p. 19). Since individuals base choices on data that are inherently subjective, the economist can identify waste in the actions of other people only by imposing his own standard of value (Buchanan, 1979, p. 61; Sowell, 1980, p. 218).[10]

A similar problem arises in identifying wasteful rent-seeking behavior where individuals attempt to achieve wealth transfers through the political process. Little attention has been devoted to the problem of identifying wasteful behavior in the rent-seeking literature. The examples of Tullock (1967) and Posner (1975), using the competitive norm as a benchmark, suggest that efforts to achieve monoplies, tariffs, and labor unions are rent-seeking waste. Bhagwati (1982), on the other hand, argues that rent-seeking behavior is not necessarily wasteful.[11] In the case of lobbying to restore free trade, for example, it is contended that rent-seeking activities may be beneficial or harmful depending upon whether "the resources used up in restoring free trade that is the lobby's economic advantage are socially more valuable than the social gains from free trade" (Bhagwati, 1982, p. 997).

In a book on income transfers, Tullock (1983) suggests that harmful redistribution can be identified by the motive.[12] The effect of government intervention, however, is not determined by the motives of those responsible for obtaining and maintaining a particular activity. The effects of minimum wage legislation, for example, are similar whether or not the motive of the proponents is self-serving. Moreover, most transfer programs involve a mix of motives; in analyzing any real life redistributive activity, there is no reliable way to determine *the* choice influencing motive.

The Bhagwati and Tullock analyses have the same shortcomings as all other approaches based on measurements of social costs and gains. The opportunity cost of any decision, as suggested above, depends upon the decision maker's anticipation of future conditions. Thus, opportunity cost is inherently subjective and distinct from data that can be objectively measured by the outside observer (Buchanan, 1969). The difficulties are magnified when the economist attempts to make interpersonal comparisons of gains and losses in utility.[13] Utility is a subjective concept and gains and losses in utility by different individuals cannot legitimately be measured or weighed against each other (Rothbard, 1982, p. 204).

Consider again the problem of identifying inefficiency on the part of the individual decision maker. If the economist identifies an activity as wasteful and the decision maker continues the activity, one cannot legitimately conclude that the activity is wasteful; instead, it might be concluded that the analyst has not measured the choice-influencing opportunity costs and benefits. Similarly, if after pointing out the wastes of rent controls, the necessary political changes are not made, what conclusion can one draw?[14] In attempting to identify institutional inefficiency, the economist faces problems similar to those in identifying inefficiency on the part of the individual decision maker.[15]

Once, it is recognized that cost and value are subjective concepts, it becomes clear that "net social benefit is an artificial concept of direct interest only to economists" (Littlechild, 1978, p. 92). Consequently, the effects of trade barriers arising through rent-seeking activity cannot be determined by comparing the gain in utility of producers at the expense of consumers. In the words of Robbins (1981, p. 5):

> [W]henever we discuss distributional questions, we make our own estimates of the happiness afforded or the misery endured by different persons or groups of persons. But these are *our* estimates. There is no objective measurement conceivable.

Thus, utilitarian approaches do not present a way of determining which activities are wasteful. Furthermore, as shown in the following section, whether or not an activity is considered to be rent seeking hinges on one's view of the legitimate role of the state.

Rent Seeking and the Role of the State

Consider first the minimal state where law and order are deemed to be the only appropriate functions of government. In this case, the lobbying and other resource costs necessary to achieve and maintain the proper level of support for these essential activities would not be rent-seeking waste. On the other hand, resources expended by teachers to enact (or preserve) a system of public education would be wasteful if education were not a proper function of the state. Thus, as in other cases of alleged inefficiency, rent-seeking waste can be identified only by substituting the observer's own standard of value.

Consider again the example of education. It is often argued (at least by educators) that education is a public good and, consequently, is a proper function of the state. If education is a proper role of the state, the use of resources devoted to lobbying efforts to improve schools and teachers' salaries would not necessarily be wasteful. Resources used in this way will appear to be wasted, however, if the real world is compared with an ideal polity where no information or transactions costs are required to initiate or maintain the appropriate functions of the state. Labeling the resource cost required to maintain legitimate political activity as rent-seeking waste ignores the problem of the "ideal benchmark" in evaluating government activities, and is another example of the nirvana approach where the real is compared with an unobtainable ideal.

A real world market will always appear inefficient when measured against the norm of perfect competition, and a real world political institution will always appear inefficient when compared to an idealized polity. The problem of identifying actual examples of "political failure" is similar to that of isolating examples of "market failure" in the sense that no one has discovered an appropriate benchmark against which to compare real world political institutions when information problems, transactions costs, and uncertainty are taken into account. In the absence of such a benchmark, there is no legitimate way to measure the efficiency of activities in the real world political process. It can be said, however, that to the extent that any particular activity is an appropriate function of government, it is not legitimate to consider all resources associated with securing and maintaining that activity as wasteful rent seeking.

In reality, there is no objective procedure for distinguishing productive from wasteful activities.[16] Consider several widely cited reasons for government intervention. The public goods model is taken by many economists to justify a wide range of activities including public education, income redistribution, publicly subsidized research, and national defense. Externality theory is used to justify a host of government programs, agencies, and activities including the Environmental Protection Agency, the Occupational Safety and Health Administration, the United States Department of Agriculture, SCS and land-use zoning. Monopoly theory is used to rationalize various antitrust policies. Many other restrictions on competition are justified on the basis of consumer ignorance. There is widespread disagreement, however, both as to when these market failure factors justify government intervention and as to which activities are legitimate functions of the state.[17] Nor is there agreement as to a benchmark against which to evaluate the efficiency of government activities in those areas where government intervention *is* deemed to be desirable.[18] Consequently, in the absence of a consensus on these issues, there is no objective basis for identifying which lobbying efforts are wasteful and which are beneficial.

Consider agricultural policy and the farm problem. The public interest model holds that the purpose of federal agricultural programs is to provide a remedy for chronic price and income instability in agriculture. Although agricultural price support programs are frequently attacked in the press and by many economists as prime examples of wasteful government activity, many agricultural economists justify these programs on market failure grounds.[19] For example, a recent analysis of the milk price support program concluded: "The relatively small implied consumer-to-producer transfers of the late 1970's resulting from classified pricing may be a small price to pay for the stabilizing aspect of classified pricing" (Song and Hallberg, 1982, p. 7).

Agricultural marketing orders are frequently justified on similar grounds. Marketing orders for fruits, vegetables, and specialty crops were provided to agricultural producers ostensibly as a tool for achieving "orderly marketing" conditions under the Federal Marketing Agreement Act of 1937. Oranges and other crops marketed under federal marketing orders are subject to quantity and/or quality controls reducing the amounts available for sale. Despite the fact that marketing orders from their inception were intended as means of increasing producer incomes (French, 1982), economists continue to attempt to justify this type of restriction on competition on the basis of economic efficiency.

> These regulations are designed to compensate for, or overcome certain characteristics of agricultural markets—imbalances in marketing power, instability, incomplete information, and the external effects of individual firms' actions—that prevent free trading from being fully efficient (U.S. Department of Agriculture, 1981, p. 81).

Opinions of economists and the public at large vary widely as to whether incomplete information, imbalances in market power, price instability, and other market imperfections provide a legitimate basis for government price support programs in agriculture. What are the implications for the theory of rent seeking? If an orange-marketing order, for example, is considered to be a legitimate function of government, lobbying efforts to maintain the marketing order would not necessarily be rent-seeking waste. If, however, it is held that restrictions on competition of this type are not justified, the activity of obtaining or maintaining the marketing order would be considered rent-seeking waste.

The situation is similar in the case of labor cartels. Richard Freeman and James Medoff (1979) contend that the cartel view of labor unions as rent-seeking organizations is seriously misleading. While accepting the idea that one goal of unions is to raise wages, they argue that by providing workers with a "voice" in the workplace as well as in the political arena, "unions can and do affect positively the functioning of the economic and social systems" (p. 70). If one agrees with Freeman and Medoff that the positive effects of unions are often more important than their negative effects, the lobbying efforts associated with obtaining and maintaining such unions would not necessarily be considered rent-seeking waste. If, however, the net effect of unions is deemed to be negative, resources devoted to unionizing activities would be considered waste.

A similar problem arises in the evaluation of lobbying activities to eliminate existing restrictions on competition. Consider the examples of interest rate ceilings and price controls on natural gas. If the restrictions are considered to be harmful distortions of the market process, lobbying efforts to eliminate them cannot legitimately be considered as waste.

A difference of opinion concerning the desirability of government intervention is evident in many areas including education and research subsidies, occupational licensing, and environmental and safety regulations. Are those programs merely due to imperfections in the political process that often favor the few at the expense of the many? Or, are there bona fide market failure reasons for such programs?[20] In the absence of a benchmark against which to measure the performance of the real world political process, there is no objective procedure for determining when government intervention is warranted or for judging the efficiency of government activities.[21] In all of the examples discussed here, an activity is beneficial or harmful depending upon the observer's values.

In reality, then, there is no objective procedure either in determining which activities of the state are illegitimate, or in determining the extent of rent-seeking waste associated with activities considered to be legitimate.[22] While economic theory is useful in explaining activities of individuals and groups in using the state to further their own ends, it does not provide an objective procedure for determining inefficiency or rent-seeking waste. Since utility and cost are subjective, they cannot be measured and aggregated by outside observers to determine social cost or utility. Consequently, on strictly economic grounds, the economist cannot reject (or advocate) any public policy (Rothbard, 1982, p. 212). Economic theory, in this sense, is not a substitute for ethical or philosophical analysis.

Decentralized markets are a necessary condition in maintaining individual freedom. The market, based on free exchange, is the only voluntary method of allocating resources. Yet, even if one agrees that the central issue is freedom and that reliance on market signals where feasible is ethically superior to known alternatives, the question just alluded to is still present, namely, what is the proper role of the state in a market economy? There are almost as many answers to the question as there are economists, philosophers, political scientists, and other analysts studying the problem. Consider Albert J. Nock's attempt to discriminate between productive and unproductive activities.

Nock suggests that man attempts to increase his welfare through two approaches—the economic and the political. The economic means is defined to involve the production and exchange of wealth whereas the political means involves the uncompensated appropriation of wealth produced by others (Nock, 1973, p. 26). The Nock approach to isolating wasteful activities is operational, however, only if one accepts Rothbard's conclusion that "no act of the State can ever increase social utility" (1982, p. 13). In this case, there is an unambiguous standard by which to identify rent-seeking activity. *All* activities by individuals and groups designed to achieve involuntary wealth transfers (programs financed by taxes, price increases through quotas, and so on) would, by definition, be labeled rent-seeking waste.

The Nock approach does not appear to be of much help, however, in the task of defining the scope of the "limited-government" market economy. Consider the example of lobbying by lawyers or police for increased appropriations for law and order. If successful, these activities clearly result in an uncompensated appropriation of wealth produced by others. If, however, law and order are legitimate functions of the state, expenditures to improve these services are not necessarily wasted. Moreover, the efficiency of production of law, order, and other services deemed appropriate by the state is not susceptible to measurement. In the words of Knight, "The question whether any type of political machinery will work 'better' or 'worse' than another is . . . a matter of opinion" (1935, p. 311). And, since opinions vary widely, the identification of rent-seeking activities is inevitably based on value judgments (often concealed ones).

The analysis of this article suggests that neither the appropriate role of government nor rent-seeking waste can be identified through the cost-benefit approach. If one accepts the limited state as the norm, there is at least a partial basis for identifying rent-seeking activities. Efforts by the steel industry to limit imports, for example, would be rent-seeking waste in the eyes of one convinced of the merits of free trade. There remains the normative problem, however, of specifying the appropriate functions of government or, alternatively, of determining *how limited* the role of the state should be.

Rent Seeking—Measurement versus Existence and Implications

The fact that wasteful government activity cannot be objectively determined does not suggest that the problem of rent seeking is unimportant. Stated differently, the fact that economists cannot identify or measure inefficiency in economic or political markets implies neither the absence of rent-seeking waste nor that political markets are efficient in the sense that there is no scope for improvement.[23] In the remainder of this article, it is assumed that use of the power of the state to achieve wealth transfers is an increasingly serious problem. Applying an insight from Kirzner's entrepreneurial analysis, there are opportunities to improve the operation of political markets because political decisions (like those of market participants) are never fully coordinated. The following analysis describes the effects of widespread rent seeking, problems in reducing redistributive activities, and reasons why a constitutional change may be required to reduce transfer activity.

There is evidence that the "special interest state" in which various segments of society organize, each seeking to get its share of government largesse, has incresed markedly in recent years.[24] In achieving their objectives, groups use their lobbying power to influence government policy bringing about an increase in the complexity and scope of government.[25] Olson (1982) argues that the effect of the increase in specialized pressure groups is to gradually strangle the economy.[26] Moreover, as special interest groups become more important and distributional issues more significant, political life tends to be more divisive.

Olson's argument concerning the harmful effects of transfers achieved through organized group activity is similar to that of F.A. Hayek. Hayek (1979) argues that the chief threat to the market order comes not from the selfish actions of individuals but rather from the selfishness of organized groups who "have gained their power largely through the assistance government has given them to suppress those manifestations of individual selfishness which would have kept their action in check" (p. 85).[27] While individual selfishness will in most instances lead the individual to act in a manner conducive to the preservation of the spontaneous order of society, the desire of individuals to become a closed group "will always be in opposition to the true common interest of the members of a Great Society" (Hayek, 1979, p. 90). The interest of organized groups is typically either to prevent entry of others wishing to share the profits or to avoid being driven out of production by lower-cost producers. Hayek suggests that more injustice is done in the name of group loyalty than from selfish individual motives and he emphasizes the implications of redistributive behavior on the political system.

> So long as it is legitimate for government to use force to effect a redistribution of material benefits . . . there can be no curb on the rapacious instincts of all groups who want more for themselves. Once politics becomes a tug-of-war for shares of the income pie, decent government is impossible (p. 150).

Thus, it might be argued that an "economic education revolution" is a necessary precondition for achieving a consensus concerning the need to limit the role of government and for devising institutional arrangements that can make these limits stick (Dorn, 1982). This approach implies that a shift in the focus of economic analysis is warranted—a shift toward political economy emphasizing the framework of institutions and rules within which people can effectively cooperate in pursuing their own diverse ends through decentralized coordination of their activities (Yeager, 1976).

Even if most people recognize the desirability of limiting government activity, however, there is a "you-first" problem in reducing transfers (Anderson and Hill, 1980). Each recipient of government aid has an economic incentive to favor a reduction in the transfers received by other people while maintaining his own. Thus, it might be argued that the need for an education revolution in ethics is no less important than in economics.[28] If individual freedom is accepted as an ethical standard, individuals have the right to engage in mutually beneficial exchange. Moreover, income redistribution through the aegis of the state inevitably involves coercive restrictions on free exchange and infringements on individual freedom. Thus, if people were convinced that it is ethically wrong to achieve wealth increases through political means, the cost of engaging in rent-seeking activities would increase with a consequent decrease in these activities. However, as discussed, the case for reducing redistributive activities has also been made on nonethical grounds. In the words of Mitchell (1983):

> Rational individual and group action will increase transaction costs, produce a smaller social product, and in the end leave most worse off. This is the disastrous dynamic of our democracy. . . . We face the dilemma of individual and collective rationality that general ruin can be the outcome of rational action (pp. 365–66).

Whether or not the problem of rent-seeking is viewed as an ethical issue, it is likely that a significant reduction in the bargaining society will require constitutional reform.[29] Buchanan (1977) suggests that the cost of the present system may become so great that the individual transfer recipient will agree to a change in an existing rule that imposes limited damages on him in exchange for a reciprocal agreement by others for another set of changes that will greatly benefit him. An analysis of alternative methods of limiting the harmful effects of special interest groups through constitutional reform is beyond the purview of this analysis. Possibilities include limits on taxation and spending, reverse revenue sharing, and Hayek's proposal to entrust the general rules of just conduct to a representative body distinct from the body entrusted with the task of government (Hayek, 1979; Lee, 1983).

Conclusions

Rent-seeking waste is a matter of opinion depending on one's view of the appropriate role of the state, which must ultimately be determined on the basis of ethics rather than economic theory. If emphasis is placed on the freedom of individual choice, there are genuine opportunities for improvements in the political system and strong reasons to reduce the current level of redistributive activity. Rent-seeking activities by organized groups are important in the growth of the bargaining society or transfer society with its stifling effect on the competitive market process and concomitant shrinking of liberty of choice. Moreover, while there can be little doubt that there has been a pronounced increase in the number of groups organized for redistributive purposes, group activities generally pose little reason for concern in the absence of government assistance. Thus, limiting the role of the state is essential in minimizing the effects of rent-seeking activity.[30] There is mounting evidence that a revision of the constitutional contract will be necessary to reduce the role of the state. Regardless of the approach taken in reducing the scope of government, however, a necessary first step is increased awareness of the economic and ethical implications of redistributive activities by individuals and groups.

Notes

1. While rent seeking is usually used to describe the effects of groups attempting to obtain wealth transfers through the aegis of the state, the term is also applied (as will be shown here) to the effects of "monopoly" not rooted in government power. In contrast to the orthodox analysis which implies that rent seeking generates social waste only in settings where *artificial* scarcities are created, Buchanan (1983) suggests in a recent paper that rent seeking emerges in any uncompensated transfer of value—notably with respect to gifts or bequests among persons.

2. This article mainly focuses on problems in *identifying* rent-seeking activities. Relatively little attention is devoted to the reasons why measurement of waste, even in principle, is not possible.

3. In the conventional approach, following a specific market event or act of government to increase or decrease competition, it is assumed that gains and losses to producers and consumers can be empirically compared. It is argued that this approach is not valid in a later section of this article.

4. Says Worcester (1982, p. 87):

> A longer run view of what may seem to be excessive profits or losses is appropriate because every successful penetration . . . because of artful foresight, scientific estimation, or plan luck—gives the entrepreneur an edge . . . that can be classified as a monopoly return. There would be no such return if buyers did not find the new superior to the old, and thus, in the large sense, the consequence of a more efficient use of resources.

5. Economic rent is defined in conventional neoclassical theory as the return in excess of opportunity cost. Since opportunity cost is subjective and profits are created through entrepreneurial activity, there is no way for an outside observer to objectively identify economic rent which, in practice, is taken to mean "excessive profits" or "unearned returns." As in the case of the distinction between profits and profiteering, the identification of economic rent depends on judgments of value (von Mises, 1974, p. 129).

6. According to Cowling and Mueller (1980, p. 134):

> Gordon Tullock and Richard Posner have argued that previous studies understate the social costs of monopoly by failing to recognize the costs involved in attempts to gain and retain monopoly power. These costs could take the form of investment in excess production capacity, excessive accumulation of advertising goodwill stocks, and excessive product differentiation through research and development.

[A]nd anyone can try to form a cartel with his competitors or, if he is a member of a cartelized industry, to engross a greater share of the monopoly profits of the industry." (Posner, 1975, p. 809).

7. The use of the concept of rent seeking for the remainder of this article is restricted to activities of this type where groups attempt to obtain wealth transfers through the aegis of the state.

8. Buchanan and di Pierro (1980, p. 699) write:

> There exists basic uncertainty . . . about the set of possibilities that might be realized upon choice or consequent to choice. In a very real sense, the entrepreneur creates his own opportunity set and the act of choice enters a new world that unfolds with choice itself. When this point is recognized, formal theories of probability have little or no contribution to make to our understanding of entrepreneurial choice.

9. "In short, when the entrepreneurial aspect of efficient allocation is taken into account, the system will *always* be in temporary disequilibrium when equilibrium is defined by static or stationary criteria" (Worcester, 1982, p. 87).

10. In efficiency measurements, welfare economists have generally finessed this information problem by implicitly assuming omniscience on the part of the observing economist (Buchanan, 1959).

11. Bhagwati (1982) proposes "directly unproductive, profit-seeking" activities as a general concept that includes conventional rent seeking as a special case.

12.

> How, then, do we tell a government action that we shall call redistributive . . . ? Essentially, we must look at the motives of the act. . . . When we observe a government that does not seem to be solely aimed at improving the efficiency of the economy, defending the country, suppressing murder, etc., we call it redistributive (Tullock, 1983, p. 13).

13. A dramatic example of the positivist approach appears in Tullock (1983, p. 7):

> Let us, for example, take a fairly clear-cut case in which income generates rather little utility: people who are seriously and permanently crippled, such as multiple sclerosis victims. It is fairly obvious that the marginal utility derived from each dollar put in the support of such people is low. If we were attempting to maximize total utility, we would surely cut back on our expenditures to them and increase our expenditures to the beach boys of Malibu.

14. Stigler (1982b) holds that although economic analyses of government intervention including minimum wages, rent controls, and so forth are "tolerably accurate" as to their effects, economists' policy advice on these issues is disregarded because economists are uninformed concerning political desires of the community: "The true account, then, is that the economists refused to listen to the society, not that the society refused to listen to economists. What the economists had to say that was relevant was heard and acted upon" (pp. 15–16). In this view, economics teaches the worthlessness of public policy advice. Studies by public choice economists, by the neoclassicists of the Chicago school, and by the Austrians, however, have helped to make the case for limited government and free markets (McKenzie, 1983, p. 53).

15. Says Buchanan (1959, pp. 137–38):

> The individual preference patterns which he incorporates into his models must be conceived as presumed or predicted, and the changes which are based on these must always be considered tentative hypotheses to be subject to testing in the polling places. The economist can never say that one social situation is more "efficient" than another.

16. Self-interest is likely to play a role in people's attitude toward particular transfers. In the words of Stigler (1982b, p. 15), "One is entitled to suspect that a person's disapproval is related to his circumstances: economists believe that federal support of their research is more desirable than federal support of industrial research."

17. For example, occupational licensing of real estate salespeople, medical doctors, and the like means that the licensed businesses are not as competitive as they otherwise would be (Tullock, 1980a, p. 17). Yet many (most?) people appear willing to pay a higher price in exchange for a perceived increase in information and decrease in uncertainty associated with such restrictions on competition.

18. Browning (1974) points out that rent-seeking behavior may be important in providing information to legislators, which further complicates the benchmark problem in identifying rent-seeking waste.

19. Gardner (1981) discusses the theory that agriculture has special characteristics that unregulated markets cannot properly handle.

20. Ruttan (1980, p. 531) argues, for example, that there is currently underinvestment in publicly supported agricultural research.

> The observed annual rates of return typically fall in the 30–60 percent range. . . . It is hard to imagine very many investments in either private or public sector activity that would produce more favorable rates of return. There is little doubt that a level of expenditure that would push rates of returns to below 20 percent would be in the public interest.

If Ruttan's conclusion were correct, the lobbying necessary to bring about this result could not legitimately be considered rent-seeking waste.

21. Worcester (1982) discusses the "forbidding task" of developing an economic model that can properly be used as a basis for policy making. He concludes: "Economic analysis suitable for policy must provide a negative answer to the first and a positive answer to the second of these questions:
a. Is any unavoidable task ignored or excluded by assumption?
b. Has an equally skeptical investigation been made of the viable alternatives?" (p. 87).

22. Rothbard (1982) explains why utilitarian approaches cannot be used to make the case for or against particular restrictions on competition.

23. There is a subtle difference between the existence and the measurement of inefficiency (or errors) by decision makers. The outside observer cannot detect error or isolate inefficiency on the part of decision makers since utilities and costs are subjective. The individual may err, however, in the sense of acting in a way so that he or she is placed on a position viewed "as less desirable than an equally available state" (Kirzner, 1979, p. 120). Moreover, as Mitchell (1983) suggests, individuals and groups may knowingly be induced by short-run considerations to engage in activities which, if widely adopted, can lead to general ruin.

24. "[T]ransfer activity, originally quite limited, has come to play a much more significant role in the lives of all Americans" (Anderson and Hill, 1980, p. 91). Johansen (1979) refers to the proliferation of groups being organized with the aim of negotiating with the state to improve their economic condition as "the bargaining society."

25. Says Olson (1982, p. 69):

> Lobbying increases the complexity of regulation and the scope of government by creating special provisions and exceptions. A lobby that wins a tax deduction for income of a certain source or type makes the tax code longer and more complicated; a lobby that gets a tariff increase for the producers of a particular commodity makes trade regulation more complex than it would be with no tariff at all.

26. Olson is ambivalent about the effects of conventionally defined monopoly power. Monopoly gains are said to arise because output is reduced to obtain a higher price (p. 45). He argues, however, that though supranormal profits are common, their source is innovation.

> But what gives rise to these temporary profits? Most notably, innovation of one kind or another. . . . And the greater the extent of the profits due to difficulties of entry and imitation, the greater the reward to the innovations that mainly explain economic growth and progress (Olson, 1982, p. 61).

27. Although Olson (1982) stresses the harmful effects of special interest groups, he fails to recognize the importance of the state in creating and maintaining such groups.

Indeed, he holds that "there often will *not* be competitive markets even if the government does not intervene. . . . There will be cartelization of many markets even if the government does not help" (Olson, 1982, pp. 177–78).

28. I am indebted to Robert Batemarco for this insight.

29. Yandle (1982) traces the roots of government to rent-seeking behavior. Government emerges as a producer and monitor of property rights because of common access problems. A useful way of analyzing the conditions giving rise to decay in the legislative process is to view public officials as rent seekers in the legislative commons.

> With representative government the legislative arena is the commons upon which property rights are formed. The legislators are the sheperds and the laws passed by them are the grazing. The constitution is the monitoring device. If the basic contract—the constitution—fails to monitor the commons, overgrazing occurs. (Yandle, 1982, p. 324).

30. "While collective choice stands in the sharpest contrast to the market, marginal improvements are possible. But of all improvements the most effective is a steady diminution of the scope of government" (Mitchell, 1983, pp. 367-68).

References

Anderson, Terry L., and P.J. Hill (1980). *The Birth of a Transfer Society*. Stanford, Calif.: Hoover Institution Press.

Armentano, Dominick (1982). *Antitrust and Monopoly: Anatomy of a Policy Failure*. New York: John Wiley and Sons.

Bhagwati, Jagdish N. (1982). "Directly Unproductive, Profit-Seeking (DUP) Activities." *Journal of Political Economy* 90 (October):988–1002.

Browning, Edgar K. (1974). "On the Welfare Cost of Transfers." *Kyklos* 2 (April):374–77. Reprinted in *Toward a Theory of the Rent-Seeking Society*, J.M. Buchanan, R.D. Tollison, and Gordon Tullock, eds. College Station: Texas A&M University Press.

Buchanan, James M. (1959). "Positive Economics, Welfare Economics, and Political Economy." *Journal of Law and Economics* 2 (October):125–38.

Buchanan, James M. (1969). *Cost and Choice*. Chicago: Markham.

Buchanan, James M. (1977). *Fredom in Constitutional Contract: Perspectives of a Political Economist*. College Station and London: Texas A&M University Press.

Buchanan, James M. (1979). *What Should Economists Do?* Indianapolis: Liberty Fund.

Buchanan, James M. (1980). "Rent Seeking and Profit Seeking," chap. 1 in *Toward a Theory of the Rent-Seeking Society*.

Buchanan, James M. (1983). "Rent Seeking, Noncompensated Transfers, and Laws of Succession." *Journal of Law and Economics* 26 (April):71–85.

Buchanan, James M., and A. di Pierro (1980). "Cognition, Choice, and Entrepreneurship." *Southern Economic Journal* 46 (January):693–701.

Buchanan, James M., R.D. Tollison, and Gordon Tullock, eds. (1980). *Toward a Theory of the Rent-Seeking Society*. College Station: Texas A&M University Press.

Cowling, Keith, and Dennis C. Mueller (1980). "The Social Costs of Monopoly Power," chap. 8 in *Toward a Theory of the Rent-Seeking Society*.

Demsetz, Harold (1969). "Information and Efficiency: Another Viewpoint." *Journal of Law and Economics* 12 (April): 1–22.

Dorn, James A. (1982). "Trade Adjustment Assistance: A Case of Government Failure." *The Cato Journal* 2 (Winter):865–905.

Freeman, Richard B., and James L. Medoff (1979). "The Two Faces of Unionism." *The Public Interest* 57 (Fall):69–93.

French, Ben A. (1982). "Fruit and Vegetable Marketing Orders: A Critique of the Issues and State of Analysis." *American Journal of Agricultural Economics* 64 (December):916–23.

Friedman, Milton (1976). *Price Theory*. Chicago: Adline.

Gardner, Bruce L. (1981). *The Governing of Agriculture*. Lawrence, Kan.: Regents Press of Kansas.

Harberger, A.C. (1954). "Monopoly and Resource Allocation." *American Economic Review, Proceedings*. 44 (May):73–87.

Hayek, F.A. (1948). "The Meaning of Competition," in *Individualism and Economic Order*. Chicago: University of Chicago Press.

Hayek, F.A. (1979). *Law, Legislation and Liberty: The Political Order of a Free People*. Chicago: University of Chicago Press.

Hirshleifer, Jac, (1980). *Price Theory and Applications*, 2d. ed. Englewood Cliffs, N.J.: Prentice-Hall.

Johansen, Leif (1979). "The Bargaining Society and the Inefficiency of Bargaining." *Kyklos* 32, no. 3: 497–522.

Kirzner, Israel M. (1973). *Competition and Entrepreneurship*. Chicago: University of Chicago Press.

Kirzner, Israel M. (1979). *Perception, Opportunity and Profit*. Chicago: University of Chicago Press.

Knight, Frank H. (1935). *The Ethics of Competition and Other Essays*. Midway Reprint 1976. Chicago: University of Chicago Press.

Lee, Dwight R. (1983). "Reverse Revenue Sharing: The Importance of Process in Controlling Government." Paper presented at Public Choice Meetings, Savannah, Georgia, March 24–26, 1983.

Littlechild, S.C. (1978). "The Problem of Social Cost," pp. 77–93 in *New Directions in Austrian Economics*, Louis M. Spadaro, ed. Kansas City: Sheed Andrews and McMeel.

Littlechild, S.C. (1981). "Misleading Calculations of the Social Costs of Monopoly Power." *Economic Journal* 91 (June):348–63.

McKenzie, Richard B. (1983). *The Limits of Economic Science*. Boston: Kluwer-Nijhoff.

Mitchell, Willim C. (1983). "Efficiency, Responsibility, and Democratic Politics," chap. 14 in *Liberal Democracy*, J. Roland Pennock and John W. Chapman, eds. New York: New York University Press.

Nock, Albert J. (1973). *Our Enemy, The State*. New York: Free Life Editions.

Olson, Mancur (1982). *The Rise and Decline of Nations*. New Haven: Yale University Press.

Pasour, E.C., Jr. (1981). "Economic Efficiency: Touchstone or Mirage?" *The Intercollegiate Review* 17 (Fall/Winter):33–44.

Posner, Richard A. (1975). "The Social Costs of Monopoly and Regulation." *Journal of Political Economy* 83 (August): 807–27. Reprinted in *Toward a Theory of the Rent-Seeking Society*.

Robbins, Lionel (1981). "Economics and Political Economy." *American Economic Review* 71 (May):1–10.

Rothbard, Murray N. (1982). *The Ethics of Liberty.* Atlantic Highlands, N.J.: Humanities Press.

Ruttan, V. W. (1980). "Bureaucratic Productivity: The Case of Agricultural Research." *Public Choice* 35, no. 5:529–47.

Schultz, T.W. (1980). "Investment in Entrepreneurial Ability." *Scandinavian Journal of Economics* 82, no. 4:437–48.

Song, D. Hee, and M.C. Hallberg (1982). "Measuring Producers' Advantage from Classified Pricing of Milk." *American Journal of Agricultural Economics* 64 (February):1–7.

Sowell, Thomas (1980). *Knowledge and Decisions.* New York: Basic Books.

Stigler, George J. (1982a). *The Economist as Preacher and Other Essays.* Chicago: University of Chicago Press.

Stigler, George J. (1982b). "Economists and Public Policy." *Regulation* (May/June):13–17.

Tollison, Robert D. (1982). "Rent Seeking: A Survey." *Kyklos* 35, no. 4:575–602.

Tullock, Gordon (1967). "The Welfare Costs of Tariffs, Monopolies and Theft." *Western Economic Journal* 5 (June):224–32. Reprinted in *Toward a Theory of the Rent-Seeking Society.*

Tullock, Gordon (1980a). "Rent Seeking as a Negative-Sum Game," chap. 2 in *Toward a Theory of the Rent-Seeking Society.*

Tullock, Gordon (1980b). "Efficient Rent Seeking," chap. 6 in *Toward a Theory of the Rent-Seeking Society.*

Tullock, Gordon (1983). *Economics of Income Redistribution.* Boston: Kluwer-Nijhoff.

U.S. Department of Agriculture (1981). *A Review of Federal Marketing Orders for Fruits, Vegetables and Specialty Crops: Economic Efficiency and Welfare Implication.* AMS Agricultural Economics Report no. 477, Washington, D.C.

von Mises, Ludwig (1966). *Human Action,* 3d ed. Chicago: Henry Regnery.

von Mises, Ludwig (1974). "Profit and Loss," chap. 9 in *Planning for Freedom,* memorial ed. South Holland, Ill.: Libertarian Press.

Worcester, Dean A., Jr. (1982). "On the Validity of Marginal Analysis for Policy Making." *Eastern Economic Journal* 8 (April):83–88.

Yandle, Bruce (1982). "Conflicting Commons." *Public Choice* 38, no. 3:317–27.

Yeager, Leland B. (1976). "Economics and Principles." *Southern Economic Journal* 42 (April): 559–71.

Some Austrian Perspectives on Keynesian Fiscal Policy and the Recovery in the Thirties

Gene Smiley

T he standard explanation for the snail-like pace of the recovery from the Great Depression was first proposed by E. Cary Brown in 1956, and was enhanced and extended by Larry Peppers in 1973.[1] Though there are a few skeptics, the story of the federal government's failure to use expansionary fiscal policy is repeated in most economic history, principles of economics, and intermediate macroeconomics textbooks.[2] Here, I suggest that this tale is wrong since it is built upon assumptions inconsistent with observed behavior during the recovery from the Great Depression. Using some insights from Austrian analysis, I conclude that a more expansionary fiscal policy would have had little effect in promoting a more rapid recovery from the Depression.

Brown and Peppers argued that the reason for the retarded recovery in the 1933–39 period was that the federal government failed to use expansionary fiscal policy.[3] This is not to say that federal government expenditures did not increase.[4] Rather, Brown and Peppers argued that the problem was that both the Hoover and Roosevelt administrations also sharply increased tax rates in attempting to "balance" the federal government's budget. The contractionary effects of increasing taxes largely offset the expansionary effects of increasing spending. With the exception of 1931 and 1936, when the federal government made "bonus" payments to veterans, Peppers's analysis indicated that the federal budget would have shown a substantial surplus if full employment had prevailed.[5] Both Brown

Substantial portions of this study were undertaken while I was a fellow at the Liberty Fund-Institute of Humane Studies 1983 summer research seminar on historical aspects of political power and individual freedom. Useful comments were provided by all of the participants as well as colleagues at Marquette University, but I wish to especially acknowledge the comments of Steven Crane, Lowell Gallaway, Thomas Humphrey, Paul McGouldrick, Murray Rothbard, Sudha Shenoy, Richard Timberlake, Richard Vedder, and several anonymous referees. All errors and omissions are, of course, my responsibility.

and Peppers argued that the appropriate policy would have been to increase federal spending without increasing taxes. Such a policy, they contended, would have increased aggregate demand and, through the Keynesian spending multiplier, more quickly restored full employment.

Apparently Brown and Peppers assumed that the money borrowed to finance such a federal government deficit would not have crowded out other spending. In Keynesian analysis, this requires that there be a highly interest-elastic demand for money balances—something approaching a Keynesian liquidity trap. Alternatively, the Federal Reserve System could have purchased the additional federal government debt and created new money by an equal amount. *If* the reason for the contraction was an insufficient stock of money, then the new money could have employed the idle resources without causing inflation or reducing real spending in any other sector in the economy.

Though the stock of money did increase from 1933 through 1939, this was due to the flow of gold into the United States, not to the actions of the Federal Reserve System. Since the FRS did not aid the federal government's financing of its deficit, and, in fact, consistently attempted to reduce the growth of the money stock, I do not consider the monetization of the deficit a viable alternative. One aspect of the question of the potential power of fiscal policy then concerns crowding out as a result of the deficit spending. My purpose in the first part of this article is to establish plausible explanations of what might have happened to the funds collected through increased taxes and increased borrowing if the government had not gained the additional funds and increased spending. This provides one part of the answer to the question of what would have been the effect of greater deficit spending by the federal government by addressing the question from the perspective of the Keynesian analysis.

In the second part of the article, I consider the question of the potential effect of greater deficit spending by the federal government during the 1930s recovery from the perspective of Austrian analysis. The procedure here is to consider the effect of increased federal spending on the structure of relative prices, an effect Keynesians and monetarists generally tend to ignore.

In 1942, the U.S. National Resources Planning Board estimated that for the 1933–39 period, 42.6 percent of the federal public aid expenditures were financed by tax revenues, and 57.4 percent financed by additional debt issues.[6] Whether financed by tax increases or additional bond sales, if the positive spending multiplier occurs, it is because some of the increased taxes or purchases of additional debt use money that otherwise would have been completely idle, or would not have existed.[7]

For federal spending financed by equivalent tax increases, the size of the Keynesian fiscal spending multiplier depends on the type of savings reduced by the tax increase.[8] Prior to World War II, Milton Friedman and Anna Schwartz's data show that the deposit/currency ratio fell to a low of just under 5 in 1933, and rose to 7.25 by early 1937.[9] Households generally held the bulk of their savings as time deposits in financial intermediaries, while demand deposit and cash holdings were largely related to household transactions.[10] The argument that banks relent most of the deposited funds will be developed here. Therefore, if the tax increase induced individuals to reduce savings by decreasing bank deposits, this would have brought about a nearly proportionate reduction in bank lending and private sector spending.[11] Even if the tax increase proportionately reduced household deposit and currency "savings," the fact that households only held $1 in currency for every $5 to $7.25 in deposits means that the fiscal multiplier would have been tiny.[12] Considering that household currency holdings were largley related to transactions demands and the progressive personal income tax system, it seems most likely that during the 1933–39 period, the federal government spending financed by equivalent tax increases would have had a multiplier close to zero—certainly not close to one.

The majority of the federal government's public aid expenditures, 57.4 percent, were financed by selling debt. Table 1 presents the ownership of the federal debt between 1933 and 1939 and the six-month (or yearly) changes in the amount held. The data show that there was virtually no monetization of the debt, especially from June 1934 on.[13] From June 1933 through December 1939, 74.7 percent of the total debt issued was purchased by member and nonmember banks, savings banks, insurance companies, and "other investors"—a category that includes other financial firms, all nonfinancial firms, all households, and any other investors. Nearly 89 percent of all the federal debt sold in the private sector was sold to banks and insurance companies. For the federal government expenditures financed by debt sold to the private sector to have a large multiplier effect, much of the debt must have been purchased by banks which largely used reserves that otherwise would not have been used for any purpose other than idle excess bank reserves, by insurance companies which mainly used money that otherwise would have been held only as idle currency balances outside of the banking system, and by "other investors" who primarily used money that otherwise would have been held as idle currency —not bank deposit—balances.

I will first examine the behavior of nonfinancial firms and individuals ("Other investors").[14] As noted, the deposit/currency ratio rose from 5 to 7.25 between 1933 and 1937, where it roughly remained for the rest of the decade. Recent empirical research suggests that there was a highly interest-inelastic demand for money balances during this period.[15] Money market and securities market interest rates (such as those on treasury bills, U.S. government and corporate bonds, major city bank commercial loans, prime commercial paper, and stock exchange time loans) were very low and relatively stable or falling slightly. Though bank commercial loans rates, outside of the largest cities, were higher and tended to rise from 1934 to 1936, particularly in the western states, the

Table 1

Ownership of U.S. Government Debt, 1933–39

(end-of-month figures in $ millions)

Date	Total Amount Outstanding	Federal Agencies and Trust Funds	Federal Reserve Banks	FRS Member Banks	Other Commercial Banks	Mutual Savings Banks	Insurance Companies	Other Investors
6/1933	22,158	690	1,988	6,887	590	720	1,000	10,300
6/1934	27,161	1,428	2,432	9,413	900	970	1,500	10,500
6/1935	31,768	1,991	2,433	11,430	1,290	1,540	2,600	10,500
6/1936	37,707	2,320	2,430	13,672	1,600	2,050	3,900	11,700
12/1936	38,362	2,432	2,430	13,545	1,790	2,250	4,500	11,400
6/1937	40,465	3,584	2,526	12,689	1,870	2,390	5,000	12,400
12/1937	41,353	4,255	2,564	12,372	1,780	2,450	5,300	12,600
6/1938	41,428	4,777	2,564	12,343	1,700	2,690	5,500	11,900
12/1938	43,891	5,333	2,564	13,223	1,850	2,880	5,700	12,300
6/1939	45,336	5,886	2,551	13,777	1,920	3,040	5,900	12,300
12/1939	47,067	6,531	2,484	14,328	1,970	3,100	6,300	12,400

Changes in the Amount of U.S. Government Securities Owned

Date	Total Amount Outstanding	Federal Agencies and Trust Funds	Federal Reserve Banks	FRS Member Banks	Other Commercial Banks	Mutual Savings Banks	Insurance Companies	Other Investors
6/33 to 6/34	5,003	738	444	2,526	310	250	500	200
6/34 to 6/35	4,607	563	1	2,017	390	570	1,100	
6/35 to 6/36	5,939	329	−3	2,242	310	510	1,300	1,200
6/36 to 12/36	655	112	0	−127	190	200	600	−300
12/36 to 6/37	2,103	1,152	96	−856	80	140	500	1,000
6/37 to 12/37	888	671	38	−317	−90	60	300	200
12/37 to 6/38	75	522	0	−29	−80	240	200	−700
6/38 to 12/38	2,463	556	0	880	150	190	200	400
12/38 to 6/39	1,445	553	13	554	70	160	200	
6/39 to 12/39	1,731	645	−7	551	50	60	400	100

Source: Board of Governors of the Federal Reserve System, *Banking and Monetary Statistics* (Washington, D.C. National Capital Press, 1943), table 149, p. 512.

Note: Components may not add to the total due to the rounding of the estimates. The estimated figures for "other commercial banks" and "mutual savings banks" were rounded to the nearest $10 million and the estimated figures for "insurance companies" and "other investors" were rounded to the nearest $100 million.

newly controlled deposit rates were low and could not rise.[16] With the roughly constant interest rates, the interest-inelastic demand for money balances, and the fact that households and firms held from $5 up to $7.25 of deposit balances for every dollar of currency, it seems most unlikely that any significant portion of the debt sold to those in the "other investors" category would have ben purchased using idle currency balances.

The evidence suggests similar behavior for insurance companies. In the interwar years, the ten largest life insurance companies operated with very low ratios of cash balances to total assets. The ratio averaged about 0.7 to 0.8 percent in the twenties, about 2.0 percent in the thirties after the Depression, and from 1.0 to 1.5 percent from 1947 to 1955.[17] The cash balances included both bank deposits and currency. Though the data on this composition are not available, surely the insurance companies would have held the bulk of their "cash" balances as bank deposits rather than currency on hand since bank deposits were the most efficient means of making payments to claimants, policyholders, agents, and employees. Table 1 shows that insurance companies increased their holdings of federal government debt by over $1 billion a year from June 1934 through June 1937.

If the insurance companies had not purchased the additional government debt, would they have held these funds in idle cash balances rather than purchasing any private or nonfederal government financial securities; if held as cash balances, would the money have been held mainly as currency holdings rather than as bank deposits? The most plausible answer to both of these questions would seem to be no. First, the life insurance companies were contractually obligated to make future payments. Surely, if they had not invested in federal government debt, they would have invested in private or local and state government financial securities. Second, even if they would have held all of the funds as "cash" balances (rather than purchasing the new issues of federal debt), it seems most reasonable to assume that they would have held most of the "cash" in bank deposits rather than currency.

Williamson and Smalley's data on Northwestern Mutual Life make possible some instructive calculations for that large life insurance company. Northwestern Mutual's "cash" holdings were $10.3 million in 1933, $10 million in 1935, and $14.0 million in 1939, or 1.03, 0.93, and 1.08 percent respectively of the admitted assets. Northwestern's holdings of U.S. government securities can roughly be estimated at $25 million dollars in 1935, $150 million in 1935, and $125 million in 1939. If the U.S. government securities had not been issued and Northwestern had then held additional cash balances of $125 and 100 million in 1935 and 1939, their cash as a percentage of admitted assets would have been 12.59 percent in 1935, and 8.82 percent in 1939. This behavior hardly seems plausible.

In his history of the Metropolitan Life Insurance Company, Louis Dublin indicated that a reduced supply of other investment opportunities, as well as the much lower risk associated with federal government debt, led insurance companies to purchase more federal bonds in the post-1933 period.[18] In their history of Northwestern Mutual Life, Williamson and Smalley provided more information on this company's investments during the thirties. The company built up its holdings of federal government bonds in 1934 and 1935," when the supply of *higher yielding* securities was limited" (emphasis added).[19] However, the absolute and relative amount of U.S. government bonds held by Northwestern Mutual Life declined from 1935 through 1941. Williamson and Smalley report that the company's investment management felt that "the most promising areas for an expansion of the Company's security holdings were state, county, and municipal bonds in the United States and the obligations in public utilities and industrial concerns."[20] They report that rather than wait for applications to come to them, the company actively sought out these types of investments. The state, county, and municipal bonds were, of course, tax exempt. According to Williamson and Smalley, Northwestern considered public utility and industrial securities the most attractive investments "largely because of their favorable showing during the Depression and their future prospects."[21]

This analysis does not suggest that the insurance companies would have held all or even much of the assets used to purchase the federal debt as idle currency balances if the additional federal debt had not been issued.

The behavior of the banks was critical since they were the dominant purchasers of the federal debt and controlled the deposited funds of insurance companies, other nonbank financial firms, and other investors. From June 1933 through December 1939, 60.2 percent of the additional U.S. debt purchased by the private sector was purchased by member and nonmember commercial banks and savings banks. For federal spending to have a large multiplier effect, as the Keynesian scenario suggests, the banks must have purchased the debt largely using funds that otherwise would have been held only as idle excess bank reserves. Friedman and Schwartz have calculated that the ratio of bank reserves to bank deposits for all banks rose continuously from 1933 through 1939.[22] Though at the time, the Federal Reserve Board asserted that the accumulating excess reserves resulted from inadequate loan demand at any reasonable interest rate, Friedman and Schwartz have argued that bankers were consciously building up the excess reserves as additional liquidity; in effect, a "Maginot line" of excess reserves against further banking crises. If the excess reserves were desired by bankers, then the purchase of federal government debt would have been made in lieu of loans and other securities purchases, rather than have been made using funds that otherwise would have been held only as idle excess reserves.

It is difficult to determine the motives of the managers of the banks. However, there are some data and clues upon which to base an analysis. In the first two years after the trough of the Depression, banks were heavy purchasers of the bonds being sold by the federal government to finance the New Deal programs. FRS member banks increased their holdings of U.S. government securities by 50.7 percent from June 1933 through June 1935, nonmember banks increased their holdings of these securities by 78.2 percent in this period, and mutual savings banks increased these holdings by 75.7 percent. Member and nonmember banks' holdings of other securities rose by only 7.4 percent and 2.9 percent respectively in this two-year period, while mutual savings banks' holdings of other securities fell. The loans of all of these banks fell during these two years. These figures are shown in table 2.

Rates on government bonds, industrial bonds, commercial paper, and New York City bank loans were very low in absolute terms, and falling through early

Table 2

Loans and Securities Held by FRS Member, Nonmember Commercial, and Mutual Savings Banks

(end-of-month figures in $ millions)

te	Loans			U.S. Securities			Other Securities		
	FRS Member Banks	Nonmember Commercial Banks	Mutual Savings Banks	FRS Member Banks	Nonmember Commercial Banks	Mutual Savings Banks	FRS Member Banks	Nonmember Commercial Banks	Mutual Savings Banks
/33	12,858	3,491	5,894	6,887	589	723	5,041	1,491	3,331
/33	12,833	3,491	5,808	7,254	na	na	5,132	na	na
/34	12,513	3,177	5,606	9,413	895	895	5,239	1,495	3,233
/34	12,028	2,960	5,451	10,895	na	na	5,227	na	na
/35	11,928	2,981	5,304	11,430	1,287	1,542	5,427	1,535	2,913
/35	12,175	2,944	5,183	12,269	na	na	5,542	na	na
/36	12,541	3,017	5,077	13,672	1,598	2,052	6,045	1,666	2,713
/36	13,360	2,998	5,001	13,545	1,789	2,253	6,095	1,685	2,719
/37	14,284	3,147	4,978	12,689	1,874	2,391	5,765	1,712	2,724
/37	13,958	3,142	4,965	12,371	1,784	2,454	5,423	1,655	2,675
/38	12,937	3,115	4.929	12,343	1,699	2,685	5,440	1,574	2,489
/38	13,207	3,156	4,897	13,223	1,848	2,883	5,640	1,594	2,382
/39	13,141	3,282	4,897	13,777	1,923	3,043	5,686	1,559	2,309
/39	13,962	3,281	4,926	14,329	1,971	3,102	5,651	1,474	2,190

Changes for the Six Months Ending

te	Loans			U.S. Securities			Other Securities		
/33	−20	−78	−86	367	153[a]	124[a]	91	2[a]	−49[a]
/34	−320	−326	−202	2,159	153[a]	124[a]	107	2[a]	−49[a]
/34	−485	−217	−155	1,482	196[a]	285[a]	−12	20[a]	−160[a]
/35	−100	21	−147	535	196[a]	285[a]	200	20[a]	−160[a]
/35	247	−37	−121	839	155[a]	255[a]	115	65[a]	−100[a]
/36	366	73	−106	1,403	156[a]	255[a]	503	65[a]	−100[a]
/36	819	−19	−76	−127	191	201	50	21	6
/37	924	149	−23	−856	85	138	−330	27	5
/37	−326	−5	−13	−318	−90	63	−342	−57	−4
/38	−1,021	−27	−36	−28	−85	231	17	−81	−186
/38	270	41	−32	880	149	198	200	20	−107
/39	−66	126	0	554	75	160	46	−35	−73
/39	821	−1	29	552	48	59	−35	−85	−119

Source: Borad of Governors of the Federal Reserve System, *Banking and Monetary Statistics* (Washington, D.C.: tional Capital Press, 1943), tables 4–7, pp. 20–23.

not available.

ver these dates only the twelve-month change could be calculated. Thus, these figures for the six-month changes one-half of the twelve-month changes.

1935. This has led to suggestions that the demand for loans and for invest-ment funds in the immediate post-Depression years was so low that if the federal government had not sold securities to finance its spending, banks, individuals, and firms would have had no choice but to hold larger idle money or reserve balances. However, there is evidence against this assertion. When bank loan rates for banks outside of the major financial centers are examined, one finds that loan rates were much higher and actually rose sharply in a number of western states in the two and a half years after the trough of the Depression.[23] The rising interest rates would not suggest such inadequate loan demand.

In addition, there is also evidence that banks rationed credit by simply refusing to make some loans. Ben Bernanke examined this evidence as part of his study of how the financial crises of the Depression raised the costs of credit intermediation and reduced the efficiency of the financial sector.[24] Lewis Kimmel's survey of credit availability during 1933–38 indicated that a large share of manufacturing firms were refused bank loans during this period; in particular, more than 30 percent of the smaller manufacturing firms reported being refused credit.[25] Relatively few of the largest manufacturing firms reported difficulty in securing bank loans. A survey of firms in the seventh Federal Reserve District in 1934–35 found "a genuine unsatisfied demand for credit by solvent borrowers," and a U.S. Dept. of Commerce survey of small firms with high credit ratings found that nearly half of them had difficulty borrowing for working capital and most were not able to obtain investment funds.[26]

This suggests that in the first two to two and a half years after the end of the Depression, banks were investing in the new issues of government securities because of the extremely low risks involved in holding these "safe" financial assets compared to alternatives, not because there were simply no other investment or loan opportunities. Under these circumstances, if the additional federal government bonds had not been issued, then banks would have turned, perhaps reluctantly, to other investments and loan demands. Private and nonfederal government spending was forced to decline because of the federal government's increased spending.

As economic activity began to recover, the authorities of the Federal Reserve System became increasingly concerned about the buildup of banks' excess reserves. They feared that with the revival of the demand for loanable funds and an increased supply of financial securities, banks would begin reducing their excess reserves, the stock of money would begin to grow faster, and there would be inflation.[27] Convinced that the excess reserves were due only to an inadequate loan demand and armed with studies showing that the excess reserves were broadly distributed across regions and sizes of banks, the Federal Reserve System used its new tool of variable reserve requirements to double demand (and time) deposit reserve requirements over a nine-month period.

The first increase, from 13 to 19.5 percent for central reserve city bank demand deposits, was announced in July 1936, and took effect on August 16, 1936. On January 30, 1937, the FRS announced two more increases to take place on March 1, 1937 and May 1, 1937. The increases raised the central reserve city bank demand deposit requirements from 19.5 to 22.75 and then to 26 percent. With these increases the Federal Reserve System had raised reserve requirements as high as the law allowed.[28]

How would one expect the banks to respond to the increase in required reserve ratios? If the rising excess reserves were due only to a lack of loan demand at any reasonable interest rate, then one would not expect the banks to attempt to restore some or all of the eliminated excess reserves. If the excess reserves were largely desired by the banks as protection against further banking crises and the riskiness of the depressed business conditions, then one would expect to see the banks taking actions to restore some or all of the excess reserves eliminated by the rise in reserve requirements.[29] This would take the form of some combination of reducing lending andor selling some securities from the banks' investment portfolios as the excess reserves were rebuilt.

The Federal Reserve System's increased reserve requirements applied to member banks only. If the excess reserves were desired, one would expect to see member banks taking actions to restore the excess reserves, but not the nonmember banks. Table 2 presents the holdings of loans, U.S. government debt, and other securities, and the changes in these holdings. In the first several years after the trough of the contraction, all three classes of banks reduced their lending. Member banks increased their lending somewhat beginning in the last half of 1935, and sharply increased their lending in the last half of 1936 and the first half of 1937. Nonmember banks largely ceased contracting their loan portfolio at the end of 1934, and sharply expanded lending in the first half of 1937. Mutual savings banks continued to contract their lending through 1938, but the rate of contraction diminished sharply at the beginning of 1937.

All three classes of banks purchased large quantities of U.S. securities through June 1936. Member and nonmember banks also purchased other securities through June 1936, while mutual savings banks sold other securities. Member banks sold U.S. securities in the last half of 1936, and nearly ceased purchasing other securities. In the first half of 1937, member banks sold large amounts of U.S. and other securities. Nonmember banks and mutual savings banks continued to purchase U.S. securities from June 1936 through June 1937; both purchased other securities in this same period. With the onset of the 1937–38 contraction (beginning about May or June 1937), all three classes of banks reduced lending and sold U.S. and other securities (except for the mutual savings banks which purchased U.S. securities).

The rapid expansion of loans by member banks in the last half of 1936, and by member and nonmember banks in the first half of 1937, as well as the sharp decrease in the rate of loan contraction by savings banks in this period are likely explained by the ending of the National Industrial Recovery Act (NIRA). Michael Weinstein has pointed out that industrial production was virtually stagnant from the last half of 1933 through the first half of 1935, and only began to increase after the NIRA was declared unconstitutional in May 1935.[30] This would indicate that during 1936 and the first half of 1937, prior to the cyclical peak, loan demand should have been increasing. It would seem, therefore, that some of the reduction in member banks' holdings of U.S. and other securities was undertaken to obtain funds to make additional loans. Notice, however, that when nonmember banks sharply expanded their loan portfolios in the first half of 1937, they did not have to sell U.S. or other securities.

It would appear that the member banks' sales of U.S. government and other securities from July 1936 through June 1937 were related both to the increase reserve requirements and the rising loan demand. The dramatic reduction in excess reserves brought about sales from the holdings of financial securities. Loans did not decline due to the rising demand for loanable funds and it is likely that some of the sales of U.S. government and other securities were undertaken to shift the banks' portfolios of earning assets toward loans—assets yielding higher rates of return. Nonmember banks and savings banks apparently experienced smaller increases in loan demand. Since their reserve requirements were not increased, they did not have to sell securities to restore excess reserves or handle the increased loan demand.

Further evidence can be found in figures 1 through 6. Figures 1 and 2 show the monthly prices of high-grade corporate and municipal bonds and U.S. government bonds as well as the prime commercial paper rate and average rate on new treasury bills. If member banks began selling securities to restore their excess reserves and accommodate increasing loan demand, the increased supply of securities should have caused bond prices to fall and interest rates to rise. The figures show that this is what occurred and the timing is consistent with banks attempting to rebuild excess reserves (after the increase in required reserves) and satisfy an increasing loan demand. Figures 3 through 6 provide further evidence on the behavior of bankers during this period. They show that all of the classes of member banks vigorously rebuilt their excess reserves after the Federal Reserve System's attempt to eliminate the excess reserves.

I return to the original question. Was the buildup of excess reserves due to a lack of loan demand and inadequate supply of financial securities? Or was the buildup the result of the bankers' conscious desires for excess reserves as a "Maginot line" of defense against further crises? I believe that my evidence clearly suggests that bankers desired the excess reserves and considered the U.S. government securities as an investment.

I conclude that bankers were relending, via loans or the purchase of securities, what they considered to be a prudent portion of funds deposited with them. Withdrawal of deposits would have resulted in some combination of reduced lending and/or sales of securities holdings. If the federal government had increased the sale of U.S. government securities as part of an expansionary fiscal policy, the purchases by banks, insurance companies, and other investors would have taken the place of purchases of private and nonfederal government securities and would have reduced lending. The Keynesian multiplier resulting from a more expansionary pure fiscal policy during the 1933–39 period would have been quite small, and might well have approached zero, but was certainly

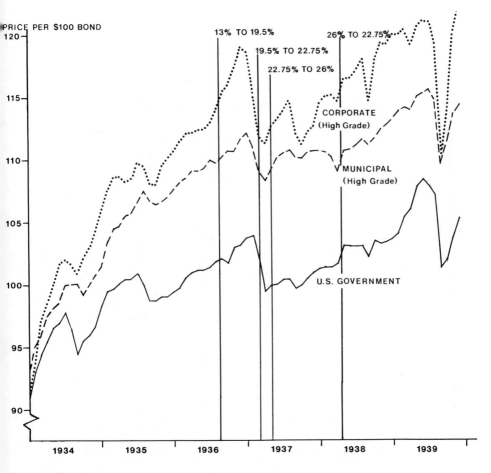

Figure 1. **Monthly Prices of High-Grade Corporate, Municipal, and U.S. Government Bonds.**

not something well in excess of one. A more expansionary fiscal policy would have done little to promote a more rapid recovery from the Great Depression.[31]

The second aspect of this question of the effectiveness of fiscal policy in the thirties deals not with crowding out, but with the effects on the structure of prices and resource allocations due to an increase in net aggregate spending resulting from expansionary fiscal policy.[32] Suppose that the increase in federal government spending had been funded by an increase in the stock of money courtesy of an accommodating Federal Reserve System policy. In such a situation, nominal spending by the private and nonfederal government sectors would

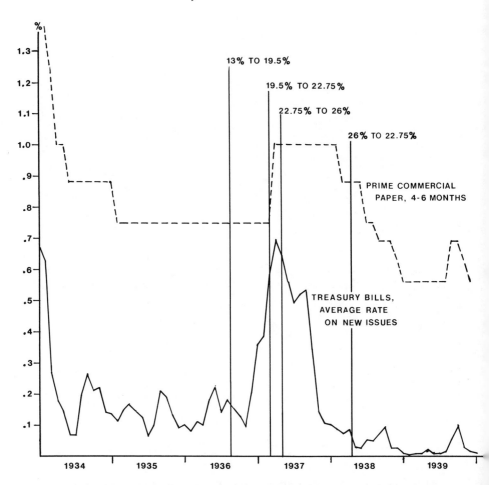

Figure 2. Prime Commercial Paper Rate and Average Rate on New Treasury Bills

not have to decline. There is still reason to expect that this expansionary fiscal policy, now accommodated by an expansionary monetary policy, would not have more quickly brought about full employment.

Macroeconomic analysis generally does not distinguish between types of expenditures made by the federal government as it pursues expansionary fiscal policy. It does suggest that the multipliers may be somewhat larger or smaller for different types of expenditures since, with constant prices, fixed coefficients of production, and idle resources, some expenditures have larger backward linkages. All expenditures, however, are assumed to have positive multipliers and the amount of the increase in federal spending is generally considered much more important than the particular types of increased federal expenditures.

The evidence, however, does not indicate that these conditions existed. Not only was there a severe price deflation during the Depression and a price inflation from 1933 on, but there were pronounced changes in relative prices during the thirties.[33] In addition, federal expenditures often have pronounced local effects which are much more important in magnitude and timing than any general economywide effects arising from the operation of the multiplier.[34]

To explain why an increase in federal spending in excess of spending declines in other sectors may well not have promoted recovery, it is useful to briefly review the role of relative prices in a market economy.[35] Austrians define an "equilibrium" as a situation where the *plans* of each and every transactor are mutually consistent. In his writings, Friedrich Hayek argued that we should speak of the tendency for mutually compatible plans to come about rather than speak of actually achieving equilibrium. With respect to this, Hayek suggested that the "division of knowledge" was *at least* as important as the division of labor, yet it had been completely neglected.

> The problem which we pretend to solve is how the spontaneous interaction of a number of people, each prossessive only bits of knowledge, brings about a state of affairs in which prices correspond to costs, etc., and which could be brought about by deliberate direction only by somebody who possessed the combined knowledge of all those individuals.[36]

The mechanism that tends to bring the plans of individual transactors into closer correspondence with each other is the price system. Hayek proposed that people consider the price system as a mechanism for economically transmitting information among transactors. It is this mechanism that has to be the focus of any study of the coordination problem that all economic systems face. Gerald P. O'Driscoll describes this as follows:

> The price system registers both the effects of changing objective conditions and the reactions of transactors to these changes. Most important, the price system is a mechanism—however imprecise—for registering the ever-changing expectations of market participants. What is important here is the argument that the price system is the cheapest possible system of resource allocation.[37]

When there are cyclical fluctuations, such as the Great Depression of 1929–33, Austrians focus on the coordination problem to explain and understand why there is a breakdown in a market system—a system that is supposed to work and previously had been working. In a cyclical contraction, discoordination of markets leads to declines in production and incomes as well as increases in idled resources (labor and capital). Relative prices are the primary economic data providing the information tending to coordinate the plans of individual transactors. To understand and ejxplain the contraction, economists

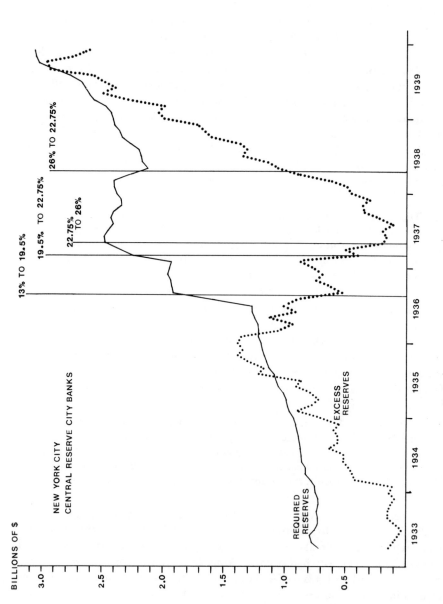

Figure 3. New York City, Central Reserve City Banks

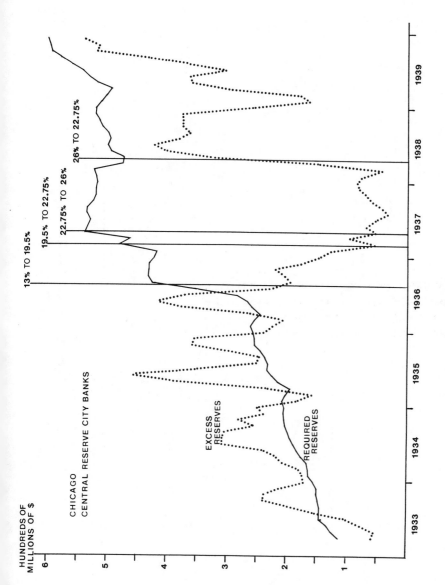

Figure 4. Chicago, Central Reserve City Banks

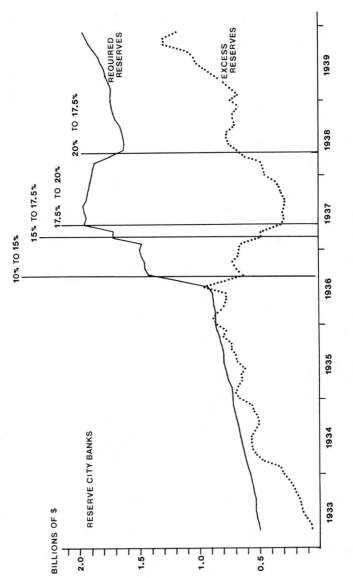

Figure 5. Reserve City Banks

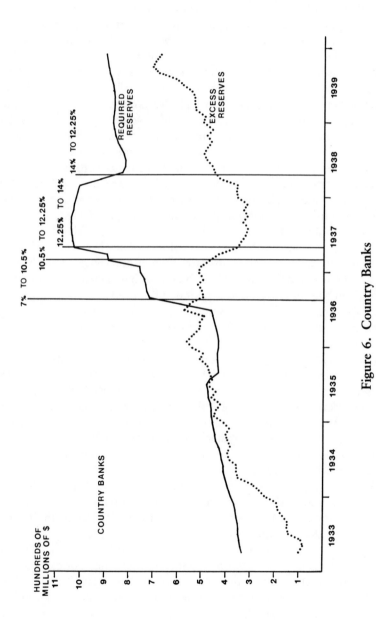

Figure 6. Country Banks

must search for the forces that alter relative prices in ways that provide incorrect information that tends to discoordinate market behavior. The recovery phase of the cycle consists of discovering and establishing the relative prices that tend to coordinate the plans of the individual transactors, and that complete the resource reallocations begun during the contraction phase of the cycle.

Several Austrian economists have examined the Great Depression. I can draw upon their analyses here.[38] Austrians point out that business cycles are "monetary disturbances [which] alter the array of relative prices by affecting market interest rates and the pattern of investment."[39] During the 1920s, the expansion of the stock of money through the banking system caused interest rates to be lower than they otherwise would have been. This inflation led to "malinvestments" as the lower discount rates induced entrepeneurs to shift productive resources toward uses further removed in time from final consumption. Since consumer preferences had not actually shifted toward future consumption, once the rate of growth of the money stock failed to increase or even slowed down, interest rates began rising and the recent investments in resources further removed from consumption proved not to be profitable.[40]

Lionel Robbins, Friedrich Hayek, and Murray Rothbard particularly blamed the Federal Reserve System's easy money policy in the last half of 1927 for leading into a more severe contraction than otherwise would have been necessary. Hayek said that until 1927, he would have expected a mild depression since in the preceding boom period, prices did not rise. However, the Federal Reserve System's expansion of the stock of money beginning in mid-1927 prolonged the boom for two more years and made the Depression more severe.[41]

When the inflationary expansion of the stock of money ceased at the end of 1928, the Depression was inevitable. Production indices began declining in the second quarter, stock market transactors recognized what was happening, and stock prices ceased rising at the end of the third quarter, and the stock market "crashed" at the end of October 1929. The "overinvestments" discovered by later analysts were not the general overinvestments, but rather the malinvestments of the boom which were shown to be unprofitable once the money growth stopped.

Murray Rothbard has made a detailed examination of the Hoover administration's actions which lengthened the Depression and made it much more severe.[42] In November 1929, Hoover met with the leaders of the major industrial firms, the heads of the leading public utilities, representatives of the building and construction industry, and leading labor union officials. He asked that money wages not be cut (to maintain purchasing power) and, when necessary, the workweek be reduced as an alternative to layoffs. These leaders were receptive to his requests. Money wage rates in twenty-five major industries remained constant until late 1930. Many businesses resisted wage rate cuts until quite late in 1931. U.S. Steel, over the opposition of its president, finally cut wage rates in September 1931. Other firms cut wages secretly "for fear of the disapproval of the Hoover Administration."[43]

This policy led to much greater declines in output and employment since holding money wage rates constant raised real wage rates as prices fell. In fact, real wage rates in June 1933 were higher than in June 1929. The primary problem was not that the policy did not allow wage rates to fall since not *all* wage rates had to decline. Rather, it did not allow the wage rates for the various occupations and for the various firms to adjust as necessary to coordinate labor and other markets.

The Hawley-Smoot Tariff was approved and put into effect in June 1930. The protective tariff raised rates to the highest in U.S. history and spawned retaliatory tariffs in many other nations. This set off a spiraling contraction of both U.S. imports and exports, and altered the demands and supplies of many products and services requiring substantial relative price adjustment and resource movements.

The Federal Farm Board, established in 1929, attempted to support the prices of wheat and many other farm products. Production rose, surpluses piled up, and world prices continued to fall. Finally the FFB began dumping its surplus holdings on world markets, driving down prices and further undermining the farmers' positions.

In 1932, Congress approved huge increases in tax rates for most federal taxes. The sharp decline in the stock of money (which began in 1931 and accelerated in late 1931, after Great Britain went off gold) continued. The Reconstruction Finance Corporation, created in 1932, made a number of loans to ailing banks. Publication of these loans led to runs on these banks as the public interpreted the loans as a sign of weakness. This, combined with the worry that Roosevelt would devalue gold (or take the United States off the gold standard), led to massive and continued bank runs by the end of 1932. With these runs there were, for the first time, specific demands for gold.

The deflationary decline in the money stock and the intermittent banking panics required further relative and absolute price adjustments. The reductions in bank lending required that interest rates be higher than they otherwise would have been. Prices of financial assets, productive resources, and goods and services had to fall in complex sequential patterns. The result was a highly complex alteration of relative prices while the declining money stock caused prices to fall.[44]

By the trough of the Depression, these shocks to the economy and the discoordination of various markets (particularly the labor markets) required large resource shifts and relative price changes to bring about higher employment and output levels. The process of recovery required these price changes and resource shifts.

This was and, of course, still is no simple task. With price searching firms, each firm has to discover each resource and product price through a trial and error process of trying different prices—a search process that can be long and difficult. In a dynamic environment, there is no simple and direct path from the prevailing disequilibrium price toward a new price consistent with all other prices.

This process is not part of the logic behind fiscal policy. The Keynesian approach simply asserts that what is necessary is to obtain a net increase in aggregate spending. Since the federal government's spending is not constrained by income, wealth, cash flows, or profitability, then it is up to the federal government to initiate the spending increase. The general logic of the Keynesian model does not suggest that it makes any important difference what type of federal spending is increased.

When one recognizes that the problem is one of price and resource adjustments to coordinate the plans of consumers and firms, fiscal policy's impact changes. It will not initiate a more rapid recovery unless the federal expenditures promote coordinating price adjustments. This, however, was as unlikely then as now. The knowledge of how relative prices should be altered to promote the appropriate resource adjustments is not something that any individual or group(s) of individuals in the government or elsewhere has. As Hayek has pointed out, it is dispersed among all of the participants in the economy.

The fiscal policies of the federal government during the recovery included a number of tax increases as well as increased spending. Much of the increased spending was on make-work jobs to give employment to those who were unemployed rather than simply provide direct relief funds, though there also was much direct relief. I can briefly note some of the projects on which the federal government increased its spending.[45] The Public Works Administration undertook a number of large-scale projects such as highway, dam, and large public building construction as well as harbor improvements. The Civil Works Administration undertook "new and improved roads; bridges; repair of 40,000 schools; drainage of hundreds of thousands of acres of malarial lands; destruction of millions of rats and ticks; 150,000 sanitary privies; 200 swimming pools; 3,700 playgrounds; new hospitals; athletic stadiums; airports; and public buildings." The Civil Works Service Program employed "nonmanual labor" on many cultural projects such as paintings, sculptures, murals, writing music, and compiling local histories. The Emergency Education Program provided work for unemployed teachers in "adult education, vocational education and rehabilitation, and nursery schools for underprivileged children." The Women's Work Program provided "homemaking" type jobs for women in such activities as "sewing clothes, making bedding, canning food, nursing, teaching, research, and making statistical surveys."[46] The Civilian Conservation Corps sent young people off to camps, especially in forests and national parks, to do conservation work.

These types of projects were continued in the Works Progress Administration. The WPA constructed streets, sidewalks, water supply systems, sewage disposal systems, parks, airports, public buildings, hospitals, penal institutions, and military establishments. It sealed mines; undertook water conservation projects and engineering surveys; set up nursery schools; provided library services; sponsored adult education, museum, music, writing, art, and theater projects; provided social, economic, housing, and national health surveys; and organized a number of other welfare projects.[47]

The Reconstruction Finance Corporation provided loans and purchased stock to prop up financial institutions. Agricultural credit was provided to farmers and the Agricultural Adjustment Administration spent funds to raise farm prices and limit farm production.

There is no evidence that these types of expenditures promoted coordination of the plans and actions of individuals and firms. Many of these projects involved "public" or conservation projects which would not have been undertaken otherwise and which were not the type that private enterprise would have undertaken. Offsetting the coordination that these federal expenditures brought about were other aspects of these and other New Deal programs.

At the time, it was noted that the labor required for many of the public works projects (such as roads, buildings, and bridges) "could not provide appropriate employment for many types of the unemployed."[48] Wage and hours policies also were controversial. There was considerable discussion of whether the wages should be at the prevailing level or lower than prevailing wages to encourage workers to seek employment in private industry. The general policy was to pay the prevailing wage rates "except where these were below the stated minimum levels" and to establish maximum hours of work.[49] Minimum wage rates and maximum hours of employment per week were written into a number of New Deal laws. Such actions certainly did not facilitate the market adjustments necessary to coordinate markets, particularly the labor markets.

Other New Deal programs severely hindered market processes. The NIRA's attempt to cartelize much of U.S. business virtually stopped the recovery. In attempting to stop price competition and raise prices, it tried to control and set uniform prices, raise and equalize wage rates, eliminate nonprice as well as price competition, and stop investment if there were any excess capacity in other firms in the industry.[50] The promotion of unionization following the Wagner Act, the late 1930s antitrust crusade, and the creation of an unending agricultural crisis through price support programs all made the coordination of markets much more difficult. By reducing the ability of prices to adjust in response to changes in market conditions, it became more difficult to bring about greater consistency in the plans of the market participants. These New Deal programs—combined with federal expenditures concentrated on producing public and cultural works and the construction of public buildings and other capital goods—lengthened the recovery from the Great Depression.

On the basis of this anlaysis, I conclude that the evidence indicates that a more expansionary fiscal policy would not have brought about a faster recovery from the Great Depression. First, the evidence suggests that an expansion of federal spending, financed by the sale of U.S. government securities rather than by tax increases and without the Federal Reserve System "monetizing" the additional federal debt, would have, for all practical purposes, have been offset by induced decreases in private and nonfederal government spending. Second, there is no reason to think that increases in net aggregate spending initiated by increased federal spending would have been likely to alter relative prices in ways that would have promoted coordinating adjustments toward higher employment and output. This would not have been an objective in the decision as to how the expenditures should have been undertaken. Even if the increased federal spending had been accommodated by an expansionary monetary policy, there is a low likelihood that the pattern of spending would have been such as to promote equilibrating price adjustments. Previous analyses of Keynesian fiscal policy in the recovery from the Great Depression have failed to adequately examine either crowding out effects or effects on the structure of relative prices, and, therefore, were misleading as to the potential effects of expansionary fiscal policy.

Appendix:
The Early 1940s Recovery

One of the reasons that Keynesian analysis became widely accepted and still has many adherents is the belief that the early 1940s proved that Keynesian expansionary fiscal policy "worked" in promoting a more rapid return to full employment. From 1940 on, the federal government rapidly expanded its spending under the impetus of preparation for and then involvement in World War II. Most economic history and macroeconomics textbooks still single out this period as evidence of the power of Keynesian fiscal policy.

This acceptance is primarily a matter of faith rather than analysis. The early 1940s recovery cannot be seen as evidence that pure Keynesian fiscal policy works since, to give just one example, the Federal Reserve System authorities dramatically changed monetary policy. Under the pressures of the war in Europe and, presumably, the likely involvement of the United States, the Federal Reserve System adopted an extremely expansionary monetary policy at the start of 1940. From January 1940 through January 1941, the stock of money grew 12.01 percent, then 22.88 percent from January 1940 through January 1942, and 44.78 percent from January 1940 through January 1943. Through 1940 and 1941, nearly 90 percent of the growth of the stock of money was due to the growth of the high-powered money, controlled by the Federal Reserve System.[51] The change in monetary policy, in effect, allowed a monetization of the debt the federal government issued as its spending rapidly increased. With such an expansionary (or inflationary) monetary policy, economists cannot conclude that it was fiscal policy rather than monetary policy that was the proximate cause of the more rapid recovery.

I have argued above that there is no reason to think that either fiscal policy with debt monetization or pure monetary policy would necessarily promote higher employment and output unless the additional expenditures tended to promote greater coordination of the plans of individual transactors through the appropriate relative price adjustments. There is, in fact, reason to believe that something such as this did occur. To understand why this is so, one needs to consider the unionization that occurred in the late 1930s.

Following the Wagner Labor Relations Act of 1935, there was an accelerated drive to unionize various firms—often all the firms in an industry. This was concentrated in the major industries containing the largest firms. For the most part, rather lengthy and bitter strikes were necessary to bring union recognition. Once the unions were recognized as the monopoly bargaining agents for the firm's workers, relatively large wage rate increases were negotiated as well as reductions in working hours. For example, when U.S. Steel and many smaller steel firms were organized in 1937, wage rates rose 19 percent (from 52.5 to 62.5 cents an hour) and overtime wage rates were installed. "Little Steel" temporarily staved off unionization by granting the same wage increase. It appears that similar types of wage and hour agreements were concluded in most cases of successful unionization in the late 1930s.

There has been little analysis of the firms' responses to these increased operating outlays. Yet, one would expect the magnitude of the wage rate changes to have noticeable effects. All else remaining the same, the increases in labor expenditures would cause the firms to discover some combination of higher prices for the products being produced as well as reduced production (because of the higher product prices). Employment in the newly unionized firms would decline because of the reduced production and because firms would begin the process of marginally substituting capital for labor due to the higher relative price of labor.

If the demands for the products of the newly unionized firms were increasing, then their product prices might not have to rise and production might not decline. In time, there would still be some reduction in employment due to the marginal substitution of capital for labor. The problem is that we do not know what the conditions were in the late 1930s. No examination of the responses of the various firms seems to have been undertaken. There are no data on product prices, labor costs, employment, and production for both the firms that underwent unionization and those that did not.

My guess is that there were no relative increases in demand for the firms being unionized. If this were the case, then those firms had to choose some combination of increased product prices and relatively reduced production and employment. This would seem likely because of the 1937–38 contraction and the slow recovery from mid-1938 to 1940, as well as the fact that there is no reason to think that the demands for the products of the unionized firms would have been growing faster than the demands for the products of firms not being unionized.[52] This would have slowed down the recovery. Workers who were employed and would have been employed by these firms would thus have had to search for employment elsewhere. Most of the firms being unionized were large, heavy industry firms and their plants dominated the communities in which they were located. It is likely that workers would have had to extend their search toward other locations to discover employment opportunities. Since the products of some of the unionized firms were inputs into final products of other firms, there would be a complex alteration of the relative prices and production of many other products. Thus, the process of firms discovering whether the demand for their output had increased or decreased (and whether this was temporary or permanent), as well as workers discovering where employment opportunities were and what were the employment conditions, would have slowed the movements toward higher employment and production.

The federal government's expenditures on war goods in 1940, 1941, and 1942 tended to be concentrated on materials produced by heavy industry firms, firms where the late 1930s unionization had been concentrated. The result was that federal expenditures on war materials largely tended to increase demands in those industries where it is likely that costs had increased without commensurate demand increases in the late 1930s. This would have allowed them to profitably expand employment and production. The federal government's war expenditures at the beginning of the 1940s, financed largely by an increasing stock of money, are likely to have unintentionally promoted a number of equilibrating price and resource adjustments. The increased coordination would have more rapidly increased employment and output.[53]

The empirical research necessary to address the question of why there was such a rapid recovery in the early 1940s has not yet been undertaken. It should be noted that the question is not one of theory; rather it is one of empirical facts.[54] What were the demand conditions in the late 1930s and early 1940s for firms that were unionized and those that were not? How did the managements of the unionized firms respond to these changes? To what firms did the federal government's early 1940s war purchases go, and in what magnitudes? This constitutes an important empirical research agenda. What is presently clear is that the rapid recovery of the early 1940s is neither evidence nor proof that Keynesian fiscal policy "works" nor evidence that it would have restored full employment much more rapidly in the 1933–39 period.

Notes

1. See E. Cary Brown, "Fiscal Policy in the Thirties: A Reappraisal," *American Economic Review* 46 (1956), pp. 857–79; and Larry C. Peppers, "Full-Employment Surplus Analysis and Structural Change: the 1930's," *Explorations in Economic History* 10 (Winter 1973), pp. 197–210.

2. For a skeptical view, see Michael R. Darby, "Three-and-a-Half Million U.S. Employees Have Been Mislaid: Or, an Explanation of Unemployment, 1934–1941," *Journal of Political Economy* 84 (February 1976), pp. 1–16. Recent restatements of the accepted view can be found in J.R. Kesselman and N.E. Savin, "Three-and-a-Half Million Workers Never Were Lost," *Economic Inquiry* 16 (April 1978), pp. 205–25; and, Bert Hickman and Robert Coen, *An Annual Growth Model of the U.S. Economy* (Amsterdam: North Holland, 1976). In their simulation model Hickman and Coen found, for the decade of the thirties, an unbelievably huge federal spending multiplier of 7.4 in the third year after the spending increase.

3. Brown, "Fiscal Policy," pp. 863–66; Peppers, "Full-Employment Surplus Analysis," pp. 209–10.

4. In 1929 dollars, federal outlays averaged $3.0 billion a year from 1922 through 1929, $4.8 billion a year from 1930 through 1933, and $9.2 billion a year from 1934 through 1939. Therefore, federal expenditures in the recovery years were triple the level during the 1920s. The data come from U.S. Dept. of Commerce, Bureau of the Census, *Historical Statistics of the United States: Colonial Times to 1970* (Washington, D.C.: U.S. GPO, 1976) series F5 and Y336.

5. Peppers, "Full-Employment Surplus Anlaysis," p. 208.

6. U.S. National Resources Planning Board, *Security, Work, and Relief Policies* (Washington, D.C.: U.S. GPO, 1942), pp. 326–27. This source and these figures were reported by Kesselman and Savin, "Three-and-a-Half Million Workers," p. 214.

7. It should be clear that federal debt purchases made by federal government agencies use taxes which have been collected, and really should be treated as additional expenditures financed by additional taxes rather than as debt-financed additional expenditures.

8. It is still common in macro texts to find expositions of the lump sum tax "balanced budget multiplier" of unity (or less than unity if taxes vary with income). It is usually not noted that this result can only hold if individuals "save" in the form of idle currency holdings, or that savings placed in financial institutions by individuals are always matched by a rise in idle excess reserves of the financial institutions. It should be noted that a similar type of rather implausible assumption underlies the full-employment balanced budget (or "high employment surplus") concept. The general idea is that if the government tax and expenditure functions are such as to produce a budget surplus at full employment, then the "drag" makes it unlikely that full employment will be achieved. This holds only if the government collects the surplus in cash and holds it in government vaults. If the surplus is used to reduce the government's debt or even is placed as deposits in financial institutions, then the funds will be transferred to individuals or firms that will spend the money, and the surplus is no longer a drag on the economy. A quick examination of the prosperous, high-employment 1920s, when the government used the huge surplus of each year to reduce the government debt, quickly illustrates the nonsense of the idea that any government budget surplus that would arise at full employment is a drag on reaching full employment.

9. Milton Friedman and Anna Schwartz, *A Monetary History of the United States: 1867–1960* (Princeton: Princeton University Press for the National Bureau of Economic Research, 1963), table B-3, pp. 803–5.

10. Though the use of demand deposits by private households was increasing prior to World War II, it was well after the war before checking account use by private households became nearly universal. In the interwar period, businesses were much more important users of demand deposits. In the 1920s, as business firms, particularly the larger ones, increasingly turned to nonbank sources of borrowed funds, short-term business lending and demand deposits as fractions of banks' assets and liabilities both sharply declined. For a discussion of this, see Benjamin Klebaner, *Commercial Banking in the United States: A History* (Hinsdale, Ill,: Dryden, 1974).

11. Since most households held savings in time deposits when the required reserve ratio was much lower, the decline in private sector spending (due to the decline in bank lending) would come very close to offsetting the rise in federal spending. (The required reserve ratio on time deposits was 3 percent through August 15, 1936; it was then raised in three steps to 6 percent on May 1, 1937. On April 16, 1938, it was lowered to 5 percent, where it remained through most of 1941.) For demand deposits, with their higher required reserve ratios, there would be a small rise in aggregate spending in the year higher required reserve ratios take place since the rise in spending effectively increases the income velocity of money in that year. In other words, there would be one additional round of final purchase transactions equal to the fraction of savings coming from reserves against the deposits (which were used to pay the increased taxes). The effect would be relatively small.

12. A simple numerical example will illustrate this. Suppose that the marginal propensity to consume is 0.9 so that the spending multiplier is 10, and the deposit/currency ratio is 7. Federal spending and taxes increase by $100 million and "savings" are reduced by $10 million. Deposit "savings" are reduced by $8.57 million and currency "savings" by $1.43 million. Since only the reduction in currency savings does not create a reduction in private spending offsetting the rise in federal spending, aggregate spending will ultimately rise by $14.3 million for a $100 million rise in federal government spending and in federal taxes. The balanced budget multiplier then is 0.143, significantly less than one. I can also illustrate the effect of temporarily putting reserves to use. Suppose that the banks held deposit reserves of 15 percent. The loss of $8.57 million of deposits would reduce banks' reserves by $1.2855 million and banks' lending by $7.2845 million. The increase in federal spending of $8.57 million in that year means that net aggregate spending would rise by $1.2855 million in that year. Therefore, in the first year, a $100 million increase in federal spending and taxes would lead to aggregate spending $1.2855 million greater than that fraction of the $14.3 million increase (due to the multiplier effect) occurring in the first year. The net spending multiplier in the first year probably would not be far in excess of zero. This result would be stronger if taxes (part or all) are made a function of the level of income, as was the case. This is the optimistic scenario since it assumes that higher tax rates will not drive more economic activity "underground" nor reduce output and income by discouraging economic activity and increasing the consumption of leisure.

13. Federal agencies and trust funds (such as the social security system) were using tax revenues they had collected to "purchase" the debt. My discussion suggests that there is little reason to think that there was a multiplier very much above

zero on federal expenditures financed by equivalent tax increases, which is what the purchase of federal debt by federal government agencies and trust funds would amount to.

14. The information in *Banking and Monetary Statistics* (Washington, D.C.: National Capital Press, 1943) did not provide any information on the distribution of the government debt held by individuals and firms in the "other investors" category.

15. See Arthur E. Grandolfi, "Stability of the Demand for Money during the Great Contraction—1929–1933," *Journal of Political Economy* 82 (September/October 1974), pp. 969–84; Arthur E. Grandolfi and James R. Lothian, "The Demand for Money from the Great Depression to the Present," *American Economic Review* 66 (May 1976), pp. 46–51; Moshin S. Khan, "The Stability of the Demand-for-Money Function in the United States 1901–1965," *Journal of Political Economy* 82 (November/December 1974), pp. 1205–19; David E.W. Laidler, *The Demand for Money: Theories and Evidence* (Scranton, Pa.: International Textbook, 1969); and John T. Boorman, "The Evidence on the Demand for Money: Theoretical Formulations and Empirical Results," pp. 315–60 in Thomas M. Havrilesky and John T. Boorman, eds., *Current Issues in Monetary Theory and Policy,* 2nd ed. (Arlington Heights, Ill.: AHM, 1980).

16. See Gene Smiley, "Regional Variation in Bank Loan Rates in the Interwar Years," *Journal of Economic History* 41 (December 1981), pp. 889–901.

17. This data on insurance companies come from Harold G. Williamson and Orange A. Smalley, *Northwestern Mutual Life: A Century of Trusteeship* (Evanston, Ill.: Northwestern University Press, 1957).

18. Louis Dublin, *A Family of Thirty Million: The Story of the Metropolitan Life Insurance Company* (New York: Metropolitan Life Insurance Company, 1943).

19. Williamson and Smalley, *Northwestern Mutual Life,* p. 266.

20. Ibid., p. 268.

21. Ibid.

22. Friedman and Schwartz, *A Monetary History,* table B-3, pp. 803–5.

23. See Smiley, "Regional Variation."

24. Ben Bernanke, "Nonmonetary Effects of the Finance Crisis in the Propagation of the Great Depression," *American Economic Review* 73 (June 1983), pp. 257–76.

25. Lewis Kimmel, *The Availability of Bank Credit, 1933–1938* (New York: National Industrial Conference Board, 1939), cited as Bernanke, "Nonmonetary Effects."

26. These data are reported in W.L. Stoddard, "Small Business Wants Capital," *Harvard Business Review* 18 (1940), pp. 265–74, as cited by Bernanke, "Nonmonetary Effects."

27. See Friedman and Schwartz, *A Monetary History,* pp. 511–34.

28. Ibid., pp. 526–27.

29. Richard Timberlake has pointed out that required reserves were not, in fact, usable by the banks. Excess reserves could be used when there were large conversions of deposits to currency holdings. Given the notable failure of the Federal Reserve System to discount member banks' assets to provide the banks with liquidity during the banking crises, he suggests that it is not surprising that excess reserves were built up to reduce the banks' reliance upon an undependable Federal Reserve System

30. Michael M. Weinstein, *Recovery and Redistribution under the NIRA* (Amsterdam: North-Holland, 1980), and "Some Macroeconomic Impacts of the National Industrial Recovery Act, 1933–1935," chap. 14 in Karl Brunner, ed., *The Great Depression Revisited* (Boston: Martinus Nijhoff, 1981).

31. Recent Keynesian research has suggested that one mechanism by which expansionary fiscal policy could have provided some additional impetus toward recovery is as follows. The government spending financed by the additional government debt will increase the demand for commodities and services, while the sale of the debt might not diminish spending elsewhere. If the government bonds are viewed as increments to net wealth, while the future taxes implied by the government debt are not perceived and discounted by private citizens, then consumption spending out of permanent income might rise so that there is less, or perhaps little, induced decrease in private consumption spending. This situation, however, did not apply in the 1930s. The mechanism requires that households purchase the debt so that the discrepancy between the perceived wealth effects and debt effects can lead to increases in consumption spending out of permanent income. As noted, nearly all of the federal debt issued was purchased by the financial intermediaries, and the data suggest that they did reduce purchases of other securities and reduce lending when this occurred. Therefore, investment spending had to decline. The discussion of this effect was reopened by Martin J. Bailey and Robert J. Barro. See Martin J. Bailey, *National Income and the Price Level* (New York: McGraw-Hill, 1962, 1971); and Robert J. Barro, "Are Government Bonds Net Wealth?" *Journal of Political Economy* 82 (December 1974), pp. 1095–1117. There are many recent articles on this subject. For a list of references, see Roger C. Kormendi, "Government Debt, Government Spending, and Private Sector Behavior," *American Economic Review* 73 (December 1983), pp. 994–1010.

32. In this analysis I am guided by the writings of a number of Austrian economists. The foundations of this analysis are: Ludwig von Mises, *Human Action: A Treatise on Economics,* 3rd rev. ed. (Chicago: Henry Regnery, 1966), chap. 20 in particular; Friedrich A. Hayek, *Prices and Production* (New York: Agustus M. Kelly, 1931, reprinted 1967); Hayek, *Monetary Theory and the Trade Cycle* (London: Jonathan Cape, 1933); Hayek, *Individualism and Economic Order* (Chicago: Henry Regnery, Gateway edition, 1948); Murray N. Rothbard, *Man, Economy, and State: A Treatise on Economics,* 2 vol. (Los Angeles: Nash, 1962, reprinted 1970), particularly chaps. 5–7 and 11–12; and Rothbard *America's Great Depression* (Los Angeles: Nash, 1963, reprinted 1970). Recent studies include the following: Ludwig M. Lachmann, "Toward a Critique of Macroeconomics," and Gerald P. O'Driscoll, Jr., and Sudha R. Shenoy, "Inflation, Recession, and Stagflation," pp. 152–59 and 185–211 in Edwin G. Dolan, ed., *The Foundations of Modern Austrian Economics* (Kansas City: Sheed and Ward, 1976); Gerald P. O'Driscoll, Jr., "Spontaneous Order and the Coordination of Economic Activities" and Roger W. Garrison, "Austrian Macroeconomics: A Diagrammatical Exposition," pp. 111–42 and 167–204 in Louis M. Spadaro, ed., *New Directions in Austrian Economics* (Kansas City: Sheed and Ward, 1978); and, Gerald P. O'Driscoll, Jr., *Economics as a Coordination Problem: The Contributions of Friedrich A. Hayek* (Kansas City: Sheed, Andrews, and McMeel, 1977).

33. The price inflation from 1933 on was the result of an increasing stock of money, as well as, initially, the NIRA. The money stock rose as bank reserves were increased due to the inflow of gold into the United States.

34. Although conventional macroeconomic analysis generally does not recognize the predominance of the local effects over the national effects arising from increases in federal spending, one does not have to listen to politicians very long to realize that they clearly recognize this. It was not different in the 1930s. Several years ago, Leonard

Arrington and then his student Don Reading used a number of economic variables in an attempt to explain the state-by-state variation in per capita New Deal spending. See Leonard J. Arrington, "The New Deal in the West: A Preliminary Statistical Inquiry," *Pacific Historical Review* 38 (August 1969), pp. 311–16; Arrington, "Western Agriculture and the New Deal," *Agricultural History* 44 (October 1970), pp. 337–53; and Don C. Reading, "New Deal Activity and the States, 1933 to 1939," *The Journal of Economic History* 33 (December 1973), pp. 792–810.

Gavin Wright later reexamined the issue, arguing that the political factor had to be taken into account. Wright's study convincingly argued that New Deal spending tended to be concentrated in those states where the spending was more likely to change the course of an election because the voting was expected to be close or there had been substantial swings in voter sentiment in the past. This brings into question one of the most fundamental assumptions of Keynesian macroeconomic analysis. See Gavin Wright, "The Political Economy of New Deal Spending: An Econometric Analysis," *Review of Economics and Statistics* 56 (February 1974), pp. 30–38.

35. The concept of the coordination of the plans of transactors as the economic problem is a fundamental one that runs all through the literature on Austrian economics. It is difficult to point to a few individuals as primarily responsible for developing the ideas. However, Friedrich A. Hayek's writings have dwelled on this somewhat more than other Austrian economists' and, for economists in general, his name is probably more closely associated with these ideas. Gerald O'Driscoll makes an excellent argument that the concept of the economic problem being really one of coordination is woven into all of Hayek's writings, ranging from monetary-business cycle theory, to capital theory, to his pathbreaking articles on economics and knowledge, and on to his work on law, legislation, and liberty. In the following brief exposition I shall draw primarily on O'Driscoll, *Economics as a Coordination Problem,* chap. 2. O'Driscoll's chapter primarily is built upon several touchstone papers by Hayek, all of which were reprinted in Hayek's *Individualism and Economic Order.* Those papers are "Economics and Knowledge," *Economica* 4 (new series, 1937), pp. 33–54; "The Use of Knowledge in Society," *American Economic Review* 35 (September 1945), pp. 519–30; and "The Meaning of Competition," the Stafford Little Lecture delivered at Princeton University on May 20, 1946.

36. Hayek, "Economics and Knowledge," pp. 50–51. This statement was quoted in O'Driscoll, *Economics as a Coordination Problem,* p. 26.

37. O'Driscoll, ibid., p. 27.

38. In particular, see Hayek, *Prices and Production,* pp. 160–62; Lionel Robbins, *The Great Depression* (New York: Macmillan, 1934); and Rothbard, *America's Great Depression.* Murray Rothbard's book is the most extensive and complete examination of the Great Depression, in terms of the monetary disturbances that created the disaster as well as the further discoordinating actions which made it become so long and so severe. Recently, Charles Wainhouse (a Ph.D. student of Gerald P. O'Driscoll, Jr., at New York University) wrote a dissertation on business cycles. Using extensive empirical techniques, his results were further support for the Austrian explanation of the Great Depression.

39. Gerald P. O'Driscoll, Jr., "Foreword" in Friedrich A. Hayek, *Unemployment and Monetary Policy: Government as Generator of the "Business Cycle,"* Cato Paper no. 3 (San Francisco: Cato Institute, 1979), p. xi.

40. It is important to emphasize several points which non-Austrian economists often misinterpret. First, the Austrian theory of the business cycle begins with monetary disturbances which disrupt prices, but the business cycle involves the misallocation of real resources. This means that the ending of the inflation (monetary disturbance) exposes the misallocation of the real capital resources. Because of the costliness of reallocating real nonhuman resources (many of which are specific to the production of quite limited products and even a particular stage of production), a contraction is inevitable. Second, the Austrian theory of the business cycle is *not* an overinvestment theory. Rather it is a "malinvestment" theory concerning investment that is misdirected. It is not necessary for the magnitude of investment to be greater than if there had been no monetary disturbances. For extended discussions of these points see Hayek, *Prices and Production* and Rothbard, *America's Great Depression,* particularly part I.

41. Hayek, *Prices and Production,* pp. 161–62.

42. Rothbard, *America's Great Depression,* especially part III, chap. 7–12.

43. Ibid., pp. 188–90 and 237–38.

44. Rothbard argues that the actions undertaken by the federal government and Federal Reserve System prolonged the time that it took for the money stock and prices to fall and to eliminate the "unsound" banks. He also argues that deflation is not as much of a problem as inflation. Inflation lowers interest rates, disturbs the prices of capital goods, and leads to malinvestments that, to be worked off, require an economic contraction. Deflation does not lead to malinvestments of capital that require a contraction to be worked off.

45. Much of these data are drawn from Lester V. Chandler, *America's Greatest Depression, 1919–1941* (New York: Harper & Row, 1970).

46. Ibid., p. 201.

47. Ibid., pp. 203–5.

48. Ibid., p. 193.

49. Ibid., p. 200.

50. Some of this is discussed in Chandler, chap. 13. A much more thorough and critical discussion can be found in Paul K. Conkin, *The New Deal,* 2nd ed. (Arlington Heights, Ill.: AHM Publishing, 1975). This is also discussed in Weinstein, *Recovery and Redistribution.* Weinstein's perspective is somewhat different. He criticizes the NIRA because it attempted (with some success) to raise prices and wages. This thwarted the expansionary effect that the increase in the stock of money (through gold inflows) would have had. He follows the view that the location of the net increase in spending (due to the increase in the stock of money) was not important; only the magntidue was important. This increasingly critical view of the New Deal can also be found in the more recent U.S. economic history textbooks. See Jonathan Hughes, *American Economic History* (Glenview, Ill.: Scott, Foresman, 1983) and Stanley Lebergott, *The Americans: An Economic Record* (New York: W.W. Norton, 1984).

51. These figures were calculated from Friedman and Schwartz, *A Monetary History.* From January 1940 through January 1942, the share of the growth in M2 due to changes in the high-powered money was 89.96 percent. The share due to changes in the deposit/reserve ratio was 36.08 percent, but, largely offsetting this, the share due to changes in the deposit/currency ratio was – 22.91 percent. The shares will not add to 100 percent due to the interaction of the deposit/reserve and deposit/currency ratios.

52. One possibility, which generally seems not to have been examined, is that the unionization surge as well as the Federal Reserve System's deflationary monetary policy brought on the contraction running from mid-1937 through mid-1938.

53. Under normal circumstances, one would expect the improvement to have been temporary since the increased demand for unionized firms would last only as long as the govermment's extraordinary expenditures continued, and the inflationary monetary policy would lead to discoordination. Of course, these were not normal times. The government's war expenditures grew rather than declined, and the federal government began to impose economic controls as early as May 1940. The first price schedule was issued in February 1941, and the Office of Price Administration and Civilian Supply was established in April 1941. Wages were brought under government control in December 1941. In April 1942, wages and prices were frozen. By that time, the extensive rationing system was imposed and it continued through the end of World War II. For a discussion of World War II wage and price controls, see Hugh Rockoff, *Drastic Measures: A History of Wage and Price Controls in the United States* (New York: Cambridge University Press, 1984).

54. One does not test an economic theory. Given the theory's premises, it is either logically true or false. Though people know that this is the case, economists seem to continually talk about "testing" theories rather than determining whether the initial conditions are consistent with the premises of the theory.

References

Arrington, Leonard J., (1969), "The New Deal in the West: A Preliminary Statistical Inquiry." *Pacific Historical Review* 38, 311–16.

———, (1970), "Western Agriculture and the New Deal." *Agricultural History* 44, 337–53.

Bailey, Martin J. (1962, 1971), *National Income and the Price Level.* New York: McGraw-Hill.

Barro, Robert J. (1974). "Are Government Bonds Net Wealth?" *Journal of Political Economy* 82, 1095–1117.

Bernanke, Ben S. (1983), "Nonmonetary Effects of the Financial Crisis in the Propagation of the Great Depression." *American Economic Review* 73, 257–76.

Beveridge, W.H. (1930), *Unemployment: A Problem of Industry.* London: Longmans, Green.

———, (1931), *Causes and Cures of Unemployment.* London: Longmans, Green.

Board of Governors of the Federal Reserve System (1943), *Banking and Monetary Statistics.* Washington, D.C.: National Capital Press.

Boorman, John T. (1980), "The Evidence on the Demand for Money: Theoretical Formulations and Empirical Results," pp. 315–60 in Thomas M. Havrilesky and John T. Boorman, eds., *Current Issues in Monetary Theory and Policy,* 2nd ed. Arlington Heights, Ill.: AHM Publishing.

Brown, E. Cary (1956), "Fiscal Policy in the Thirties: A Reappraisal." *American Economic Review* 46, 857–79.

Brunner, Karl, ed. (1981), *The Great Depression Revisited.* Boston: Martinus Nijhoff.

Chandler, Lester V. (1970), *America's Greatest Depression, 1929–1941.* New York: Harper & Row.

Conkin, Paul P. (1975), *The New Deal,* 2nd ed. Arlington Heights, Ill.: AHM Publishing.

Darby, Michael R. (1976), "Three-and-a-Half Million U.S. Employees Have Been Mislaid: Or, an Explanation of Unemployment, 1934–1941." *Journal of Political Economy* 84, 1–16.

Dolan, Edwin G., ed. (1976), *The Foundations of Modern Austrian Economics.* Kansas City: Sheed and Ward.

Dublin, Louis (1943), *A Family of Thirty Million: The Story of the Metropolitan Life Insurance Company.* New York: Metropolitan Life Insurance.

Friedman, Milton, and Anna Schwartz (1963), *A Monetary History of the United States: 1867–1960.* Princeton: Princeton University Press.

Gallaway, Lowell, and Richard Vedder (1985), "Wages, Prices, and Employment: Von Mises and the 'Progressives'." Manuscript, Ohio University, 1985.

Gandolfi, Arthur E. (1974), "Stability of the Demand for Money during the Great Contraction—1929–1933." *Journal of Political Economy* 82, 969–84.

Gandolfi, Arthur E. and James R. Lothian (1976), "The Demand for Money from the Great Depression to the Present." *American Economic Review* 66, 46–51.

Garrison, Roger (1978), "Austrian Macroeconomics: A Diagrammatical Exposition," pp. 167–204 in Louis M. Spadaro, ed., *New Directions in Austrian Economics.* Kansas City: Sheed and Ward, 1978.

Havrilesky, Thomas M., and John T. Boorman, eds., (1980), *Current Issues in Monetary Theory and Policy,* 2nd ed. Arlington Heights, Ill.: AHM Publishing.

Hawley, Ellis W. (1965), *The New Deal and the Problem of Monopoly, 1933–1939.* Princeton: Princeton University Press.

Hayek, Friedrich A. (1931, 1967), *Prices and Production.* New York: Agustus M. Kelly.

———, (1933), *Monetary Theory and the Trade Cycle.* London: Jonathan Cape.

———, (1948), *Individualism and Economic Order.* Chicago: Henry Regnery, a Gateway edition.

———, (1979), *Unemployment and Monetary Policy: Government as Generator of the "Business Cycle,"* Paper no. 3. San Francisco: Cato Institute.

Hickman, Bert, and Robert Coen (1976), *An Annual Growth Model of the U.S. Economy.* Amsterdam: North-Holland.

Hughes, Jonathan R.T. (1977), *The Governmental Habit: Economic Controls from Colonial Times to the Present.* New York: Basic Books.

———, (1983), *American Economic History.* Glenview, Ill.: Scott, Foresman.

Kesselman, J.R., and N.E. Savin (1978), "Three-and-a-Half Million Workers Never Were Lost." *Economic Inquiry* 16, 205–25.

Khan, Mohsin S. (1974), "The Stability of the Demand-for-Money Function in the United States 1901–1965." *Journal of Political Economy* 82, 1205–19.

Kimmel, Lewis H. (1939), *The Availability of Bank Credit, 1933–1938.* New York: National Industrial Conference Board.

Kindleberger, Charles P. (1973), *The World in Depression, 1929–1939.* Berkeley: University of California Press.

King, Wilford I. (1938), *The Causes of Economic Fluctuations.* New York: Ronald Press Co.

Kirzner, Israel M. (1973), *Competition and Entrepreneurship.* Chicago: University of Chicago Press.

——, ed. (1982), *Method, Process, and Austrian Economics: Essays in Honor of Ludwig von Mises.* Lexington, Mass.: Lexington Books.

Klebaner, Benjamin (1974), *Commercial Banking in the United States: A History.* Hinsdale, Ill.: Dryden.

Kormendi, Roger C. (1983), "Government Debt, Government Spending, and Private Sector Behavior." *American Economic Review* 73, 994–1010.

Lachmann, Ludwig M. (1976), "Toward A Critique of Macroeconomics," pp. 152–59 in Edwin G. Dolan, Ed., *The Foundations of Modern Austrian Economics.* Kansas City: Sheed and Ward, 1976.

Laidler, David E.W. (1969), *The Demand for Money: Theories and Evidence.* Scranton, Pa.: International Textbook.

Lebergott, Stanley (1984), *The Americans: An Economic Record.* New York: W.W. Norton.

Leuchtenberg, William E. (1963), *Franklin D. Roosevelt and the New Deal.* New York: Harper & Row.

Lyon, LeVerett S., et al. (1935), *The National Recovery Administration: An Analysis and Appraisal.* Washington, D.C.: The Brookings Institution.

Mitchell, Broadus (1947), *Depression Decade: From New Era Through New Deal, 1929–1941.* New York: Rinehart.

Mises, Ludwig von (1966), *Human Action: A Treatise on Economics,* 3rd rev. ed. Chicago: Henry Regnery.

Nash, Gerald D. (1979), *The Great Depression and World War II: Organizing America, 1933–1945.* New York: St. Martin's.

O'Driscoll, Gerald P., Jr., (1977) *Economics as a Coordination Problem: The Contributions of Friedrich A. Hayek.* Kansas City: Sheed, Andrews, and McMeel.

——, (1978), "Spontaneous Order and the Coordinaton of Economic Activities," pp. 111–42 in Louis M. Spadaro, ed., *New Directions in Austrian Economics.* Kansas City: Sheed and Ward, 1978.

O'Driscoll, Gerald P., Jr. and Sudha R. Shenoy (1976), "Inflation, Recession, and Stagflation," pp. 185–211 in Edwin G. Dolan, ed., *the Foundations of Modern Austrian Economics.* Kansas City: Sheed and Ward, 1976.

Peppers, Larry C. (1973), "Full-Employment Surplus Analysis and Structural Change: The 1930's." *Explorations in Economic History* 10, 197–210.

Reading, Don C. (1973), "New Deal Activity and the States, 1933 to 1939." *Journal of Economic History* 33, 792–810.

Rizzo, Mario J., ed. (1979), *Time, Uncertainty, and Disequilibrium: Explorations of Austrian Themes.* Lexington, Mass.: Lexington Books.

Robbins, Lionel (1934), *The Great Depression.* New York: Macmillan.

Rockoff, Hugh (1984), *Drastic Measures: A History of Wage and Price Controls in the United States.* New York: Cambridge University Press.

Rothbard, Murray N. (1962, 1970), *Man, Economy and State: A Treatise on Economics,* 2 vols. Los Angeles: Nash.

——, (1963), *America's Great Depression.* Kansas City: Sheed and Ward.

Schlesinger, Arthur M., Jr. (1957–60), *The Age of Roosevelt,* 3 vols. Boston: Houghton Mifflin.

Schumpeter, Joseph A. (1939), *Business Cycles,* 2 vols. New York: McGraw-Hill.

Smiley, Gene (1981), "Regional Variation in Bank Loans Rates in the Interwar Years." *Journal of Economic History* 41, 899–901.

Spadaro, Louis M., (1978), *New Directions in Austrian Economics.* Kansas City: Sheed and Ward.

Stein, Herbert (1969), *The Fiscal Revolution in America.* Chicago: University of Chicago Press.

Stoddard, W.L. (1940), "Small Business Wants Capital." *Harvard Business Review* 18, 265–74.

U.S. Dept. of Commerce, Bureau of the Census (1976), *Historical Statistics of the United States: Colonial Times to 1970.* Washington, D.C. U.S. GPO.

U.S. National Resources Planning Board (1942), *Security, Work, and Relief Policies.* Washington, D.C.: U.S. GPO.

Viner, Jacob (1935), *Balanced Deflation, Inflation, or More Depression?* Minneapolis: University of Minnesota Press.

Weinstein, Michael M. (1980), *Recovery and Redistribution under the NIRA.* Amsterdam: North-Holland.

———, (1981), "Some Macroeconomic Impacts of the National Industrial Recovery Act, 1933–1935," chap. 14 in Karl Brunner, ed., *The Great Depression Revisited.* Boston: Martinus Nijhoff.

Williamson, Harold G., and Orange A. Smalley (1957), *Northwestern Mutual Life: A Century of Trusteeship.* Evanston, Ill.: Northwestern University Press.

Wright, Gavin (1974), "The Political Economy of New Deal Spending: An Econometric Analysis." *Review of Economics and Statistics* 56, 30–38.

GNP, PPR, and the Standard of Living

Robert Batemarco

Over the past two decades, economists have observed and become professionally concerned with falling rates of economic growth. To many young people today trying to establish homes and raise families, that concern is not merely professional. Despite their greater investment in education than any previous generation and despite the extent to which two-earner households have become the norm, this generation, by all indications, is likely to be the first in U.S. history not even to maintain, let alone improve upon, the standard of living enjoyed by their parents.[1]

Standard measurements of economic activity conceal much of this development. Gross national product since 1960 has exhibited seldom-interrupted growth even in real per capita terms.[2] Either the perception described in the first paragraph is amiss or standard measurements are faulty. My aim in this article is to examine alternative measurements which accord with these perceptions to a greater extent than do the standard ones. Such an alternative has been developed by Murray Rothbard.[3] In the second section of this article, I describe that measurement and explain the analytical insights from which it was derived. In the third section, I calculate its values from 1947 to 1983, and compare its growth rates over that period. The fourth section examines the assumptions underlying that measure and indicates the consequences of making them less restrictive. Concluding comments constitute the fifth section.

Austrian economics places great emphasis on the subjective nature of value. In his "Toward a Reconstruction of Utility and Welfare Economics," Murray Rothbard draws the implication that the valuations individuals place on economic goods are revealed only by their actions.[4] Thus, the only way economists can place a monetary value on some commodity is by observing an individual voluntarily exchanging a certain amount of his own money for that commodity. A person who pays $20 for a shirt reveals that he values the shirt more than he values the $20.

While this concept is by no means unique to the Austrian school,[5] hardly any non-Austrian economist has cared to push it to its logical conclusion as far as national income accounting is concerned.[6] This is just what Rothbard does, however. Because government output is, with few exceptions, not sold on the market, one cannot accurately measure its value. Furthermore, the fact that such output must be financed coercively (through taxation) creates at least a presumption that those unwilling to pay for such output do not place *any* value on it.

Rothbard treats government output as if this were precisely the case in defining his measurements "gross private product" (GPP) and "private product remaining with producers" (PPR). Gross private product is defined as gross national product less income originating in government and government enterprises.[7] To the extent that government enterprises charge fees for their output, it seems that deducting only the subsidized part of their income would be more consistent with the considerations just discussed than deducting all of them, as Rothbard does. Private product remaining with producers is computed by deducting the higher of government expenditures and tax revenues plus interest received from gross private product.[8] Transfer payments as well as exhaustive expenditures are deducted since they too wind up in the hands of nonproducers. Rothbard characterizes these expenditures as depredations upon private output.[9]

Rothbard anticipates the criticism that first subtracting income originating in government and then substracting government expenditures is a form of "double counting."[10] An example may clarify this issue. Suppose there were a very simple economy, in which farmers produced 1,000 bushels of wheat and the government collected 200 bushels in taxes to support workers whose output was not sold to the farmers on the market. GNP would be 1,200 bushels (private output plus costs of producing government output), GPP would be 1,000 bushels, and PPR would be 800 bushels. Indeed, 800 bushels of wheat is all that remains in the hands of the farmers who produced it, which would be the definition of PPR in this case.

Table 1 shows the calculation of GPP and PPR. I first calculate nominal GPP and PPR, and then use the GNP deflator to calculate real PPR.

The figures in table 1 corroborate to some extent the impressions described in the introductory paragraphs of this article. This can be more clearly seen when the figures are expressed in terms of growth rates. While real GNP grew at an annual rate of 3.5 percent between 1947 and 1983, real PPR grew by only 2.4 percent annually. This gap widens when one looks at more recent periods. Between 1965 and 1983, real GNP grew at a 3.2 percent rate compared to 1.6 percent for real PPR. Between 1973 and 1983, the figures are 2.8 percent and 1.0 percent for real GNP and real PPR respectively. Finally, from 1978 to 1983, real PPR fell by 0.4 percent per year while real GNP growth rose by 2.7 percent.

Table 1
Measures of Output
(measured in billions of current dollars except for real PPR, which is measured in billions of 1972 dollars)

	GNP	Income Produced by Government and Government Enterprises	GPP	Government Depredations[a]	PPR	Real PPR
1947	233.1	19.3	213.8	56.9	156.9	316.6
1948	259.5	20.2	239.3	58.9	180.4	340.5
1949	258.3	22.5	235.8	59.3	176.5	336.2
1950	286.5	23.8	262.7	70.2	192.5	359.4
1951	330.8	30.8	300.0	85.6	214.4	375.5
1952	348.0	35.3	312.7	93.9	218.8	377.8
1953	366.8	36.4	330.4	101.7	228.7	388.8
1954	366.8	36.9	329.9	97.0	232.9	391.1
1955	400.0	38.5	361.5	102.4	259.1	425.9
1956	421.7	40.7	381.0	110.6	270.4	430.6
1957	444.0	44.0	400.0	117.6	282.4	434.9
1958	449.7	47.1	402.6	127.6	275.0	416.4
1959	487.9	50.0	437.9	131.0	306.9	454.0
1960	506.5	53.4	453.1	142.8	310.3	451.7
1961	524.6	56.7	467.9	149.1	318.8	459.8
1962	565.0	61.1	503.9	161.0	342.9	485.6
1963	596.7	65.9	530.8	172.8	358.0	499.5
1964	637.7	71.2	566.5	181.9	384.6	528.5
1965	691.1	76.7	614.4	193.4	421.0	566.2
1966	756.0	86.4	669.6	220.1	449.5	585.6
1967	799.6	96.3	703.3	242.4	460.9	583.0
1968	873.4	108.1	765.3	273.8	488.5	591.8
1969	944.0	118.2	825.8	305.0	520.8	600.1
1970	992.7	130.5	862.2	315.3	546.9	598.0
1971	1077.6	141.8	935.8	344.6	591.2	615.8
1972	1185.9	155.4	1030.5	396.8	633.7	633.7
1973	1326.4	167.8	1158.6	433.1	725.5	686.0
1974	1434.2	182.7	1251.5	483.8	767.7	667.1
1975	1549.2	202.0	1347.2	539.8	807.4	641.9
1976	1718.0	220.4	1497.6	591.5	906.1	684.7
1977	1918.3	237.2	1681.1	675.3	1005.8	718.2
1978	2163.9	259.1	1904.8	740.8	1164.0	773.8
1979	2417.8	279.6	2138.2	821.5	1316.7	805.7
1980	2631.7	308.1	2323.6	949.9	1373.7	769.9
1981	2957.8	338.1	2619.7	1082.4	1537.3	785.9
1982	3069.3	364.7	2704.6	1193.0	1511.6	728.9
1983	3304.8	392.1	2912.7	1291.1	1621.6	753.0

Source: *The Economic Report of the President, 1985*, pp. 236, 244, 275, 320, and 312.
[a]The higher of government expenditures or tax receipts plus interest received at federal level plus the same variables at state and local level.

Of perhaps more relevance to the question of what has been happening to the U.S. standard of living is the PPR per person. Rather than taking a simple per capita PPR, I divide PPR by the number of producers responsible for it. This means that I subtract government employees from total employment to obtain nongovernment employment. PPR per person employed not by the government is given in table 2.

These figures make it clear that steady growth of real PPR per producer ceased after 1966. Since that time the trend has, with some interruption, been downward. The 1983 figure is approximately the same as that for 1964. This tells a far different story than does the 2.3 percent annual rate of increase in the standard measure, per capita GNP, during that same period.

Table 2
Real PPR per Person Employed by the Private Sector

	Real PPR (billions of 1972 dollars)	Employment (Nongovernment) (millions)	Real PPR/Employment (Nongovernment) (1972 dollars)
1947	316.6	51.3	6,172
1948	340.5	52.7	6,461
1949	336.2	51.8	6,490
1950	359.4	52.9	6,794
1951	375.5	53.6	7,006
1952	377.8	53.6	7,048
1953	388.8	54.5	7,134
1954	391.1	53.4	7,324
1955	425.9	55.3	7,702
1956	430.6	56.5	7,621
1957	434.9	56.4	7,711
1958	416.4	55.2	7,543
1959	454.0	56.6	8,021
1960	451.7	57.4	7,869
1961	459.8	57.2	8,038
1962	485.6	57.8	8,401
1963	499.5	58.5	8,538
1964	528.5	59.7	8,852
1965	566.2	61.0	9,282
1966	585.6	62.1	9,430
1967	583.0	63.0	9,254
1968	591.8	64.1	9,232
1969	600.1	65.7	9,134
1970	598.0	66.1	9,047
1971	615.8	66.5	9,260
1972	633.7	68.8	9,211
1973	686.0	71.3	9,621
1974	667.1	72.6	9,189
1975	641.9	71.2	9,015
1976	684.7	73.9	9,265
1977	718.2	76.9	9,339
1978	773.8	80.4	9,624
1979	805.7	82.9	9,719
1980	769.9	83.0	9,276
1981	785.9	84.4	9,312
1982	728.9	83.7	8,708
1983	753.0	85.0	8,859

Rothbard's definitions of GPP and PPR are both consistent and clear enough to not be misleading. To give a reliable description of economic reality, however, it is necessary that the assumptions on which their relevance is based be grounded in reality. Anyone not sharing Rothbard's anarchocapitalist leanings, however, would recoil from the assumption that the government produces nothing of value. Indeed, even anarchists are aware that the undesirability of government provision of some service does not in and of itself make the provision of that service undesirable. The fact that the government provides armed forces, a court system, and police makes it extremely difficult to measure the value of those services but does not deprive them of their value. The nonexclusivity of such services (their being public goods) means that people will not demonstrate their true preferences because they are never faced with the alternative of forgoing such services if their value fails to exceed the costs. This is what economists call the free rider problem.

Even allowing for the public goods nature of certain items produced by government, their exclusion from PPR is made less difficult by a fact that would lead us to question their inclusion in GNP: government output that is truly valuable very seldom provides direct utility to ultimate consumers. Rather, much of it is actually an intermediate good. National defense can be thought of in this way.[11] The definition of GNP deliberately excludes intermediate goods. Thus, it is possible without denying the value of some of the services produced by government to exclude them from GNP and thus *a fortiori* from GPP and PPR.

On the other hand, there is no doubt that many people find much government activity useless if not downright objectionable even if they disagree on which activities fall into these categories. Lipset and Schneider cite the median response of people asked what percentage of their tax money is wasted by the federal government to be 48 percent.[12] David Boaz estimates that at least 35 percent of 1982 federal expenditures are of no value to anyone except the special interests which got them enacted in the first place.[13] The Grace Commission, which directed most of its scrutiny to the efficiency with which the federal government provides services rather than to the desirability of the services themselves, was able to find one-third of taxes to be "consumed by waste and inefficiency."[14]

What I have shown is that to the extent that government spending consists either of waste or of intermediate goods, measurement of the standard of living of those working in the private sector is rendered much more accurately by Rothbard's measurement of PPR per private sector worker than by the Department of Commerce's per capita GNP. The former indicates that the standard of living for workers in the private secort has been at a standstill since 1964, while the latter exhibits growth in the 2 percent per annum range. Nevertheless, there are two possible interpretations of these facts. The one presented in the introduction to this article is simply that the U.S. standard of living has stopped rising. The other possibility is that economic activity has quickened its shift into the underground economy. While such unreported production is counted in neither GNP nor PPR, it does contribute to the standard of living of those responsible for it. The underground economy renders any measurement of aggregate economic activity suspect.

Notes

1. Phillip Longman, "The Downwardly Mobile Baby Boomers," *Wall Street Journal,* April 12, 1985, p. 28.

2. Per capita real GNP rose from $4,080 in 1960 to $6,544 in 1983 (a 2.1 percent annual rate). Derived from *Economic Report of the President, 1985* (Washington, D.C.: U.S. Government Printing Office, 1985), pp. 234, 265.

3. Murray Rothbard, *America's Great Depression* (Kansas City: Sheed and Ward, 1963), pp. 224–26, and 296–304.

4. Rothbard in Mary Sennholz, ed., *On Freedom and Free Enterprise* (Princeton: D. Van Nostrand, 1956), pp. 224–62. He calls this principle "demonstrated preference."

5. Oscar Morgenstein applies it in his classic discussion of the treatment of government spending in *On the Accuracy of Economic Observations,* 2d ed., completely revised (Princeton: Princeton University Press, 1963), pp. 247–48.

6. Tom Bettell is one exception. See his "Taxes and GNP," *National Review,* September 17, 1982, p. 1134.

7. Rothbard, *America's Great Depression,* p. 296.

8. Ibid., p. 297. I have disaggregated into federal, and state and local and taken the higher for each.

9. Ibid., p. 296.

10. Ibid., p. 335.

11. Morgenstein, p. 247.

12. Lipset and Schneider, *The Confidence Gap* (New York: Free Press, 1983).

13. David Boaz, "How to Really Cut the Budget," *Inquiry,* April 12, 1982.

14. J. Peter Grace, *War on Waste: President's Private Sector Survey on Cost Control* (New York: Macmillan, 1984), p. vii.

Review Essays

The Economics of
Time and Ignorance:
A Review

Charles W. Baird

T his is a very difficult review for me to write, for my overall assessment of *The Economics of Time and Ignorance* is strongly negative. Jerry O'Driscoll got me started in Austrian economics, and I have over the years learned much of value from him. Both he and Mario Rizzo have excellent track records of significant contributions to the revival of the Austrian school in the 1970s and 1980s, and I am certain they will make such contributions in the future. The present book, however, is not such a contribution. In it the authors make much of the distinction between typical and unique features of events. Regretfully, the book is not typical of the authors' work, and its problems, as I will relate, are quite unique.

The dust jacket of the book calls it:

> The first contemporary account of [the Austrian school's] foundations. In it [the authors] present an integrated view of its themes and make an original contribution to our understanding of uncertainty and dynamic processes.

In the acknowledgments, the reader is told that the book was originally conceived as an exposition of standard contemporary Austrian school economics. It was to be an extension of the paper "What Is Austrian Economics?" the authors delivered at the 1980 American Economic Association meeting. Most Austrian economists who knew that the book was being written expected that it would be precisely that; and most of them, especially this reviewer, looked forward to having just such an authoritative exposition available to open-minded neoclassical economists and for their own classroom use.

If the authors had stuck to their original intentions and focused their energies on producing a lucid exposition of standard Austrian theory together

T he Economics of Time and Ignorance by Gerald P. O'Driscoll, Jr., and Mario J. Rizzo. Oxford and New York: Basil Blackwell Ltd., 1985.

with clear and convincing illustrations setting out the many advantages of the Austrian perspective over the dominant neoclassical orthodoxy, they would have indeed advanced the Austrian resurgence. But they fell prey to the temptation to focus on what the dust jacket calls their "original contribution." As they put it at the beginning of chapter 1, they came to feel they had to "go beyond" standard Austrian theory.

That was a most unfortunate decision. Economists are all much the worse for it. They should have saved the original contribution for a separate book, for in their attempt to do both tasks in one volume they offer many confusing expositions of standard Austrian economics, and they present a most unconvincing case in support of their original contribution.

The first five chapters of the book are devoted to theory, and the remaining five chapters discuss applications. Chapters 7–9 are the best. Here the authors exposit standard Austrian theory unencumbered by their original contribution. Chapters 4–6 are the worst in the volume. Here the authors seem literally to strain for originality. In so doing, they suggest spurious distinctions between standard Austrian theory and their own approach, and they discuss the work of Hayek (and, to a much smaller extent, of von Mises and Kirzner) in a misleading and confusing way.

It soon becomes apparent that the key ideas in their original contribution involve several distinctions hitherto unknown even to Austrian economists. Two such distinctions are introduced in chapter 1, "An Overview of Subjectivist Economics"—the distinction between static subjectivism and dynamic subjectivism, and between static (or Newtonian) time and real time. Since these distinctions are novel even to Austrian economists, it behooves the authors carefully and clearly to set out their points right from the beginning. They do not.

To an Austrian, the subjectivist nature of economics refers to the fact that economics is about the formulation and consequences of the plans and actions of people as they attempt to do the best they can for themselves within a context of imperfect information and scarcity. The focus of attention is on the subjects, not the objects, of human action. Each individual's plans and actions are formulated on the basis of perceived costs and benefits. Both costs and benefits are subjective. That is, they both have whatever significance the individual's mind attaches to them. Neither costs nor benefits are objectively observable or measurable by third parties. As the authors phrase it, "for the Austrians, and for subjectivists generally, economics is first and foremost about the thoughts leading up to choice, and not about things or objective magnitudes" (p. 2).

So far, so good. But then the reader is told that there are two kinds of subjectivism—static and dynamic. No explanation is offered. The reader is simply told that "[s]ubjective probability . . . reflects subjectivism in its static form; while unbounded possibility sets reflect the essentially dynamic aspect of subjectivism" (p. 4).

Neoclassical models typically handle uncertainty by positing the existence of known probability distributions of possible future events. Austrian economists have long argued that such known probability distributions merely replace one version of the perfect knowledge assumption with a more sophisticated version of the same assumption. In the real world, however, there is genuine uncertainty. As Frank Knight long ago pointed out, not even the probability distributions are known; that is, in the words of the present authors, human action takes place within the context of "unbounded possibility sets."

That is fine, but it is nothing new. And it certainly is insufficient justification for creating a hitherto unknown distinction between static and dynamic subjectivism. An Austrian, to say nothing of a neoclassical economist, is left bewildered. Perhaps, however, the authors' intent is to whet the reader's appetite for chapter 2, "Static versus Dynamic Subjectivism."

Austrian economists have also long objected to what they perceived to be an abuse of time in much neoclassical analysis. In that analysis, time is represented by t and treated as a mathematical variable, different values of which can be plugged into mathematical equations. The analyst assumes a godlike posture of comprehending all time—past, present, and future—at once, usually as positions along an axis labeled t. The past can be retrieved at any instant by picking a value of t that represents the past and plugging it into an equation. Similarly, the future can be realized at any instant by picking a value of t that represents the future. From the perspective of the present, the future already exists in determinate form. It merely has to be reached as another place on an axis. Functions are even held to be continuous and at least twice differentiable in t.

In reality, of course, time is not an objective entity that can be treated as an independent variable in a function in the same way that own price is treated as an independent variable in a demand function. Time exerts no influence in its own right in economic transactions. It is what people do in time, including the contracts they enter into that involve the elapse of specific periods of time, that influences economic transactions. Time is subjectively experienced by each individual as, in the words of the authors, "a flow of events." The future does not already exist to be reached; the future becomes what it is as the result of actions taken in the present. Since those actions are indeterminate, so too is the future. Real time is merely time treated as it is actually experienced and as it actually enters into individual decision making. Static or Newtonian time (time treated as an independent mathematical variable) is artificial and can shed no light on the formulation and consequences of human action. Such is standard Austrian fare.

But the present authors again bewilder the reader, especially the neoclassical reader, by stating that when time is conceived in purely static terms, it is "analogized to space: Just as an individual may allocate portions of space (land) to certain purposes, he can also allocate portions of time to certain activities"

(p. 3). Do the authors mean to suggest that people do not allocate time in that fashion? Economists of both the Austrian and neoclassical varieties surely will object. I, for example, have allocated a specific period of time to writing this review. But here again, perhaps the authors merely intend to whet the reader's appetite for chapter 4, "The Dynamic Conception of Time."

Contrary to reasonable expectations generated by its title, chapter 2 does little to clarify the distinction between static and dynamic subjectivism. The reader is reminded that the subjectivist realm is that of "purposes, plans, valuations, and expectations" (p. 18). Then static subjectivism, the kind that "is most closely related to the traditional subjective theory of value," is explained as that approach in which "the mind is viewed as a passive filter through which the data of decisionmaking are perceived" (p. 22).

Now, if one interprets "the traditional subjective theory of value" to mean the neoclassical model of Hicks et al. with its ordinal utility, indifference curves, and budget constraints, one is led to think that "static subjectivism" refers to decision making within a given and fixed means–ends framework. That view seems to fit in well with the authors' explanation of dynamic subjectivism which "views the minds as an active, creative entity in which decision-making bears no determinate realtionship to what went before" (p. 22). This could be taken as a roundabout way of saying that the means–ends framework itself is constantly changing as individuals' beliefs, knowledge, and perceptions change. If that is what the authors mean, "dynamic subjectivism" is the subjectivism of the standard Austrian analyses of Carl Menger, Ludwig von Mises, Friedrich A. Hayek, Israel Kirzner, Murray Rothbard, and others.

But that cannot be. The authors must intend something else by "dynamic subjectivism." They go on to say that static subjectivism is akin to the covering law model of scientific explanation of which von Mises's "apodictic praxeological theorems" are suggested as examples (p. 23). Von Mises, then, does not qualify as a dynamic subjectivist. But von Mises's praxeological theorems are "apodictic" only in the sense that as deductions from axioms they are implicit in the axioms. There is nothing in von Mises that says that decision making is preordained or predetermined by what went before. So what *is* "dynamic subjectivism"? No clear answer can be found in chapter 2, or in the rest of the book.

The confusion does not stop there. On pp. 22–27, the authors discuss the nature of explanation and prediction in economics. The trouble is that they switch back and forth between explanation and prediction without giving the reader any warning. In so doing, they implicitly subscribe to the "symmetry thesis" of covering law models—explanation and prediction are exactly the same, except temporally.

But surely explanation and prediction are *not* the same. Some event happens, and an analyst wants to explain it. In order to explain it completely, the analyst would have to know all the antecedent conditions and all the relevant chains of cause and effect that gave rise to the event. Such is, as the authors convincingly demonstrate, impossible. Even neoclassical economists deny the possibility of explanation in such a radical sense. The best that can be done is to come up with an explanation that makes the event more intelligible than it would be without that explanation. Prediction, on the other hand, as long as it is limited to what Hayek calls "pattern prediction," is not only possible, it is a major part of standard Austrian analysis. For example, from the action axiom (a covering law) and scarcity (a pervasive antecedent condition), it is possible to predict that there will, ceteris paribus, always be an inverse relationship between own price and quantity demanded. The "pattern" is the inverse relationship. Precise quantitative prediction of a particular instance of that pattern is, an Austrian economist would say, impossible because of the impossibility of being certain the ceteris paribus conditions hold.

The authors' discussion is at best a confusing and misleading exposition of the standard Austrian critique of neoclassical methodology. Austrians hold that explanation and prediction in economics are not, and cannot be, the same as what positivists assert they are in the natural sciences.

The chapter concludes with a section entitled "Relationship between Static and Dynamic Subjectivism" which, on its own, is clear and informative. Unfortunately, it seems to be unrelated to the rest of the chapter. According to this section,

> The static subjectivist view is that four factors determine choice: (1) the ordinal ranking of goals or wants, (2) knowledge of the relationship between courses of action . . . and want satisfaction, (3) knowledge of prices, and (4) knowledge of the income constraint (p. 28).

This corroborates my earlier interpretation of static subjectivism. It is the neoclassical approach to value theory.

Dynamic subjectivism, in addition to applying a more thoroughgoing subjectivist interpretation to the foregoing four factors, recognizes a fifth: "What an individual decides to do depends, in large part, on what he expects other individuals to do" (p. 29). Since such expectations are never held with certainty, good models of choice cannot be deterministic. This corroborates my earlier suspicion regarding dynamic subjectivism. It is the subjectivism of standard Austrian economics.

Chapter 3, "Knowledge and Decisions," is fairly clear and helpful. It points out that the knowledge problem in economics is never the acquisition of a fixed stock of information. There is in human action a continual increase in knowledge. There is no equilibrium stock of knowledge. Knowledge is divided up and distributed unequally among economic actors; because different people face different problem settings, different people will not ultimately learn the same things. Knowledge is communicated between transactors by prices (both equilibrium and disequilibrium prices) and by institutions. All of this is standard Austrian (mainly Hayekian) fare, and the authors exposit it well.

Their best exposition comes in the chapter's last section, "Subjectivism as Weighing of Alternatives." It summarizes many of the points made by Buchanan in *Cost and Choice* on the subjective nature of costs, pointing out that Marshall was wrong when he claimed that demand is subjective and cost is objective. Both blades of the Marshallian "scissors" are subjective categories. The authors also construct a helpful schematic to illustrate "a thoroughly subjectivist view of value theory" (p. 46). They carefully distinguish (1) between commodities and projected want satisfaction and (2) between projected and realized want satisfaction, pointing out that in the static neoclassical approach to value theory, all three of these collapse into one.

I have only two complaints about chapter 3. The authors correctly say that learning in the real word is neither deterministic nor random, but something in between. They note that in the "in-between" view, the analyst asserts a priori that learning does take place, and then they say:

> Second, given the overall context of a change in knowledge, we can show how the move from framework 1 (F1) to framework 2 (F2) is intelligible, in the sense that a metatheory can be constructed in which a loose dependency on F1 is shown. F2 is more likely (though not necessarily highly likely or probable) given F1 than it would be given some other $F1_9$. On the other hand, we might say that, given F1, many possible alternative frameworks can be ruled out and that only a class of subsequent frameworks (which includes F2) can be determined (p. 38).

All that seems to mean is that perceptions tomorrow are, affected by perceptions today, but to different degrees depending on the circumstances at hand. Why the authors choose to dress up this obvious point in the formalistic garb of mathematical symbols and language is a puzzle. As Austrians, they surely realize that no analytical progress is ever made by converting plain English into mathematics which then must be restated in English to be comprehended. Could it be that the authors' intent here is merely to appeal to the prejudices of possible neoclassical readers?

My second complaint in this chapter is a recurring one throughout the book. In discussing Hayek's notion of institutions as routine courses of action that embody efficient adaptations to the environment, they point out that one problem with such a "Darwinian" view is that "[s]ome clearly inferior routines must be maintained in order to permit those clearly superior (but dependent) to exist" (p. 40). It would have been most helpful if they could have illustrated this proposition. No example is given. The point is, in the abstract, interesting and (I think) novel. Its validity and usefulness are another matter. Only a good example from the world of economics would convince me of its value. I shall refer to other instances of missing or unhelpful examples in other chapters.

Chapters 4 and 5 present the theoretical core of the authors' original contribution. They are key chapters, for if the analysis therein fails, there is nothing to their original contribution; and, inasmuch as the authors' exposition of what is standard Austrian analysis is, at least until chapter 7, so confusing, most of the book then fails.

Chapter 4 begins with a very good exposition of what is wrong with the standard uses of time in neoclassical models. It would have been better, I think, to refer to the static uses of time as "neoclassical time" rather than "Newtonian time," for the latter suggests that more is at stake than the misuse of time in economic analysis. But that is a quibble. The last subsection of their discussion of Newtonian time, "The Measurement of Time" (pp. 58–59), is dressed up in mathematical garb and is very difficult to understand; but it adds nothing to their argument, so little is lost.

The meat of the chapter is found in pages 59–67. Here it is explained that real time—or the authors' "dynamic conception of time"—is time as it is experienced by the economic actors whose plans and actions are what economics is all about. For every economic actor, each present moment is connected to the past by memory and to the future by expectation. The future can never be known with certainty; it can only be anticipated. Moreover, the anticipation cannot be in the form of a complete list of all possible future events weighted by known probabilities of occurrence. The probabilities themselves are unknowable, and any list must be incomplete.

Consider the following statement (which is not a direct quote from the text): "A transactor's expectations of the future are changed as his present knowledge changes." The statement seems to be correct. However, suppose that the change in his present knowledge is merely that what had hitherto been only expected is now fact (that is, an expectation is ratified by experience). Would that change in present knowledge necessarily alter the transactor's already existing expectations concerning that which has not already happened? For example, suppose that yesterday I expected the annual inflation rate for the coming two days to be 10 percent, and that todays inflation rate *is* 10 percent. Would my expectation of tomorrow's inflation rate necessarily change? I do not see why it must. I do not see how the authors can conclude that the passage of time *necessarily* changes expectations, and thus *necessarily* always changes the plans and actions of economic agents. Yet a very important part of what the authors later claim is their original contribution—their idea of unavoidable endogenously generated forces which preclude equilibrium—rests on that conclusion.

Consider the following direct quotes from the text:

> As we contemplate a course of action and project its consequences, we [must?] continually refine and refocus our tentative plans (p. 63).

> In the process of acting . . . the individual experiences things. These experiences are novel if only because he approaches the world from subjective

standpoints [necessarily?] continually change by the memory of what has been occurring (p. 63).

[G]rowth in the stock of experience [necessarily?] leads, via growth in the stock of knowledge, to alterations in both memory and expectations (p. 64).

Real time is important because in the course of planning and acting the individual acquires new [necessarily unanticipated?] experiences. These new experiences then [must?] give rise, in a non-deterministic way, to new knowledge. On the basis of this new knowledge, the individual [necessarily?] changes his future plans and actions.Thus the economic system is propelled by purely endogenous [and necessarily disequilibrating?] forces (p. 64).

If each of the bracketed questions I inserted in these quotes is answered in the negative, the quotes are reasonable and can be used quite effectively in the argument against the standard neoclassical treatment of time. In some passages this is what the authors do. However, the authors also seem strongly to suggest that all of the bracketed questions should be answered in the affirmative. And on those grounds, they later seem to assert, there is no tendency to equilibrium in real world markets.

In chapter 5, "Uncertainty in Equilibrium," the authors demonstrate that equilibrium in the standard neoclassical sense (Walrasian general equilibrium as formalized by Arrow and Debreu, as well as Marshallian partial equilibrium) is logically flawed and totally irrelevant to any real world economy. For that they deserve applause. However, from time to time—although it is hard to be sure— the authors also seem to suggest that *any* concept of equilibrium must be logically flawed. They seem to flirt with the adoption of the extreme view of Shackle on equilibrium—namely there is no reason to think that there exist any systematic tendencies toward coordination or equilibrium in real world economies.

They do not adopt that view wholeheartedly for, as they correctly say, "some idea of equilibrium is important. Indeed it would be difficult to imagine a viable economics without one" (p. 71). Von Mises would replace "difficult" with "impossible" because, as he points out in *Human Action*, if there are no systematic tendencies toward coordination in an economy, an economist can derive no general principles of economics at all. Economists would be reduced to writing ex post descriptions of actual events on a one-by-one basis and methodological essays proclaiming that economic theory is impossible.

Moreover, the authors say that while "the endogeneity of uncertainty in real time" is incompatible with "standard notions of equilibrium" (p. 72),

A suitably reformulated equilibrium construct can be consistent with our real-time framework, and can also be the analytical source of the uncertainty and endogenous changes that pervade market processes (p. 71).

They name their reformulated version of equilibrium "pattern coordination" (p. 72). So the authors apparently do not want, as Shackle does, to rule the whole idea of equilibrium out of order. They just want to do away with "standard notions" of equilibrium.

Hayekian equilibrium—plan coordination, the notion that most Austrians consider useful—is one of the standard notions to be done away with. Consider the following quotes taken from subsections "Equilibrium as Exact Coordination" and "Inadequacy of Exact Coordinaton," respectively:

> Austrians generally follow Hayek in thinking of equilibrium in terms of compatibility of individual plans (p. 80).

> Hayek's avowed intention in developing his concept of equilibrium as the consistency of individual plans was to marry time and equilibrium. Since plans are forward-looking, he reasoned that plan coordination must entail time. Unfortunately, he did not fully understand the distinction between the Newtonian and real-time constructs. Hayekian equilibrium incorporated only Newtonian time (p. 81).

I am aware of nothing in Hayek's work that even remotely suggests that he ever treated time as it is treated in the standard neoclassical models. Hayek was always mindful that it is what people do and learn during the passage of time, not the passage of time itself, that matters. Hayek has never been guilty of the mathematical abuse of time customarily found in neoclassical analyses.

Remember, the authors' whole idea of "real time" is that the present is connected to the past by memory and to the future by anticipation. As time goes by, expectations are confirmed or falsified, and "memory swells." Thus each individual continually adopts a new knowledge perspective from which to view the unknowable, but not unimaginable, future. Time is not a mathematical variable; it is experienced by each individual as a flow of events. Hayek has always treated time in this way. His notion of plan coordination is based on this view of time.

For Hayek, however, the constantly changing perspective with which transactors view the future—the process of real learning—does not mean that those transactors constantly must change their future plans and actions. If expectations are confirmed, there is nothing in the swelled memory of the changing perspective to force plans and actions to change. Indeed, the process of approaching plan coordination involves the gradual changing of expectations and perceptions until mutually consistent plans are formulated. When that happens, transactors will no longer learn anything that forces them to change their expectations, plans, and actions. That is Hayek's plan coordination.

There is a second, closely related, Hayekian notion—pattern prediction—involved in the authors' exposition. Hayek's point here is simply that economic science can never generate precise quantitative predictions of future events. Although complete detailed descriptions of future events are beyond the reach of economics, the prediction of important qualitative, common characteristics of a class of event is possible. For example, economics can make the prediction that effective price ceilings will all share a common (typical) feature—they will all cause shortages. The detailed quantitative description (the unique attributes) of any specific future instance of effective price ceilings cannot be predicted.

The authors sometimes seem to recognize that Hayek's notion of pattern prediction is consistent with their reformulation of the idea of equilibrium, but sometimes they do not. In chapter 4, they say that Hayek's pattern prediction "echo" their insight that "[t]heories of complex phenomena can be expected to predict only the overall pattern of outcomes . . . rather than the exact outcome" (p. 66). Yet in chapter 5 they assert that:

> The inadequacy of exact Hayekian equilibrium for the analysis of processes in real time means that we are faced with two alternatives: either (1) revise the equilibrium construct so as to incorporate time and uncertainty, or (2) abandon equilibrium altogether. . . .
>
> The only feasible alternative is to revise our notion of equilibrium. . . . We propose . . . pattern coordination. This makes use of both the original Hayekian "compatibility of plans" and the distinction between typical and unique aspects of future events. The plans of individuals are in a pattern equilibriuim if they are coordinated with respect to their typical features, even if their unique aspects fail to mesh (p. 85).

For the record, see what Hayek has to say about equilibrium. In his 1968 essay "Competition as a Discovery Procedure" (reprinted in *New Studies in Philosophy, Politics, Economics and the History of Ideas,* University of Chicago Press, 1978), Hayek states that the capacity of the theory of competition:

> [T]o predict is necessarily limited to predicting the kind of pattern, or the abstract character of the order that will form itself, but does not extend to the prediction of particular facts (p. 181).

> While an economic equilibrium never really exists, there is some justification for asserting that the kind of order of which our theory describes an ideal type is approached in a high degree.
>
> This order manifests itself in the first instance in the circumstance that the expectations of transactions to be effected with other members of society, on which the plans of all the several economic subjects are based, can mostly be realized (p. 184).

I fail to see how this notion of equilibrium is "inadequate for the analysis of processes in real time."

To get a handle on what the authors have in mind, one has to understand the force of their notion of endogenously generated changing knowledge. Their position is that "exact equilibrium," even Hayek's plan coordination, is impossible because the market process necessarily always generates unexpected knowledge which must cause transactors constantly to change their plans. No equilibrium set of plans (plans that, in the absence of shocks, would not be revised) can be formulated because transactors are necessarily constantly bombarded with endogenous shocks to which they must constantly adapt.

This is certainly an important idea. One naturally hopes that the authors will explain this point with careful argument and good examples which make it clear and convincing. But they do no such thing. The point is illustrated by two scenarios having little to do with the world of economics, and these illustrations are taken as sufficient argument to establish the point.

The first scenario is Keynes's beauty contest—which Keynes originally used to illustrate a point concerning the stock market.

> A hundred photographs are reproduced in a newspaper. Each contestant must choose the six prettiest or handsomest faces. The winner will be that contestant whose choices most closely approximate those of "average opinion." The goal of each contestant is therefore not to choose the six most attractive to him or her . . . , or even to guess what average opinion believes to be the most attractive. . . . Rather, the object must be to guess what average opinion believes that average opinion will choose (pp. 72–73).

> [B]ecause the individual is making predictions of predictions rather than of tastes, resource availability, and so forth, the relevant information will be what others are predicting. Therefore, knowledge gained over time by market participants will necessarily affect the object of each agent's prediction. These considerations enable us to conclude that the very activity designed to cope with uncertainty (i.e., the acquisition of knowledge) is responsible for its continued existence (p. 74).

I think their conclusion is not sufficiently supported by the example. It is instructive that the illustration does not come from the usual world of economics. In typical market settings (not the stock market), the relevant pattern predictions that agents must make do concern "tastes, resource availability, and so forth." The only market setting I can think of wherein "predictions of predictions" are crucial is the Cournot oligopoly model. The authors referred to that model briefly on pp. 61–62 when discussing real time and promised that a "similar example" would be used later to discuss dynamic uncertainty. The "similar example" offered is the beauty contest. I infer from this that they, too, could not come up with anything more germane to the customary concerns of economists.

Moreover, in the beauty contest, the ends of the contestants are mutually inconsistent. Each contestant wishes to win, but there can be only one winner. It is a zero-sum game. Most market interactions, on the other hand, are positive-sum games. One must be careful to avoid coming to strong general conclusions regarding the competitive market process on the basis of examples of zero-sum games. Yet the authors do precisely that. I will not be convinced "that the very activity designed to cope with uncertainty is responsible for its continued existence" in the competitive market process until the authors either come up with an effective a priori argument or many pertinent examples. They have done neither.

The second scenario (also a zero-sum game) is Morgenstern's Holmes-Moriarity story, which, as the authors say, is worth quoting in full. (Curiously, the authors give a better example, one from the world of economics, illustrating the point of the Holmes-Moriarity story in a footnote.)

> Sherlock Holmes, pursued by his opponent, Moriarity, leaves London for Dover. The train stops at a station on the way, and he alights there rather than travelling on to Dover. He has seen Moriarity at the railway station, recognizes that he is very clever and expects that Moriarity will take a faster special train in order to catch him in Dover. Holmes' anticipation turns out to be correct. But what if Moriarity had been still more clever, had estimated Holmes' mental abilities and had foreseen his actions accordingly? Then obviously he would have travelled to the intermediate station. Holmes, again, would have had to calculate that and he himself would have decided to go on to Dover. Whereupon, Moriarity would have "reacted" differently. Because of so much thinking they might not have been able to act at all or the intellectually weaker of the two would have surrendered in the Victoria Station, since the whole flight would have become unnecessary (p. 84).

This example shows that when *A* and *B* are adversaries, when *A*'s plan depends on *B*'s plan, and when both *A* and *B* have perfect foresight concerning the plans of the other, no stable set of plans can be formulated. There is no process by which equilibrium can be established. True enough, but largely irrelevant to the issue at hand. Surely, the authors do not mean to imply that any form of Hayekian equilibrium is precluded by such an example. Perfect foresight has never been a part of any Hayekian analysis of which I am aware.

The conclusion the authors reach from the Holmes-Moriarity story is that:

> [I]mperfect foresight is a necessary, although not sufficient, condition for a process to result in an equilibrium. This equilibrium cannot, however, be a position of exact coordination. A process in which there must be errors cannot, except by chance, culminate in an errorless equilibrium (p. 85).

How does one know that there "must be" errors in market processes? Presumably the beauty contest was to have convinced people of that. At least now people know that in the view of the authors, "exact coordination" is "errorless equilibrium." From the rest of the chapter, one knows, that "errorless" here means formulated on exactly correct predictions of all typical and unique features of future actions. But since Hayekian equilibrium notions are not "errorless" in that sense, the reader is forced to the conclusion that "pattern coordination" is merely standard Austrian coordination correctly understood, or it is a well-disguised denial of any meaningful coordination at all.

It is difficult to tell which of those two options characterizes the authors' "pattern coordination" because they never really do a clear job of explaining what they mean. The idea fails for want of instructive and clear illustrations. The only example offered to explain what this key notion really means is, just like the beauty contest and the Holmes-Moriarity story, unrelated to the world of economics.

Pattern coordination, they tell us, is when future events are coordinated in their typical features but not in their unique features. They explain what they mean by asking the reader to consider the case of two professors working on a jointly authored book. The professors achieve pattern coordination of their plans when they know when they each will be available for joint discussions of their project. The unique features of these future events (joint discussions)—the actual details of who will say what and when he will say it—are uncoordinated. The knowledge necessary to achieve *ex ante* coordination of the unique features is unobtainable.

Try as I may, I cannot, from this example, see that pattern coordination is anything new at all. I know of no Austrian—certainly not von Mises, Hayek, or Kirzner—who ever maintained that plan coordination required coordination of all the unique features of future events. The content of "unique features" suggested by the authors' example is irrelevant to any sort of plan coordination. It is even irrelevant to many notions of neoclassical equilibrium. It seems to me that the authors, by misspecifying the requirements of "standard" notions of equilibrium, have trapped themselves into thinking that a whole new idea of coordination is needed to save a viable economics. In straining to differentiate "pattern coordination" from Hayekian coordination, they have led themselves toward the nihilistic views of Shackle that no viable economics is possible.

Chapter 6, "Competition and Discovery," begins the "Applications" half of the book. Inasmuch as I have always found that the examination of applications is the surest route to understanding points of theory, I had high hopes for the final five chapters of the book. And I was not totally disappointed. There is much that is excellent in chapter 6. The authors' present an effective exposition of the deficiencies of perfect competition in "A Parable on Competition," which likens perfect competition to a sports contest wherein the judges insist in repeated replays until the foreordained "correct" outcomes emerge. Their explanation of the logical and practical superiority of defining "competition" as rivalry rather than a state of perfectly competitive equilibrium is as good as I have seen. Their insistence that good economic analysis requires competition to be anlayzed as a process rather than as an equilibrium state should be at least credible to all but the most closed-minded neoclassical readers. Of course, the sports contest analogy, like all analogies, is not exact. Inasmuch as there is only one winner in a sports contest, such contests are zero-sum games. While some features of interfirm rivalry may be characterized as a zero-sum game, the voluntary exchange basis of most of the competitive market process makes it a positive-sum game. In perfect competition, however, there is no rivalry at all. Perfect competition is in no sense a zero-sum game.

The section "Knowledge and Competition" examines the "five general characteristics of knowledge with which a Hayekian view of competition is concerned" (p. 104). The authors do a superb job of spinning out the implications of the fact that the relevant knowledge is sometimes private, often consists of information of temporary but crucial significance, is frequently tacit, and is often the source of surprise. Moreover, much of the relevant knowledge is communicated by nonprice signals such as evolved rules and customs.

The best section is "Process Theories and Normative Economics." I especially liked the discussion of the relationship between neoclassical general equilibrium theory and Adam Smith. The beliefs that modern neoclassical theory has identified the necessary conditions for the validity of Smith's laissez-faire conclusions and that those necessary conditions do not exist in the modern world are dead wrong. Adam Smith's views were based upon his process theory of competition. His laissez-faire conclusions in no way depend on the conditions of perfectly competitive equilibrium. They rest on the key insight that unhampered market processes are the best means available for the discovery and correction of economic error. Here the authors do an excellent job of debunking.

However, chapter 6 is not without its faults. And those faults are tied to the authors' notion of "pattern coordination." First, the authors reiterate their assertion that Hayek had a faulty notion of equilibrium which he later discarded in favor of a better notion that resembles the authors' pattern coordination. Here, at least, the reader gets a better idea of what they mean:

> Hayek originally defined as an equilibrium a situation in which there is both *ex ante* plan consistency, and no information disruptive of plans that agents are bound to learn in the course of executing their plans. [In chapter 5, the authors characterize this as "exact equilibrium."] Exogenous disturbances might occur before these plans are executed, and upset the equilibrium. As long as agents did not themselves bring about these disturbances by the very execution of their plans, their plans were coordinated and consistent (p. 100).

The last sentence of the quotation is, of course, where the authors believe that they have made an original contribution—the notion of endogenous learning precluding "exact equilibrium."

Hayek's later (1968) view of equilibrium, the authors say,

> embodies endogenous learning and entrepreneurship. Moreover it captures that essential element of competition that is absent from alternative economic conceptualizations: the element of surprise or the unexpected (p. 102).

I have already explained why I did not think there was an early Hayek and a later Hayek on the question of equilibrium. My view is supported by the passages quoted earlier from Hayek's 1968 essay "Competition as a Discovery Procedure" concerning the nature and usefulness of equilibrium. Any apparent differences between an early and a later Hayek on the question of equilibrium are due to differences in the expositions of his unchanged view.

But here another issue emerges:

> In his work on entrepreneurship, Kirzner has consistently adhered to Hayek's early view. Yet by focusing on entrepreneurship, we can understand better the reasons that surely entered into Hayek's revised approach to competition, coordination, and equilibrium. The fundamental problem is that the "tendency to equilibrium" view does not take time seriously. The latter is, of course, as serious an internal criticism as one could level against a subjective analysis (p. 100).

The unmistakable implication is that Kirzner, of all people, does not take time seriously and so ignores the elements of surprise and the unexpected in his work on entrepreneurship. In so doing, the authors assert, Kirzner makes himself out to be a poor subjectivist. This suggestion is simply beyond comprehension. Surprise, the unexpected, and unanticipated learning are all parts of Kirzner's analysis. That "endogenous learning" makes any difference at all has not been demonstrated. Keynes's beauty contest, the only argument the authors offer to support their contrary position, proves nothing.

The second fault with chapter 6 lies with the authors' discussion of rent control to illustrate the superiority of their concept of pattern coordination.

> After effective controls are imposed, housing services will be *temporarily* [emphasis in original] in excess demand. Lessors and lessees cannot make their plans mesh. *Over time, however, the housing stock will deteriorate until housing services supplied satisfy observed demand at the controlled rental prices* [emphasis added]. Even with market excess demand eliminated, plans continue to be frustrated, however, for renters cannot bid higher prices for the higher-quality units that they prefer (p. 115).

Now, what the authors should mean by the underlined sentence is that as the housing stock deteriorates, at any fixed rent per dwelling unit, the price per unit of housing services in those units increases. The tenants in such dwellings do not pay lower prices per unit of housing services because of the rent control. The higher price per unit of housing services eliminates the excess demand for housing services *in those units*. But the excess demand for housing services in better-quality dwelling units is *not* eliminated. In no sense is the "market excess demand" for housing services eliminated. The authors' statement that deterioration of the housing stock eliminates the market excess demand for housing services is an example of poor expositional judgment in the pursuit of originality.

In that same pursuit the authors go on to outline all the customary indirect effects of rent control—diminished mobility, growing demands for new controls such as condominium conversion restrictions, and so forth. That is all right, but they assert that only their analysis permits such insights to be gained. The truth is, of course, that such indirect effects of rent control have long been recognized even in neoclassical analysis.

There is much of value in chapter 7, "The Political Economy of Competition and Monopoly," which concerns such issues of law and economics as antitrust, pollution regulation, property rights, and deregulation. In fact, I think chapter 7 is excellent. Perhaps that is because nothing in it depends on the three dubious concepts of the theoretical chapters—pattern coordination, real time, and dynamic subjectivism. Any reasonably informed neoclassical or Austrian economist could read, understand, and benefit from chapter 7 without having read any of the rest of the book.

The chapter begins by pointing out that those who disapprove of the outcomes of the competitive market process without also disapproving of the process itself are logically inconsistent. Outcomes and the processes that produce them cannot be thought of as separate entities. "In objecting to market outcomes, one is in reality objecting to market processes" (p. 131). The authors note that among the outcomes frequently objected to by many who claim to approve of the market process are income and wealth distributions, various forms of market structure, and product differentiation. Some neoclassical economists characterize outcomes of which they disapprove as "market failures."

The authors do a splendid job of criticizing the standard neoclassical approaches to pollution regulation and antitrust policy on the same grounds that von Mises and Hayek used to criticize socialism in the socialist calculation debate—namely, the informational and calculational dilemma. The informational and calculational requirements of both pollution regulation (whether the command or "tax price" variety) and antitrust policy based on neoclassical notions of competition and monopoly cannot be met. Moreover, as Arrow pointed out in 1959, even in the neoclassical framework, except in equilibrium, all firms must be price searchers. The basic distinctions upon which U.S. antitrust policy is based are, therefore, meaningless.

The superiority of a process view of competition over the traditional static equilibrium view is well illustrated by the examples of deregulation of the airline and telecommunications industries. In these instances, several predictions based on static analysis (for example, that small towns would lose airline service and that the average cost of home phone service would rise because of the loss of economies of scale) were clearly proven wrong by events. What actually happened after deregulation is, however, easily understood using a standard Austrian market process analysis.

The final section of the chapter, "Property Rights Theory of Monopoly," argues effectively that the nature and source of entitlements to market shares should replace downward-sloping demand curves and welfare loss triangles as the focus of analytical attention in antitrust. In other words, and I wish the authors had used these words, the focus of attention ought to be on the positive and normative analysis of "rent seeking." Austrians and a good many neoclassical economists have long understood that government favor is the only source of durable monopoly. The authors are remiss in failing, even briefly, to discuss the theory of rent seeking. Of course, the economics of rent seeking is usually not thought of as an Austrian innovation. It is usually associated with the public choice school.

There is one curiosity early in the last section of the chapter. There the authors assert:

> A monopoly right can encompass a great deal of economic activity or apply to a wide geographic area. . . . When monopolists holding market share or operating jointly in a territory or market cooperate, we call this a "cartel." Cartels are shared monopolies. There is thus no separate oligopoly theory (p. 149).

I think this is a non sequitur. Why should the analysis of shared monopolies preclude an oligopoly theory? More importantly, recall that the only obvious example from the world of economics that corresponds to Keynes's beauty contest is the Cournot oligopoly model. If there is no separate oligopoly theory, the authors lose their best illustration of endogenous uncertainty.

Chapter 8, written by Roger Garrison, is entitled "A Subjectivist Theory of a Capital-Using Economy." As its title suggests, it is about Austrian capital and interest theory. It is exceptionally well done. It is the only chapter in the book that gives von Mises the attention he deserves in any exposition of Austrian economics. A neoclassical economist who knows nothing about Austrian economics can learn a lot by reading this chapter. The author patiently explains each concept as he introduces them. It is all here: a brief historical sketch of the development of Austrian capital theory; a clear statement of why it is a subjective theory; and precise explanations of the structure of production, the period of production, roundaboutness, capital heterogeneity, intertemporal coordination, and the time-preference theory of interest.

For Austrians, capital and interest theory is the basis of legitmate macroeconomic theorizing. Garrison explains the connections between the two. He then discusses the effects of changes in preferences for liquidity and leisure on the structure of production through entrepreneurial adaptations to those changes. Finally, he traces through the normal adaptations to changes of time-preference and points out that although there is likely to be entrepreneurial error in the process of adaptation to such changes, there is no reason to expect a "clustering of error." He thus sets the stage for chapter 9, which exposits the von Mises-Hayek monetary theory of the trade cycle.

In the last section of chapter 8, "Subjectivism Revisited," Garrison puts the Cambridge "reswitching" argument against Austrian capital theory to rest.

He points out that because of the subjectivist definitions of period of production, roundaboutness, earlier and later investment programs, and original factors of production, the reswitching phenomenon implies nothing about Austrian capital theory. The Cambridge attribution of those categories to physical objects and techniques, rather than to the planning perspectives of decision makers, makes its critique irrelevant to the real world as well as to Austrian capital theory.

Chapter 9, "The Microanalytics of Money," discusses Menger's view of the evolution of money, the von Mises-Hayek monetary theory of the trade cycle, and rational expectations. The exposition is very good. Austrians and neoclassical economists alike will find much of interest in the chapter. Neoclassical economists can learn a lot here about the Austrian views of these matters, and Austrians can learn about Wainhouse's sophisticated econometric testing of the von Mises-Hayek model. Statistical evidence turns out to be consistent with six empirically testable hypotheses derived from that model.

I did get a scare when I read:

> In our analysis, we adopt Hayek's view of the cycle as a disequilibrium phenomenon. We restate his analysis, however, in terms of our own formulation of process theory. In particular, we argue that the distinction between typical and unique aspects of phenomena is especially useful in analyzing economic fluctuations (p. 199).

But it turns out that the authors never go beyond standard Austrian analysis. They use the words "typical" and "unique" on pp. 222–23, but in so doing they merely put standard Austrian analysis into slightly different words. There is no substantive difference between their exposition of their theory and standard Austrian theory of misdirection of resources, malinvestment, and clustering of entrepreneurial error.

Chapter 10, "Some Unresolved Problems," is the brief, final chapter of the book. In it the authors suggest three possible areas of research where the principles of the book might profitably be put to work: law and economics, the analysis of money, and the competitive market process. I agree that effort in these areas, especially the first and the third, could greatly benefit from the incorporation of the standard Austrian perspective. Unfortunately, there is little in this book that successfully promotes that incorporation.

In conclusion, I cannot recommend this book to either neoclassical or Austrian readers. A neoclassical reader cannot attain a clear understanding of the basic principles of Austrian economics from it. An Austrian reader will be bewildered by the authors' apparent inability to settle their own position on the question of the possibility of equilibrium or even the tendency to coordination that is central to any viable economics. It is sadly ironic that the authors, who have done so much to foster the Austrian revival, may have, in this atypical book, set it back. Austrians can take comfort in the knowledge that the damage is not irreparable.

Method versus Methodology:
A Note on
The Ultimate Resource

M.W. Sinnett

> Science appears but what in truth she is,
> Not as our glory and our absolute boast,
> But as succedaneum, and a prop
> To our infirmity. No officious slave
> Art thou of that false secondary power
> By which we multiply distinctions, then
> Deem that our boundaries are things
> That we perceive, and not that we have made.
> —William Wordsworth, "The Prelude"

I n discussing the thought of Albert Einstein in the second course of his Gifford Lectures at Edinburgh, Professor Stanley L. Jaki draws an important distinction between the great physicist's method and his methodology. On the one hand, says Jaki, Einstein represented himself as an advocate of the "sensationism" of Ernst Mach, according to which view the existence of an objective cosmos underlying the subjective sensations of the physicist was expressly denied; whereas, on the other hand, the spectacular breakthrough represented by special (and later, general) relativity was the result of Einstein's conviction of the existence of a universal natural order, which was intelligible to man in a manner quite independent of his cultural or historical position.[1] Thus, the manner of Einstein's approach to reality (his method) was not at all consistent with his own reflection on the manner of his approach to reality (his methodology).

The possibility of such confusion as this is but one result of the fact emphasized by William James that the process of our consciousness is one thing and our critical reflection (through the vehicle of memory) on that process quite another.[2] Just as "systematic reflection on the consciousness is a late event in

The Ultimate Resource by Julian L. Simon. Princeton, N.J.: Princeton University Press, 1981.

the biography of [a] philosopher," as Eric Voegelin observed,[3] so also, quite often, does method (the way people do things) antedate methodology (their understanding of the way they do things), both in the biographies of particular scholars as well as in the histories of scholarly disciplines. The resulting possiblities for confusion are considerably augmented nowadays by the equivocation of these two terms, which is nearly universal in popular usage. One will hear a new instructional technique, for example, described as "an interesting new educational *methodology.*"

Indeed, the so-called social sciences are particularly liable to such difficulties. A particularly instructive example is to be found in Julian L. Simon's book, *The Ultimate Resource.* The goals of this essay are to demonstrate the existence of a glaring inconsistency between Professor Simon's method and his methodology, and then to draw out several important implications of this situation. In the process readers will gain some acquaintance with the concrete problems which Simon addresses as well as with his approach to the, both matters being important and instructive in and of themselves. More specifically, one will find (1) that Simon's optimistic conclusions concerning world resources are entirely justified, (2) that his method (from the Austrian perspective) is correct and appropriate, but, (3) that in discussing various methods he has given credit for his success to a method that he does not actually employ, a method which, (4) had he actually put it into practice, would have produced only the most complete confusion.

The next section briefly indicates the concrete issues with which Simon is primarily concerned. It also presents Simon's methodology, that is, his own understanding of the method he has employed to achieve his results. The following three sections, show that his methodology does not match his method. This will be accomplished through the successive examination of three technical concepts central to Simon's effort: the concepts of "scarcity," "resource," and "finiteness." I hope that my discussion of these terms will have value, not only in clarifying understanding of Simon's important work, but also as a contribution to future discussion of world resources. The final section offers concluding reamrks.

Issues and Methodology

Popular opinion has it that mineral resources are becoming increasingly scarce. This claim, in common parlance, is not simply an assertion of the economic character of mineral resources,[4] in which case it would be entirely unobjectionable, but rather, the prediction of their impending exhaustion.[5] It is Simon's burden to refute this claim. (He also provides an illuminating analysis of world population growth and a survey of some of the rather irresponsible publicity techniques employed by proponents of population control. My purpose will be best served by restricting attention to Simon's discussion of rsources—particularly mineral resources.) He begins his assault by arguing that the proper standard for the scarcity of a mineral resource is its price, or, even better, the ratio of its price to some other benchmark such as wage rate or consumer price index. Then, in discussing trends in such resource prices, he asks whether data from the past can serve as a basis for prediction of future conditions. In the process of providing an affirmative answer, Simon says:

> The question facing us is a problem in scientific generalization. A good general principle is that you should generalize from your data if you can reasonably regard them as a fair sample of the universe about which you wish to generalize. It is prediction that concerns us, however, and prediction is not quite the same as generalization. Prediction is a special type of generalization, a generalization from past to future. Prediction is always a leap of faith; *there is no scientific guarantee that the sun will come up tomorrow* (emphasis added).[6]

The "fair sample of the universe" he seeks to generalize from consists of the price trends he has been discussing, which (like the rising and the setting of the sun), it is implied, constitute the objective truth, the "truth with the bark on it," the unshakeable rock upon which he proposes to build his scientific house. Later, in a systematic discussion of the concept of "finiteness," to which I shall have occasion to return, Simon remarks that "scientific subjects [such as economics, he implies here]are empirical rather than definitional, as twentieth-century philosophers have been at great pains to emphasize." He goes on, "Mathematics [unlike economics] is not a science in the ordinary sense because it does not deal with facts other than the stuff of mathematics itself" (p. 48). The point is that Simon regards his discipline as an empirical natural science. He understands the "facts" of his subject to be the particular configurations (resource prices per unit wage rate, say) that he has identified in the marketplace, and his goal to be the construction of "scientific generalizations" based upon them.

In fact, however, despite Simon's confident suggestion of concensus, there remains considerable disagreement among "twentieth-century philosophers" as to the nature of the "empirical" natural sciences and even as to whether or not the natural sciences can be described as "empirical" in any meaningful way. Certainly, it poses no difficulty to find serious philosophers of science who would attach little value to the sort of naive inductive method Simon here attributes to natural scientists.[7]

On the other hand, there is no question that practicing members of the scientific community have long maintained that their method *is* this naive empiricism and have "urged the representatives of other disciplines to imitate [it]," with the result that "many social scientists are still trying to imitate what they wongly believe to be the methods of the natural sciences."[8] The situation presented by Simon's work, however, is slightly more complicated. For, as I shall now proceed to argue, he does not actually "imitate . . . the methods of the natural sciences." He merely says that he does. In the course of this discussion I employ the three phrases ("scarcity," "resource," and "finiteness") mentioned in the introduction. One must now carefully inquire as to Simon's understanding of these terms. In so doing one will find that Simon's *method*—as opposed to his *methodology*—is unobjectionable from an Austrian perspective.

Scarcity

The crucial issue may be revealed by asking where Simon's analysis of resource supply begins. If one agrees with him that his is an empirical method, then one must be able to argue that his "data" represents a bare-handed grasp of reality; in other words, that it is comprised of "facts" which are "other than the stuff of [economics] itself." This, however, is clearly not true. His consideration of the data is preceded by his examination of "an unexciting but crucial matter, the *definition* of 'scarcity' " (p. 17) (emphasis added). He goes on to say:

> Upon reflection perhaps you will agree that a complete absence of the material will *not* be a sign of scarcity. We will not reach up to the shelf and suddenly find that it is completely bare. It is obvious that the scarcity of any raw material would only gradually increase. Long before the shelf would be bare, individuals and firms, the latter operating purely out of the self-interested drive to make future profits, would be taking steps to hoard supplies for future resale so that the shelf would never be completely bare. Of course the price of the hoarded material would be high, but there still would be some quantities to be found at some price, just as there always has been some small amount of food for sale even in the midst of the very worst famines.
>
> The preceding observation points to a key sign of what we generally mean by scarcity: a price that has persistently risen. More generally, cost and price . . . will be our basic measure of scarcity.

It is only at this point, *having already decided what he is looking for,* that Simon turns to an examination of the data and concludes, inescapably it seems, that "raw materials have been getting increasingly available—less scarce—relative to the most important element of life, human work time" (p. 25). Now, Simon's conclusion that the resource future is increasingly bright relies for its validity on his data, that is, on the trends in resource price he quotes. Readers are entitled, however, to reject his data and hence his conclusion, unless he can persuade them to accept his definition of "scarcity," which he does, of course, very convincingly. How does he do this? By a further appeal to market data? Not at all. He asks, instead, that one *reflect* on the actions and motivations of people in the marketplace. Consider again some of the language with which he makes his appeal:

Long before the shelf would be bare, individuals and firms, the latter operating purely out of the self-interested drive to make future profits, would be taking steps to hoard supplies for future resale so that the shelf would never be completely bare.

He is arguing from the principles of praxeology—the science of human action.[9] The point is that Simon has not only reasoned *from* his "data," he has also reasoned *to* his data. His "facts" are themselves the result of economic theory. He has not simply discovered them or observed them; *he has created them.*[10]

It is instructive to consider here an analogy which Simon employs to clarify his line of argument, but in which, I submit, the same methodological confusion persists. He likens himself to a fellow making observations of the level of water in a communal tank. This fellow sees people steadily consuming, but not replenishing the water supply; he is accordingly surprised when each of his observations finds the water level higher than before. Simon asks of this situation:

> Would not a prudent person, after a long train of rises in the water level, conclude that perhaps the process may continue—and that it therefore makes sense to seek reasonable explanations? . . . Whatever the real explanation, it makes sense to look for the cause of this apparent miracle, rather than cling to a simple-minded fixed-resources theory and assert that it cannot continue (p. 23).

It is Simon's argument, and of course one ought to agree with him, that the rise in the water's level is analogous to the fall in the price of a resource. Therefore, as one might expect, he goes on to suggest that:

> The fall in the costs of natural resources decade after decade, and century after century, should shake us free from the idea that scarcity must increase *sometime.* Instead, it should point us toward trying to understand the way technological changes are induced by the demand for resources and the services they provide, and the way that such changes reduced scarcity in the past.

The crucial issue is that, while I agree that the two processes—the measurement of the water's level and the computation of a resource's price per unit work time—are analogous, they are not methodologically equivalent. The first is the action of an empiricist properly so called, requiring no a priori understanding whatsoever; whereas the second, as already shown, is the theoretically informed action of an economist. Indeed, Simon's ability to present his analogy at all is contingent on his persuading readers that the two quantities measured—water level and resource price per unit work time—actually bear some relation to one another. One is therefore reduced, once again, to his argument for his definition of "scarcity."

In the passages just quoted, one encounters a further difficulty. In both cases, it is suggested that the observation of persistently recurring configurations ("a long train of rises in the water level" and "the fall in the costs of natural resources decade after decade, and century after century") comes first and persuades (or should persuade) readers to seek out a suitable mechanism to explain them ("to look for the cause of this apparent miracle" and "[to try] to understand the way technological changes are induced by the demand for resources and the services they provide"). This suggestion of an advance from knowledge of stable or recurrent configurations to the elucidation of an explanatory mechanism evokes the global procedure of a natural scientist, but it cannot be the procedure of an economist and, in particular, it is not the procedure which Simon has employed himself. For, he cannot have drawn any conclusions from his price data until he knew the price of a resource to be the proper measure of its scarcity. He cannot have known *that,* however, prior to understanding the action of people in the face of rising resource prices. That is, in what constitutes an exact reversal of the normal procedure of a natural scientist, Simon has advanced from his knowledge of market process (or mechanism) to a correct identification of stable market configuration.[11]

A still more subtle distinction to be made between the methods of the natural and social sciences is nicely illustrated by Simon's effort. This lies in the fact that, contrary perhaps to popular perception, the natural scientist endeavors to "explain the known in terms of the unknown."[12] By way of illustration, an organic chemist will elucidate his familiar experience of various chemical reactions in terms of reaction mechanisms which will draw heavily from existing formulations, or he will elicit new formulations in physical chemistry and theoretical physics which will be relatively less familiar or even somewhat unintelligible to him. Social scientists, on the other hand, are confronted with problems of such immense complexity as to "require a reversal of what has been described as the standard procedure of [natural science]; [they] have to proceed in [their] deductions, not from the hypothetical or unknown to the known and obsevable, but—as used to be thought to be the normal procedure [in natural science]—from the familiar to the unknown."[13] In particular, Simon's discoveries, and arguments for the relevance, of stable configurations in the marketplace have flowed from his knowledge of the characteristics of human conduct of which he has a relatively more intimate knowledge.

It is in this light that the perplexity of the fellow at the water tank seems somewhat misplaced. Simon seems to require that this poor fellow oppose his intuitive understanding with a somewhat paradoxical and logically untenable induction;[14] whereas, it is in fact Simon's own praxeological anlaysis that persuades his readers not only that his price trends *are* stable configurations, but that readers should have expected this to be true from the very beginning. One is confronted, after all, not with the mysterious machinations of an inanimmate universe, but with the purposeful conduct of human beings within the "life-world"

(*Lebenswelt*).[15] (One also encounters here the issue of "teleology," to which I shall return.) Unless one expects some radical transformation of the nature of humankind, therefore, one may safely dispense with Simon's leap of faith. Herein lies the advantage of treating man anthropomorphically.[16]

Thus, by way of summary, one finds that Simon's praxeological analysis of the meaning of "scarcity" yields conclusions in which one can have great confidence, while, at the same time, rendering rather problematic his methodological claim of empiricism.

Resources

It is manifestly of the greatest importance, in such a discussion as this, that there should be agreement as to the meaning of "resource." Despite the fact, moreover, that there seems to be no explicit definition of this word in *The Ultimate Resource*, there does seem to prevail among all parties a general understanding as to its meaning. How has this understanding been effected? Why is it that copper, say, is regarded as a mineral "resource"—and no questions asked? In consideration of its color? Or its specific gravity? Or perhaps its spectral properties? Is there—in short—some empirical procedure that will yield an objective classification of copper as a "resource"? Hardly. In point of fact, as Hayek has written,

> [S]uch things as tools, food, medicine, weapons, words, sentences, communications, . . . acts of production [and, I may add, resources], or any one particular instance of any of these . . . are all instances of what are sometimes called "teleological concepts," that is, they can be defined only by indicating relations between three terms: a purpose, somebody who holds that purpose, and an object which that person thinks to be a suitable means for that purpose. If we wish, we could say that all these objects are defined not in terms of their "real" properties but in terms of opinions people hold about them.[17]

And, of course, one understands the "opinions people hold" about the objects of their action through knowledge of their action itself. Simon's last hope for an empirical understanding of "resource," therefore, is that it may prove possible to assign some objective meaning to one's observations of people's action. Alas, the hope is in vain. For, as Hayek continues:

> [I]n discussing what we regard as other people's conscious actions, we invariably interpret their action on the analogy of our own mind: that is, . . . we group their actions, and the objects of their actions, into classes or categories which we know solely from the knowledge of our own mind. We assume that the idea of a purpose or a tool, a weapon or food, is common to them with us, just as we assume that they can see the difference between different colors

or shapes as well as we. We thus always supplement what we actually see of another person's action by projecting into that person a system of classification of objects which we know, not from observing other people, but because it is in terms of these classes that we think ourselves.[18]

This is not to say that such knowledge as this is divorced from our experience of the external world (which assertion would contradict the results of the previous section). It is in fact Hayek himself who has elsewhere asserted that such knowledge as this "constitute[s] the truly empirical factor in the social sciences."[19] It is simply that such knowledge as this—knowledge of "the relations between men and things or the relations between man and man"—is qualitatively different from knowledge of "the relations between things."[20] The latter may be understood as "empirical" in the sense in which Simon has employed the term; while the former, though referred to by Hayek as being "empirical," may perhaps be better described as "intersubjective." It is a part, not of one's knowledge of the world of objects standing over against one, but of one's "lived-experience" (*Erlebnis*).[21] Thus, while people may continue to locate the basis of economic science in their ("lived") experience, and hence to regard it as "empirical" (in the intersubjective sense), it remains true that people are very far indeed from the empirical method Simon claims to have borrowed from natural science.

Once again, however, this claim is not consistent with Simon's practice. For he notes himself that in understanding the availability of a resource, the crucial consideration is not the supply of a particular mineral, but one's ability to achieve particular goals:

> What is relevant to use is not whether we can find any lead in existing mines but whether we can have the services of lead batteries at a reasonable price; it does not matter to us whether this is accomplished by recycling lead, by making lead batteries last forever, or by replacing lead batteries with other contraptions (p. 49).

As suggested above, one is faced here with one's irredeemable inability to classify a substance as a resource without reference to those human purposes for the achievement of which somebody regards the material as a suitable means. This recognition by Simon of the relevance of "purpose" to his analysis clearly demonstrates the radical discontinuity between his actual praxeological method and his methodological claim of empiricism.

Furthermore, in recognizing the teleological dimension of his undertaking, Simon has implicitly denied the applicability of the techniques of natural science generally speaking (that is, over and above the more specific issues of what one may or may not directly observe). For not only, as argued above, are the sciences of human society *necessarily* teleological, *the sciences of nature cannot be.* Jaki has shown that the assumption, at various times in the history of science, of purchase immanent in the workings of nature has invariably led to a scientific blind alley. As in the case, he says, of the classical Greek philosophers, teleologists have "built ways to the ultimate in intelligibility, only to find themselves at the end of those ways."[22]

Finally, Simon has made it his purpose to remind readers—may it henceforth be shouted from the rooftops!—that "the ultimate resource," the fountainhead of all other resource, is the human imagination. In his introduction (pp. 9–10), he describes himself in 1969, in Washington, D.C., discussing with an Agency for International Development official a project intended to lower fertility rates in less developed countries.

> I arrived early for my appointment, so I strolled outside in the warm sunshine. Below the building's plaza I noticed a sign that said "Iwo Jima Highway." I remembered reading about a eulogy delivered by a Jewish chaplain over the dead on the battlefield at Iwo Jima, saying something like, "How many who would have been a Mozart or a Michelangelo or an Einstein have we buried here?" And then I thought, Have I gone crazy? What business do I have trying to help arrange it that fewer human beings will be born, each one of whom might be a Mozart or a Michelangelo or an Einstein—or simply a joy to his or her family and community, and a person who will enjoy life?

Is it possible that it is here, so far removed from the austere machinery of empirical science, that one at last finds the true beginning of Simon's analysis?

I have now carefully examined the conceptions of "scarcity" and "resource." Three results have emerged: first, that the problems with which readers are concerned properly demand a praxeological method for their solution; second, that Simon has in fact successfully undertaken such a praxeological analysis of these problems; and therefore, third, that he may be regarded as an empiricist (according to his own use of this term) in a Pickwickian sense only. Further confirmation of these results emerges in the following examination of the concept of "finiteness."

Finiteness

Simon seeks to deny that supplies of resources are finite, with which conclusion readers ought to agree. It is in the course of his analysis of this issue, as I noted earlier, that he claims his method is "empirical rather than definitional," with which one ought not to agree. In order to clearly locate the point of departure for this erroneous methodological claim, it will be necessary to follow the sequence of Simon's argument in some detail. It will become quickly apparent, once again, how crucial is a proper understanding of the concepts of "scarcity" and "resource."

Simon begins by suggesting that people are misled in using "finite" by the term's own inherent ambiguity:

The word "finite" originates in mathematics, in which context we all learn it as schoolchildren. But even in mathematics the word's meaning is far from unambiguous.. It can have two principle meanings, sometimes with an apparent contradiction between them. For example, the length of a one-inch line is finite in the sense that it is bounded at both ends. But the line within the endpoints contains an infinite number of points; these points cannot be counted, because they have no definite size. Therefore the number of points in that one-inch segment is not finite (p. 47).

But this is an error. In fact, there is only one criterion of finiteness employed in the example Simon provides, namely, if a positive real-valued quantity, or function, is finite, then one can display, among the positive integers, say, an upper bound. (The contrapositive, of course, is that if one cannot display an upper bound, then one cannot claim finiteness.) In the first case, he observes that the length, or "Lebesgue measure," of the one-inch line is finite (since its value is a positive real number and there exists a plentiful supply of upper bounds) and, in the second case, that the number of elements, or "counting measure," of the same set is infinite (since one cannot display an upper bound).[23] That which is different in these two cases is not the criterion of finiteness, but the definition of the "measure" of the set to which the criterion is applied: Lebesgue measure, in which case the criterion is satisfied, and counting measure, in which case the *same* criterion fails to be satisfied.

There is, moreover, no reason for "finite" to be any less applicable to a discussion of resources. Indeed, among other things, Simon says, "[A] reason that the term 'finite' is not meaningful [in a discussion of resources] is that we cannot say with any practical surety where the bounds of a relevant resource system lie, or even if there are any bounds" (p. 48). But, the inability to say "where the bounds of a relevant resource system lie" does not imply the meaningless or ambiguity of "finite" in such a context; it simply implies that the criterion of finiteness is not satisfied. This point may be reinforced by considering a brief passage from a delightful afternote to chapter 3, entitled "A Dialogue on 'Finite' " (p. 51), where Simon writes:

> PS [*Peers Strawman*]: Finite means "limited."
> HW [*Happy Writer*]: What is the limit for, say, copper?
> PS: I don't know.
> HW: Then how can you be sure it is limited in quantity?

Precisely so. If Strawman cannot display an upper bound on the quantity of copper, much less on the ability to provide the services of copper, he cannot claim to have satisfied the criterion of finiteness. There is no ambiguity here: Strawman is unambiguously wrong.

Now, however, Simon seems to change his ground. He argues that ambiguities in discussions of resource supply have resulted from the different means of measuring resource supply to which the concept of finiteness has been applied (which, in the mathematical context, is essentially what I suggested above). There are, he says, two principal methods of making such measurements, the "technologic" and the "economic." The first of these, the technologic method, consists of the effort to determine the quantity of a particular mineral physically extant in the earth's crust, or, of what is slightly more sophisticated, the effort to determine the quantity of the material recoverable given certain assumptions about available technology. Having made such a determination, the technologist, by means by some extrapolation of current rates of usage, computes the "years of consumption" remaining.

But against this technologic method Simon favors the economic method, the attempt to predict the availability of a resource in the marketplace *at different price levels*. Since the price of a particular mineral will be affected by one's ability to achieve its services by other means, this economic method automatically takes into consideration countless possibilities of substitution of which people can have no personal knowledge. Under Simon's expert tutelage, moreover, this economic perspective reveals gaping holes in the technologic analysis. The technologist remains stubbornly unaware of the fact, that the availability of a resource is dependent on its market price, and *that the resource worth looking for will invariably be found.*

Indeed, the technologist's own estimates of the supply of a material is dependent on the willingness of various people to search for it—which is to say, dependent on the demand for the mineral in the marketplace—which is to say, dependent on the price of the mineral. In any case, what is important is not how much of a particular mineral there is, but the extent to which, in some way or another, the services it performs can be provided at a given price. (To reinforce an earlier point, the foregoing analysis clearly reveals the methodological confusion in Simon's "water tank" analogy. This may now be described, using Simon's own terminology, as the confusion of the *technologic* measurement of the water's level in the tank with the *economic* computation of the water's price per unit work time.)

It is in continuing this argument for his economic method of measurement that Simon makes his "empirical rather than definitional" claim. The technologists' mistake, he says, is to have "define[d] the subject of discussion suitably, and sufficiently closely [via technologic measurement] so that [the supply of resources] can be counted." (p. 50), and hence, has the appearance of being finite. His response is to deny the applicability of such definitions to the subject matter by claiming that the proper method is one of empiricism.

That this response is an overreaction is demonstrated (as if any further demonstration is required) by Simon's restatement of his "economic" or "operational" definition of the quantity of a resource:

> A satisfactory *operational* definition of the quantity of a natural resource, or
> of the services we now get from it, is the only sort of definition that is of any

use in policy decisions. The definition must tell us about the quantities of a resource (or of a particular service) that we can expect to receive in any particular year to come, at each particular price, conditional on other events that we might reasonably expect to know (such as use of the resource in prior years) (pp. 47–48).

Once again, I have no difficulty in agreeing with his definition and the conclusion he draws from it, namely, that the supplies of mineral resources are without bound. At the same time, I can see little use in his asserting the necessity of an "operational *definition* of the quantity of a natural resource," and then going on to argue, *on the same page*, that economics is "empirical rather than *definitional*." In reality, the technologist's problem is not that he "defines the subject of discussion," but that he does so erroneously.

I return, therefore, to the first three of the four conclusions asserted in the introduction: (1) I have agreed with Simon's conclusion; (2) I have agreed with Simon's method; and (3) I have shown that his method is not what he says it is. Having now introduced the technologic measure of resource supply, I am in a position to establish my fourth conclusion.

Nothing can be more clear than that Simon's technologist adversaries have been led into error precisely by the practice of the empirical method Simon has (wrongly) claimed for himself. The scientist who insists on confronting these questions of resource supply *as a scientist* will proceed by making precisely those technologic measurements which, as Simon has phrased it, have so "muddle[d] public discussion and [brought] about wrongheaded policy decisions" (p. 47). Desiring, for example, to forecast the future availability of copper, he will begin by determining how much copper there is. Why should a good empiricist begin anywhere else? Having subsequently "observed" the rate at which this "finite" supply is being consumed, he will conclude that copper is becoming increasingly "scarce" and go on to forecast its imminent exhaustion. Notice again how crucial is a proper understanding of "scarcity" and "resource."

Again, the problem is not the presence of definitions, but the presence of definitions (and methods) that are inappropriate to the subject matter. There is a sense in which the technologist's problems stem from his having *not* "define[d] the subject of discussion suitably, and sufficiently closely." He will have missed all those considerations to which Simon will have been led by his praxeological analysis to attach the most significance. For example, although there will be more than one means of achieving the services of copper, most of these opportunities for substitution will lie beyond the technologist's knowledge, and even beyond his interest.[24] He will not see them because he did not begin by knowing that he should look for them. Also, since his effort fails to be graced by an economic theory that tells him to do so, there is no reason to expect him to consider the price of copper—much less, the price of copper per unit work time—much less still, decades (or centuries) long trends in the price of copper per unit work time.

Indeed, understanding himself to be a scientific empiricist, it is precisely the technologist who will insist that to admit such considerations into his analysis would be to impose abstract and artificial definitions on his subject matter. "Scientific subjects," he will gravely explain, "are empirical rather than definitional." And precisely because he "disdains to make use of the models worked out for him by the theorists, he is almost certain to come to grief."[25]

Thus I have used Simon's critique of his technologist adversaries to establish my fourth conclusion. By simply glancing around at the innumerable technologic studies of resource supply, one sees how dismal the results could have been had Simon really put into practice the empirical method demanded by his methodology. (There remain many other starting points for the practical realization of Simon's empirical methodology, one of which I shall now discuss.)

Conclusion

It is clear that Simon's topic is an important one and my objections to his methodology notwithstanding, that his contribution to a proper understanding of these issues is extremely valuable. It remains, however, by way of conclusion, to show how important it is that a praxeological method be matched with a praxeological methodology.

But perhaps it is still unclear how a divergence between method and methodology is possible. How is it possible, it might still be asked, for an empirical methodology to be conjoined with a praxeological method? How is it possible for a single mind to do one thing and yet understand itself to be doing quite another? One may ask this question without doubting that what it refers to is characteristic of most of one's thought throughout one's life.

An adequate discussion of this general issue is beyond the scope of this brief review, but I can offer the following warning against what William James called the "psychologist's fallacy."[26] The foregoing references to Simon's praxeological method will have brought to the attention of Austrian minds the complex of praxeology-as-a-method-consciously-chosen. They will have called to economists' attention, that is, their own reflective knowledge of praxeology as they have learned it from the method and methodology of the great Austrian teachers. And it is in this form in which the praxeological method absolutely precludes an empirical methodology. The psychologist's fallacy results when one projects one's understanding of praxeology-as-a-method-consciously-chosen into Simon's thought, where it does not actually exist. In fact, Simon's praxeological knowledge must be said to exist, not as the result of a-method-consciously-chosen, not as something of which he is methodologically self-aware, but as a part of his "tacit"[27] or "common-sense"[28] knowledge. As I have shown, moreover, Simon's possession of praxeology as "tacit knowledge" has not prevented him from deploying it with extraordinary power. Nevertheless, I will now seek to show the importance of entertaining such knowledge as this at the level of *methodology* as well.

In the first place, a praxeological methodology would strengthen several of Simon's concrete arguments. It would reinforce, as I have shown, Simon's analysis of all three of the concepts discussed in the three previous sections. Indeed, in more than one instance, little remained to be done after the terms of discussion had been suitably clarified through praxeological analysis. This clarity, however, was achieved *in spite of* Simon's claim of empiricism.

Finally, a praxeological methodology would lessen the possibility that readers of *The Ultimate Resource* might take Simon's claim of empiricism more seriously than they do the context of praxeological analysis from which his results have emerged. Nor is the method of technologic measurement discussed in the previous section the only, or even the most immediate, fashion in which Simon's empirical methodology could be translated into practice. For, recall that the "facts" that Simon understands to be the irreducible basis of his "empirical" analysis are the trends in resource prices that he reports (as opposed to technologic measurements of resource "reserves"). In other words, he has presented stable and recurrent configurations—never mind, just now, how they have been discovered—and advocated the construction of "scientific generalizations" based upon them.

Now, given these stable and recurrent configurations (and ignoring their praxeological grounding), the next step in the logic of empirical scientific procedure is to attempt a symbolization, perhaps through mathematical methods, of the process that produces these configurations. Simon, of course, has not actually taken this step, but this would not prevent someone else from taking up the "empirical" task where he left off. One can easily imagine, for example, someone seeking to understand the graph of the price of a particular resource plotted with respect to time as the graph of a "price function," itself an eigenfunction of a "price equation," and so on. Indeed, for one having some training in mathematics, the temptations presented by such a situation might well prove irresistible.

The point is, of course, that there is no need—and indeed, no room—for a fresh symbolization of the process that has produced these configurations. Readers already know the process, having *begun* by knowing the process. It is Simon's analysis of human action that has revealed these configurations in the first place, *and it is this underlying praxeological context that must be asserted at all costs*. Let this context once be dropped, as it would be Simon's claim of empiricism were allowed to stand—let these price trends once assume the appearnace of self-contained, freestanding, empirical "data"—and there will be no end of "models," "scientific generalizations," and "mathematical methods" offered by those far more consistent and ambitious than Simon in pursuing practical applications of his empiricical methodology.

On the other hand, let the praxeological context of "the facts of the social sciences" be recognized and preserved—let praxeological method be matched with praxeological methodology—and the superimposition of such superfluous and inconsistent layers of process will henceforth be undertaken with only the most embarrassing results. For there shall then be *two* layers of process: one underlying and engendering the configurations, which is symbolized praxeologically; and another overlaying and purporting to explain these same configurations, symbolized (probably) through mathematical formalism. The former shall be known with great "warmth and intimacy"[29] and the latter only rather dimly and at (at least) two removes from immediate experience.

Accordingly, one shall have the right to ask the empiricist what relation his second layer of process has to the first and more fundamental layer. In so doing, one shall merely be translating into economic terms the requirement known in physics as the "correspondence principle."[30] It will simply be required that the two symbolizations of process, being descriptions of the same reality, be continuous with one another. It will be most interesting to learn, for example, how the empiricist's differential equations can help thinkers to interpret their experience of the "life-world." And when they find, as they must, that these equations are of no help at all, then the path shall lie clearly ahead, and readers shall not hesitate to reject this scientistic deformation of economic reality.

The motto must be (with apologies to Edmund Husserl): "To the facts themselves!" For if economists clearly understand the nature of the facts of economic science, then they shall have occupied the high ground, from which, though pitifully few, they shall turn back hosts.

Notes

1. Cf. S.L. Jaki, *The Road of Science and the Ways to God* (Chicago: University of Chicago Press, 1978), pp. 182f. See also M. Polanyi, *Personal Knowledge* (Chicago: University of Chicago Press, 1962), pp. 9f.

2. Cf. William James, *The Principles of Psychology*, vol. 53 of *Great Books of the Western World*, R.M. Hutchins, ed., 54 vols. (Chicago: Encyclopedia Britannica, 1952), especially chap. X.

3. E. Voegelin, "On the Theory of Consciousness," in *Anamnesis*, G Niemeyer, trans. and ed. (Notre Dame, Ind.: Notre Dame University Press, 1978), p. 33.

4. Cf. Carl Manger, *Principles of Economics*, James Dingwall and Bert F. Hoselitz, trans. (New York: New York University Press, 1981), especially pp. 101f. See also L. Robbins, *An Essay on the Nature and Significance of Economic Science*, 3d ed. (London: Macmillan, 1984), pp. 13f.

5. Cf., for example, D.H. Meadows, et al., *The Limits of Growth* (New York: Universe Books, 1972), pp. 55f.

6. J.L. Simon, *The Ultimate Resource* (Princeton, N.J.: Princeton University Press, 1981), p. 22. All references to this work will be given, parenthetically, in the body of the review.

7. Cf., for example, K.R. Popper, *The Logic of Scientific Discovery*, 2d ed. (New York: Harper and Row, 1968), especially chaps. 1, 3, 5. For a readable and succinct discussion of the methodological debate and its relation to the social sciences, see Homa Katouzian, *Ideology and Method* (New York: New York University Press, 1980), especially chaps. 2–4.

8. F.A. Hayek, *Studies in Philosophy, Politics, and Economics*, Midway Reprint (Chicago: University of Chicago Press, 1980), p. viii.

9. This concrete situation is illustrative of the "aprioristic" character of praxeological knowledge: one is unable even to conceive of some market "data" which could shake one's confidence in Simon's use of market price as the measure of resource scarcity. That is, "we cannot think of the truth of its negation or of something that would be at variance with it" (L. von Mises, *The Ultimate Foundation of Economic Science: An Essay on Method*, 2d ed. (Kansas City: Sheed, Andrews, and McMeel, 1978), p. 4; see also, by the same author, *Human Action*, 3d rev. ed. (Chicago: Contemporary Books, 1966), especially pp. 38–41, 64–69.

Note, however, that this does not necessarily deny "the broadly empirical nature of the praxeological axioms" (M.N. Rothbard, "Praxeology: The Methodology of Austrian Economics,") in E.G. Dolan, ed., *The Foundations of Modern Austrian Economics* (Kansas City: Sheed and Ward, 1976), p. 26.

10. Cf. F.A. Hayek, "The Facts of the Social Sciences," in *Individualism and Economic Order*, Midway Reprint (Chicago: University of Chicago Press, 1980), p. 72:

> [The theories of the social sciences] are not *about* the social wholes as wholes; they do not pretend to discover by empirical observation laws of behavior or change of these wholes. Their task is rather, if I may so call it, to *constitute* these wholes, to provide schemes of structural relationships which the historian [or the economist] can use when he has to attempt to fit together into a meaningful whole the elements which he actually finds.

11. Cf. F.A. Hayek, *The Counter-Revolution of Science: Studies in the Abuse of Reason*, 2d ed. (Indianapolis: Liberty Press, 1979), pp. 102–3:

> In biology we do indeed first recognize as things of one kind natural units, stable combinations of sense properties, of which we find many instances which we spontaneously recognize as alike. We can, therefore, begin by asking why these definite sets of attributes regularly occur together. But where we have to deal with social structures, it is not the observation of the regular coexistence of certain physical facts which teaches us that they belong together or form a whole. We do not first observe that the parts always occur together and afterward ask what holds them together; but it is only because we know the ties that hold them together that we can select a few elements from the immensely complicated world around us as parts of a connected whole.

12. K.R. Popper, quoted in Hayek, "Degrees of Explanation," in *Studies*, p. 5.
13. Hayek, ibid., p. 9.
14. "Logically untenable," that is, as presented here. Cf., for example, K.R. Popper, "Two Faces of Common Sense," in *Objective Knowledge: An Evolutionary Approach*, rev. ed. (Oxford: Clarendon Press of Oxford University, 1979), especially pp. 81f.
15. Cf. M. Natanson, *Edmund Husserl: Philosopher of Infinite Tasks*, Northwestern University Studies in Phenomenology and Existential Philosophy, J.M. Edie, ed. (Evanston, Ill.: Northwestern University Press, 1973), chap. 7.

16. Cf. Hayek, "The Facts of the Social Sciences," in *Individualism*:

The tendency [of the development of scientific thought in modern times] has been correctly described as one toward the progressive elimination of all "anthropomorphic" explanations from the physical sciences. Does this really mean that we must refrain from treating man "anthropomorphically"—or is it not rather obvious, as soon as we put it this way, that such an extrapolation of past tendencies is absurd? (p. 65).

17. Ibid.,pp. 59–60.

18. Ibid., p. 63.

19. Hayek, "Socialist Calculation I: The Nature and History of the Problem," in ibid., p. 126.

20. Hayek, *Counter-Revolution*, p. 41.

21. Cf. A.Schutz, *The Phenomenology of the Social World*, Northwestern University Studies in Phenomenology and Existential Philosophy, J. Wild, ed. (Evanston, Ill.: Northwestern University Press, 1967), chaps. 2, 3; "Common Sense and Scientific Interpretation of Human Action," in *Collected Papers, vol. I: The Problem of Social Reality*, M. Natanson, ed. (The Hagüe: Martinus, Nijhoff, 1962), pp. 3–40; "Phenomenology and the Social Sciences," in ibid., pp. 118–39; "The Dimensions of the Social World" in *Collected Papers, vol. II: Studies in Social Theory*, A. Brodersen, ed. (The Hague: Martinus Nijhoff, 1976), pp. 20–63.

22. Jaki, *Road of Science*, p. 33. See also E.A. Burtt, *The Metaphysical Foundations of Modern Science* (New York: Doubleday, 1954), especially pp. 18f.

23. These are but two of many examples of measures. Lebesgue measure is due to the French analyst, Henri Lebesgue, and has the property that it extends the usual notion of length. That is, while it is applicable to a much larger class of subsets of the real line, Lebesgue measure assigns to each interval its usual length. The counting measure of a set, on the other hand, coincides with the number of elements, or cardinality, of the set. For a thorough treatment of measure theory, see Edwin Hewitt and Karl Stromberg, *Real and Abstract Analysis* (Berlin: Springer-Verlag, 1965), especially chap. 3.

24. Cf. Hayek, *The Constitution of Liberty* (Chicago: University of Chicago Press, 1960):

We know little of the particular facts to which the whole of social activity continuously adjusts itself in order to provide what we have learned to expect. We know even less of the forces which bring about this adjustment by appropriately co-ordinating individual activity (p. 25).

25. Hayek, "The Facts of the Social Sciences," in *Individualism*, p. 72.

26. Cf. James, *Principles*, pp. 128–29.

27. Cf. Polanyi, *Personal Knowledge*, pp. 62–63.

28. .Cf. Voegelin, "About the Function of Noesis," in *Anamnesis*, pp. 211f.

29. The defining characteristic, for William James, of "the stream of consciousness." Cf. *Principles*, 213.

30. This is the requirement, first explicitly stated by Niels Bohr, that the postulates of quantum mechanics must yield classical results when applied to classical systems (mechanical systems for which the quantum number, n, is large). Cf. J.D. McGervey, *Introduction to Modern Physics* (New York: Academic Press, 1971), pp. 80f.

Reviews

The Evolution of Cooperation

Reviewed by Roger Arnold

Robert Axelrod's *The Evolution of Cooperation* is destined to find its way into hundreds of scholarly footnotes over the next decade. It is, quite simply, a book that will be widely read and discussed within the academic circles of many fields.

There is a reason for this. It is a book that in simple and straightforward language addresses a major and long-standing question that, it so happens, is peripherally related to a long list of interesting topics. The question, as Axelrod notes, is "Under what conditions will cooperation emerge in a world of egoists without central authority?" A few of the peripherally related topics include: trench warfare in World War I, biological systems, the golden rule, nuclear warfare, government's raison d'être, family feuds, stereotyping, economic protectionism, congressional politics, morality, taxes, and international cooperation.

The sum around which the book revolves is the game strategic prisoner's dilemma. Prisoner's dilemma, as Axelrod tells us, "is simply an abstract formulation of some very common and interesting situations in which what is best for each person individually leads to mutual defection, whereas everyone would have been better off with mutual cooperation." The recognition of which has predictably led many persons to ask, "So, what is the solution?" Axelrod, armed with the computer tournament results of prisoner's dilemma experts, answers that in iterated prisoner's dilemma games it is Tit for Tat: the behavioral response that seeks to do to others (good or bad) what others have done to you.

A little background is necessary. Axelrod asked persons who had written on prisoner's dilemma (persons in the fields of biology, computer science, economics, mathematics, physics, political science, psychology, and sociology) to submit a computer program they thought would obtain the most points when pitted against other computer programs within the prisoner's dilemma setting. The winner was Tit for Tat, submitted by Anatol Rapoport.

The Evolution of Cooperation by Robert Axelrod. New York: Basic Books, 1984.

This is interesting in and of itself. But there is more. First, and most importantly, there is the fact that the winner of prisoner's dilemma is also the solution to it—Tit for Tat generates mutual cooperation, the slippery and supposedly unobtainable goal of prisoner's dilemma. Second, Tit for Tat, while designed as a strategy for winning, appears to have admirable characteristics: it is nice (it is not the first to make trouble), it is retaliatory (thus providing an incentive to the person who starts trouble to desist), it is forgiving (which means it shows good faith, a key ingredient for mutual cooperation), and it is clear (thus making a communication foul-up between persons unlikely).

All this is interesting and simple enough, and Axelrod does an exceptionally good job at reporting the rsults of the computer tournament, describing some of the high-scoring strategies other than Tit for Tat, and bringing out the subtle points behind Tit for Tat. It is when he tries to interpret what Tit for Tat means for some important policy questions, though, that Axelrod does less than an exemplary job. In fact, here he might be faulted for muddled thinking.

One important case in point in his discussion of government. As no doubt many persons have heard by now, and Axelrod makes clear by citing Hobbes and quoting Rousseau, it has long been acknowledged that government is the solution to prisoner's dilemma. The story line is familiar: (1) in some cases, individuals would be better off cooperating than not cooperating; (2) uncertainty and general human nature sometimes make cooperation a difficult outcome to achieve; and (3) government enters the picture, and through it individuals get what they want but could not obtain on their own.

In game theory language, government solves the prisoner's dilemma by "changing the payoffs." Axelrod notes that

> Large changes in the payoff structure can transform the interaction so that it is no longer even a prisoner's dilemma. If the punishment for defection is so great that cooperation is the best choice in the short run, no matter what the other player does, then there is no longer a dilemma.

Government's "changing the payoffs" obviously does not disturb Axelrod, for in chapter 7, he advises the reader on how to promote cooperation—government is not one of the ways ruled out. On the contrary, it is one of the ways ruled in. Speaking of government-imposed taxes, Axelrod says: "But everyone may be better off if each person has to pay so that each can share the benefits of schools, roads, and other collective goods."

This is a rather odd statement from one who, up until this point, appears to have been quite excited over the discovery that Tit for Tat offers a noncoercive way out of prisoner's dilemma settings. Axelrod might be saying that there are two ways to remove oneself from the grasp of the prisoner's dilemma: the coercive way and the noncoercive (or free) way. Or he might be saying that the noncoercive way only works in some prisoner's dilemma situations and not in others—it might work when the goal is the removal of international trade barriers, but not when the goal is the provision of a public good. In either case, Axelrod leaves people hanging; he leaves them without information that directly relates to answering the question he starts his book with: "Under what conditions will cooperation emerge in a world of egoists without central authority?"

In Axelrod's defense it needs to be said that he does say that in a prisoner's dilemma setting, the more people believe that they will come into contact with each other in the future, the more likely cooperation is to naturally emerge. While this answer to his introductory question is better than no answer, it is not a full answser, and in that it is not, one is left with no more objective knowledge to aid in deciding where the line between government and the market should be drawn than one had before reading the book. To go one step further back, no answer is provided for Axelrod's question, which is a proxy for what Robert Nozick calls the "fundamental question of political philosophy"—namely, should there be any state at all?

The Evolution of Cooperation ends up being a mixed bag. It is topical and well written; additionally, Axelrod is superb as reporter and analyzer of prisoner's dilemma strategies and computer tournament results. It is only when Axelrod sets out (one senses somewhat timidly) to look at what prisoner's dilemma and the winning strategy, Tit for Tat, mean within the larger context, that things come up short. This book would have been much improved if Axelrod had taken greater pains here, if he had only focused on answering the question that begins his book. Robert Axelrod needs to seriously think about writing *The Evolution of Cooperation: Part II*.

Competition versus Monopoly: Combines Policy in Perspective

Reviewed by Roger Arnold

T here are numerous well-known definitions of economics, but the one that best captures what economics is about is James Buchanan's definition, namely: "Economics is the science of markets or exchange institutions."

Sadly, most economists do not "do economics" with this definition in mind. They "do economics" in the same way that one would imagine an engineer "does engineering." It is all very mechanical.

Donald Armstrong is not like most economists. He is an economist who knows that economics is first and foremost about markets, about exchange. And with that proper focus, he has created a splendid work—a work rich in the nuts and bolts of everyday economic life, a work that cannot be summarized (much to its credit) in a handful of equations and curves.

This book is about many things, but mostly it is, as the title notes, about competition and monopoly. Specifically, it is a constructive criticism of the neoclassical two-dimensional price theory which looms large in the discussions of the firm and market structures in the best-selling economics textbooks. More specifically, it offers a replacement for the orthodox structuralist theory of competition.

The replacement—the behavioral theory of competition—is grounded in an emphasis on process rather than outcome, a Hayekian view of competition, a rather Rothbardian view of monopoly, and a place (thankfully) for the entrepreneur. This is all new stuff to anyone who has not utilized his peripheral vision and looked beyond the mainstream discussion of the firm, perfect competition, and monopoly found in most economics textbooks. In fact, to this person it is an entirely new language. But it is a language that accurately conveys what is happening in the real world when it comes to the firm, competition, and monopoly.

One senses that if Donald Armstrong could have his way, the model of perfect competition would tomorrow disappear from center stage of the theory

---

Competition versus Monopoly: Combines Policy in Perspective by Donald Armstrong.

ɔf prices and markets. It is too bad Armstrong cannot have his way. The model, as he points out, is not only totally artificial, but it is misleading. It implicitly ɛmphasizes the number of firms in an industry (which is difficult to define) as the sole determinant of whether or not competition exists. In the limited framework of neoclassical two-dimensional price theory, more firms in the industry mean more competition. Nothing else matters. Nonsense. There are other dimensions to competition, as Armstrong clearly points out.

Furthermore, there is the fact that this totally artificial market structure of perfect competition—which, by the way, many orthodox economists will admit is not even close to being descriptive of the real world—is put forth by these same economists as the proper benchmark for other market structures to be measured up against. (How else could it be that economists speak about "dead weight losses"?) What must first-year economics students think when presented with all this hullabaloo?

What also must they think when they encounter monopoly? As Armstrong points out in his book, they probably think that monopoly is something that it is not. This is because the students' teachers probably think that monopoly is something that it is not. Chapter 5, which deals with monopoly, is a must to read for anyone who thinks that a monopolist is a single seller of a good, is interested in the easy life, and can and will charge a price for his good that is above the competitive level. The theme here is: What you think monopoly is, and how you think it behaves, are probably all wrong.

An important message of this book is that government policy, based on a wrongheaded notion of competition and monopoly, is bound to create more problems than it solves. Take, for instance, the most common and blatant example. A government official, thinking that the model of perfect competition is the ideal, notes that in the model, in equilibrium marginal cost is equal to price, and that in the long run economic profits are zero. Greatı What next? Well, armed with this information the government official can undertake a policy of search and destroy: search for those firms selling above marginal cost and making greater than zero economic profit, and destroy them. Either that, or get them to toe the perfect competition line—all in the name of economic justice and consumer sovereignty, of course.

Economics professors and university students have the most to benefit from this book. It offers a trenchant and correct criticism of much of what they are teaching and learning. One can only imagine how things might be different today on the economic front if Armstrong's ideas had been taught in the colleges, universities, and law schools of this country over the past three to four decades. If one makes the reasonable assumption that ideas based on reality are better than those based on fantasy, then it follows that things would have been much better. And that should tell the person thinking of reading Armstrong's book just how important it is to follow through.

A Response to the Framework Document for Amending the Combines Investigation Act

Reviewed by Roger Arnold

I t is sad that Walter Block had to write this essay. If politicians were less interested in power, if bureaucrats were less interested in meddling in the affairs of the economy, and if the majority of academic economists were less starry-eyed over statistics and more knowledgeable of the way free markets work, then this essay would not have had to have been written. But, alas, the world is what it is, so this essay did have to be written. Walter Block was certainly up to the task.

First, a little background. The *Combines Investigation Act* is one of those pieces of economic legislation seeking to bureaucratize and politicize the Canadian economy. It is part of the rationalist-constructivist mindset that implicitly assumes that if government officials do not have a hand in what happens in the economy, well then, nothing good can naturally happen. To the rationalist-constructivist, the only good hand is a visible hand. To them, Adam Smith's invisible hand truly is invisible.

Specifically, the *Combines Investigation Act* addresses issues such as competition, industry concentration, mergers, price fixing, cartels, vertical integration, and price cutting.

In Spring 1981, along came the Canadian Minister of Consumer and Corporate Affairs, André Ouellet, who put forth his "Proposals for Amending the *Combines Investigation Act*: A Framework for Discussion." Briefly, Minister Ouellet's proposals for reform sought to make the *Combines Investigation Act* more interventionist and meddling.

Enter Walter Block, senior economist for The Fraser Institute. Block specifically set out to criticize Minister Ouellet's proposals, to criticize the *Combines Investigation Act* in general, and to teach some good economics in the process. It is the latter goal that is likely to be the most interesting to the reader of this essay.

Walter Block is a master at destroying economic myths in a simple, understandable, and convincing way. He proved this beyond a doubt in his book

---

"A Response to the Framework Document for Amending the Combines Investigation Act" by Walter Block.

Defending the Undefendable. No economic myth is left with an ounce of life in it after Block has taken aim at it. Just two of the many myths that Block pulverizes in "A Response to the Framework Document for Amending the Combines Investigation Act" are: (1) Economic concentration is the antithesis of economic competition; and (2) Government, manned with benevolent individuals and economics experts, promotes competition. (Yes, Virginia, there still are millions of individuals who believe this foolishness.)

As to the concentration-competition issue, Block convincingly shows that concentration ratios and the number of firms in an industry have nothing to do with competition. As he colorfully notes, "Industrial concentration is as much related to competition as fish to bicycles." As Block points out, concentration ratios—statistical artifacts—overlook much of the nitty-gritty of real economic life. They, or rather the individuals who construct such things, either overlook or are ignorant of the facts that goods and markets can either be defined narrowly or broadly, that competition does not stop at a nation's borders, that the size of the economy is relevant to the discussion, and most of all, that competitive behavior does not pay any attention to silly numbers that many academic economists and government bureaucrats come up with. It is motivated by something much more fundamental. As Block correctly points out, firms with high concentration ratios are some of the most competitive firms to be found. A quick glance at a good financial newspaper or magazine generally illustrates this fact. One would have thought that most politicians, who usually vie for office alongside only one or two other individuals, would have known this. Political competition, after all, is known for its ferocity.

As to the second myth, Block shows a series of government interventions in the economy which, although their stated intention many times is to increase competition, do just the opposite. Most of these interventions can be summarized by the phrase "barriers to entry." The Block message: If the Canadian government is truly interested in promoting competition and in advancing the standard of living of its people, it should eliminate legal barriers to entry and forget all this nonsense about promoting competition by checking a firm's concentration ratio and then acting (usually) in a rationalist-constructivist way.

It is the same message advanced by other economists who understand the workings of free markets. But Block advances the message particularly well. He does it in such a way that even if the government officials or politicians do not pay heed, at least they cannot walk away feeling smug in their ignorance or hypocrisy.

This is an essay that is of interest to the educated layman, the government bureaucrat, the politician, and the academic economist. The issues covered are of immediate and lasting importance. The essay is of particular interest to the person who wants to know what competition is and is not, how politicians behave, and why they behave as they do. With respect to the latter issue, there is enough public choice theory to make the entire discussion complete. There are few essays written today from which one can learn so much so quickly and be so thoroughly entertained along the way.

Writing History: Essay on Epistemology

Reviewed by Edward H. Kaplan

R eaders of von Mises's *Theory and History* or *Epistemological Problems of Economics* will find little to affront their sensibilities in this extended essay by a French historian on what historians ought to and (equally important) ought not to do when they write history. Veyne even cites von Mises and Hayek for some key aspects of his argument. Other aspects, though both plausible and vividly expressed, may leave many historians and economists uneasy.

Veyne denies that history can be a social science. Any true science creates a set of abstractions as its object. History fixes on concrete particulars. The historian composes these into "true novels," and so resembles the novelist more than the scientist. Because the novelist creates fictions which strive for versimilitude—the form or appearance of truth—he may have to perform the kind of research into documents one normally associates with the historian. The historian, of course, must not make up characters or incidents, but like the novelist he has to decide upon a "plot" which fits his narrative. Various plots will, however, fit a given set of documents, depending on what sort of story the historian wants to tell, and different plots will send the historian scurrying off after different sets of documents. "Facts" do not lie around in documents like so many irreducible atoms. The needs of his plot determine what facts the historian will construe out of which documents.

The historian explains what he is writing about by giving an account of it—by unfolding the plot he has selected for that narrative. Abstractions as such cannot be historical explanations. Socrates was not killed by demagogy, not even Athenian demagogy. Particular demagogues did the deed and they did it not with demagogy but with hemlock.

As it was for Aristotle and Aquinas, the historian's causation remains an uncertain mixture of physical or social law, chance, and human free will. History is, therefore, an open system, and neither the economist's equilibrium nor historical laws are possible for it.

Writing History: Essay on Epistemology by Paul Veyne (Trans. Mina Moore-Rinvolucri). Middletown, Conn.: Wesleyan University Press, 1984 (orig. French ed. 1971).

Even such "intuitive abstractions" as "enlightened despotism" are not approximations of historical laws, but mere verbal shortcuts, "only the summary of a plot." (p. 118). Such historical types, unlike biological species, are wholly subjective. Any particular enlightened despotism, for example, surely has enough unenlightened aspects as to oblige the historian to create a new type should his plot require him to notice them. General labels for concepts such as "direct taxation" or "hereditary monarchy" are no more than building blocks for historical types. To make these types sufficiently general as to approximate scientific laws is to spill over into the ridiculous (for example, the Marshall Plan as an instance of potlatch).

Not even Max Weber's "ideal types" are instances of historical laws. Ideal types are actual historical individuals or events rendered in the historian's mind as perfect examples of themselves so as to lay bare their inner logic. Would-be social scientists have stripped away the rich vestments of historical context which Weber so carefully provided for such ideal types as the "Protestant ethic" or "capitalist spirit" and thereby reduced them to bland abstractions useful neither to history nor true social science.

The historian can at least use historical types to draw analogies to roughly similar events at other times or places for which more or better documentation exists, and can thereby help "retrodict" a past cause for some later event. As the historian broadens his "historical culture," more and more apt analogies may occur to him, and his historical types may gradually turn into Weberian ideal types. By easy stages the history of specific events in particular places and times will evolve into the comparative history of what Veyne calls "non-events"—cities or direct taxes, for example—rather than "events"—Paris or direct taxation in modern France.

A science of man is possible and to some degree already exists, but history is not and cannot be that science. Such a science must, Veyne argues (citing von Mises, Hayek, and Schumpeter) be praxeological. If the objects of history are specific events (and nonevents), the objects of a true human science must be abstractions that can be manipulated in the mind independently of the world from which they were drawn. Veyne also believes they must be put into mathematical terms, a notion that he surely did not get from the Austrians, but otherwise his view is quite congruent with theirs: Just as Galileo did not infer the role of gravity from the unworkable and probably mythical experiment of simultaneously dropping a ball and a feather from the leaning tower of Pisa, but from a mental experiment conducted on the interaction of the abstractions "force" and "mass" on each other, so too economics does not base its law of declining marginal utility on data provided by psychological observations, but on the logic of a carefully delimited imaginary situation wherein people apply the firt unit of a good to the use they most favor, and each successive unit to less favored uses.

Veyne believes economics to be the best-developed human science, at least in its truly scientific neoclassical form (within which he places the Austrians), rather than in its historicist and institutionalist forms. But even economics is of mainly negative use to the historian—to explain (under certain narrowly defined circumstances) why some people did not obtain some results they expected. Laborers, for example, may never move toward actually obtaining their DMVPs for their wages because of any number of possible political interventions and/or customary freezings of relative wages; it is the historian's main business to focus on these particular events rather than on the never-achieved tendency for wages to converge on DMVPs. Indeed Veyne quotes with approval (p. 254) von Mises's dictum that the historian need only know as much of some science relevant to his topic as does an average educated man. The historian, Veyne keeps insisting, must always return to the specificities of his documents. Dwelling too long in the realm of even a valid science's abstractions must either turn him from historian into scientist or tempt him into the vain search for valid historical types that are also scientific laws.

Truly praxeological sociology barely exists as yet, Veyne argues. "General sociology" of the sort done by writers such as Talcott Parsons is merely solipsistic. It uses nominally universal vocabulary merely to label entities without turning them into abstractions that could be meaningfully manipulated as such in people's minds. To the extent that Marx attempted a general sociology, his work is no more valid than that of the Parsonians. Marx and Weber went beyond this to write "noneventworthy" history, and so both are still worth reading. Because noneventworthy history may appear to deal with abstract universals, it may fool the sociologist into thinking he is doing social science.

Veyne treats Marx as something of an extinct volcano, but Weber still excites his interest and admiration. Like Marx, Weber thought he was doing historical science. In the quarrel over methods between Carl Menger and the German historical school, Weber sided with the latter, arguing that classical economics was merely the ideal type of economic thought produced under liberal capitalism. But if economics was both ideal type and science, Weber implicitly reasoned, his own sociology of ideal types must also be a valid historical science. Weber's work has survived, Veyne insists, because he was actually pioneering noneventworthy history.

Aside from noneventworthy history, about all that is validly left to the sociologist is contemporary history, usually also of the noneventworthy sort. The history of the present and of the noneventworthy past are often left to sociologists because historiography began as the community's memory and as the handmaiden of kings and conquerors, the specific events of whose lives it commemorated. Veyne is content with this division of labor, though by calling comparative and noneventworthy history the logical completion of national and eventworthy history, he would clearly not object to either historians or sociologists poaching on each other's territories.

There is little to criticize in this English-language edition of an early 1970s book. The translation occasionally falters, but even without the original French in hand, there is no real difficulty in surmising what Veyne must have intended.

The translation nicely captures what must have been the epigrammatic touches of the original.

The most serious omission, which might serve Veyne as the topic for some subsequent essay, is that he introduces the notion of "plot" without discussing in any detail what that term implies. In a series of essays of the 1960s and 1970s collected in *Topics of Discourse: Essays in Cultural Criticism* (Baltimore: Johns Hopkins, 1978) and in detail in *Metahistory: The Historical Imagination in Nineteenth-Century Europe* (Baltimore: Johns Hopkins, 1973), the American scholar Hayden White approached this problem of the "emplotment" of factual historical narratives as an exercise in pure literary genre analysis, with results as intriguing as they are disconcerting.

Following Levi-Strauss (who is also one of Veyne's prime sources) but also literary critic Northrop Frye and linguistic theorist Roman Jacobson, White suggested that, at least for Western man and perhaps for humanity at large, there are really only four basic kinds of plot: romance, comedy, tragedy, and satire, and that each of these is associated with its own characteristic "trope" (in the sense of figure of speech): metaphor, metonymy, synecdoche, and irony, respectively. White even linked these plots and tropes to specific ideological positions: anarchist, conservative, radical, and liberal, respectively. Only mediocre and doctrinaire historians, White hastened to add, stay rigidly within this pattern. The great historians always attempt to mediate between pairs of these tropes and plots because they can see how they can all be true.

The historian has to fit his work into one or another of these sets of categories or flit back and forth between them—first, because he is using language and these categories may in fact constitute the rules for using language; and, second, because his readers, however unconsciously, attempt to recognize one of these categories in his work, and it is only when they discover the plot he is using that they grasp his explanation of the story. "Aha," in effect the reader exclaims. "Now I see what the historian is getting at here. He is recounting a tragedy. Now I understand what is going on."

If only four basic plots exist, there may be at least rough limits to the degree of complexity that the historian need embrace. White even suggests that when a revisionist historian changes plots, he is doing what a Freudian analyst does when he encourages his patient to recast his subconscious emplotment of the events that cause his neurosis into some other, more innocuous, plot. This, however, may be of more comfort to beleaguered Freudians than to historians embarrassed by such company.

White's analysis of particular historical narratives reads disconcertingly like the "deconstruction" or "unpacking" of literary texts of literati of the deconstructionist school. Flashes of insight often come wrapped in opaque technical jargon as barbarous as anything committed by the disciples of Talcott Parsons. Worse, judgments about which of two tropes dominates a particular segment of narrative sometimes seem arbitrary.

Though historians, like novelists and poets, can continue to do their jobs without benefit of literary deconstruction even if they are, in fact, writing true novels, one may wonder (to commit some trope or other) whether Professor Veyne's intriguing book has snatched the historical profession from the palsied hands of the sociologists only to inadvertently drop it into the ravening jaws of the English professors.

The Unseen Dimensions of Wealth: Towards a Generalized Economic Theory

Reviewed by Edward H. Kaplan

D espite the large claims implied by its subtitle, this is not a theoretical treatise. Nor does it succeed in laying bare the principles of how an economy behaves under normal, that is, nonequilibrium, conditions. That is just as well, since such principles almost certainly cannot be discovered anyway. Much better, it is a slightly disguised but interesting and useful economic history which succeeds in raising the economic experience of post-1949 Hong Kong almost to the level of a Weberian ideal type of a particular sort of market economy.

If Henry Woo, a talented Hong Kong economic journalist, is more nearly like George Gilder than Israel Kirzner, this is not to be despised. Like Gilder, he has read some of the Austrians, and appreciates them, at least for their understanding of the nonreality of equilibrium, but (also like Gilder) he has not entirely mastered Austrian principles. Sometimes this leads him to reinvent the wheel, at other times to reinvent the triangle and call it the wheel.

Woo's notion of "human capital," for example, is blessedly free of the narrow focus on formal education of Schulz or Becker, whose work has been so mischievously exploited by apologists for a bloated U.S. tertiary education system. Informal learning on the job and by thoughtfully scanning the evolving market is, for Woo, much more important. Indeed, without quite indicating whether he has derived it from the Austrians, he recapitulates the notion epitomized by von Mises and Rothbard that there is no homogeneous Labor, but only a congeries of particular laborers, most of whose services constitute unique goods.

Woo also incorporates the von Mises-Hayek theory of the business cycle into his analysis, but because he does so from the more visible perspective of demand for credit rather than central-bank–induced increased supply of credit, his argument is far less clear than the Austrian original both to the reader and (one suspects, from his neglect of the role of government-induced increases in the money supply as a cause of inflation) to himself as well.

The Unseen Dimensions of Wealth: Towards a Generalized Economic Theory by Henry K.H. Woo. Fremont, Calif.: Victoria Press, 1984.

Of course, the good parts as well as the theoretically murky parts of his general treatment are the consequence of Woo's frankly announced decision to generalize from the modern Hong Kong experience. Hong Kong has barely enough land to stand on. The adaptability of its labor force has counted for far more than its relatively sparse and simple supply of capital goods. Its banks are relatively free to respond to domestic and foreign pressures to create money, so it is natural for Woo to focus on these pressures rather than on the increased money supply itself.

Though in principle it need not be so, in practice it is reasonable for Woo to emphasize the tendency of an unfettered market to spontaneously grow. Woo's general stages of growth—a long stasis before the market is unchained, a relatively short burst of unconstrained growth, followed by a long period of constrained growth (caused by, first, compounding manipulation from outside the market and, second, a constantly shifting disequilibrium permitted by inefficient manipulation within the market)—all faithfully reflect the stages of Hong Kong's actual economic history.

The book is also seeded with a number of bits of illuminating narrative, such as Woo's suggestion that the recent appearance of better housing across the waters in the New Territories may be making for greater inefficiency because workers commuting so far to their jobs can no longer as easily carry piecework home during the busy season to be worked on by the grannies and children. A bit of comparative historicizing on this point (which Woo does not do) will allow one to recognize that the Hong Kong experience is not entirely unique, and that even diligent Chinese at some stage begin to favor the leisure of a decent apartment over labor, just as did diligent and then prosperous Jewish refugees from the Russian Pale after 1920, when they abandoned the slums of the Lower East Side of New York for the comparatively palatial apartment houses of the South Bronx.

About the Contributors

Roger Arnold is associate professor of economics at the University of Nevada, Las Vegas.

Charles W. Baird is professor of economics at California State University at Hayward.

Robert Batemarco is professor of economics at Manhattan College in the Bronx.

Walter Block is director of academic affairs at the Fraser Institute, Vancouver, British Columbia, Canada.

Lowell Gallaway is distinguished professor of economics at Ohio University in Athens.

Henry Hazlitt is the author of many books, including *Economics in One Lesson, The Critics of Keynesian Economics*, and *The Failure of the New Economics*.

Edward H. Kaplan is professor of history at Western Washington University in Bellingham, Washington.

William Keizer is professor of economics at the Free University of Amsterdam, The Netherlands.

E.C. Pasour, Jr., is professor of economics and business at North Carolina State University at Raleigh.

M.W. Sinnett is lecturer in economics at St. Mary's College, University of St. Andrews, Scotland.

Gene Smiley is associate professor of economics at Marquette University in Milwaukee.

Richard H. Timberlake, Jr., is professor of economics at the College of Business, University of Georgia, Athens.

Richard K. Vedder is professor of economics at Ohio University in Athens.

Leland Yeager is the Ludwig von Mises distinguished professor of economics at Auburn University, Auburn, Alabama.

About the Editor

Murray N. Rothbard is the S.J. Hall Distinguished Professor of Economics at the University of Nevada, Las Vegas. Dr. Rothbard is also vice president for academic affairs of the Ludwig von Mises Institute of Auburn University and editor of its *Review of Austrian Economics*. He received his B.S., M.S., and Ph.D. in economics from Columbia University, where he studied under Joseph Dorfman. He also studied under Ludwig von Mises at New York University. Dr. Rothbard is the author of more than one hundred scholarly articles and fifteen books, including: *Man, Economy, and State; America's Great Depression; The Panic of 1819; Power and Market;* and *Conceived in Liberty.*